Let's Pretend

A HISTORY OF RADIO'S BEST LOVED CHILDREN'S SHOW BY A LONGTIME CAST MEMBER

by ARTHUR ANDERSON

with a foreword by Norman Corwin

McFarland & Company, Inc., Publishers
Jefferson, North Carolina, and London

British Library Cataloguing-in-Publication data are available

Library of Congress Cataloguing-in-Publication Data

Anderson, Arthur, 1922–
    Let's pretend : a history of radio's best loved children's show by
a longtime cast member / Arthur Anderson; with a foreword by Norman
Corwin.
      p. cm.
    Includes bibliographical references and index.
    ISBN 0-89950-967-3 (lib. bdg. : 50# alk. paper)
    1. Let's pretend (Radio program) I. Title.
PN1991.77.L48A53 1994
791.44′72 – dc20   94-16142
                                                              CIP

Manufactured in the United States of America

McFarland & Company, Inc., Publishers
  Box 611, Jefferson, North Carolina 28640

Dedicated to the memory of
Nila Mack
whose creation "Let's Pretend" brought joy to a
generation of children and raised the standards
of American radio broadcasting

Acknowledgments

I have been able to dig out the facts for this history of "Let's Pretend" and put them together in a meaningful way only with the help of many professionals and many interested friends.

I am most grateful to the Performing Arts Research Center at the Lincoln Center branch of the New York Public Library, and its knowledgeable and patient librarians. Without the availability of its wealth of books, clippings, photographs, and other materials, among which are Nila Mack's own scrapbooks, this book would literally not have been possible.

The information provided by the surviving Let's Pretenders, and their encouragement, have also been invaluable. Each one I interviewed, on tape or in person, provided some new fact or jogged my own memory to help make more authentic this chronicle of a portion of radio's golden age. Foremost among them have been Gwen Davies, Sybil Trent, Miriam Wolfe, Jack Grimes, and Daisy Aldan. Miriam carefully read the manuscript and saved me from what would have otherwise been some gaping omissions.

Longtime friends Russell Jehn and his wife Caye went over the manuscript with an editorial magnifying glass, and I thank them for hours of careful analysis. But perhaps I was able to help them, too, with some valuable information. Think of it – neither had ever been introduced to the word "smarmy"!

Tireless old-time radio historian Anthony Tollin obliged with articles and facts about Nila Mack, the program, and some of its actors, and the loan of photographs. I am indebted also to Betty Sybrant, writer and historian of Arkansas City, Kansas, Nila Mack's hometown, for many facts about her background and childhood. Thanks are also due to Miss Mack's former secretary Mary Ponterio, whose personal memories were a great help, and Harley Flaum of Penny Lane Recording Studios, for technical information about radio. Valuable assistance also came from Ron Lackmann, a prolific author who has produced seven books about old-time radio, and the many loyal old-time radio buffs who responded quickly to my letters to various publications asking for information.

Most of all I am grateful to Norman Corwin, one of radio's foremost writers and directors, for providing the Foreword to my book.

Last but by no means least, my wife Alice showed endless patience in holding up dinner innumerable times while just one more deathless thought was put into the word processor. Her useful criticism and loving support enabled me to successfully finish my project.

Contents

Foreword

By Norman Corwin

"Please send me free a fairy," wrote a child listener to "Let's Pretend." In one simple stroke this went beyond suspension of disbelief to total abdication of it, something which has been a fond dream of drama from the Greeks onward.

The most recent setting for dispensation of drama is the unwalled theatre introduced by radio and expanded by video. Television is the undisputed champion of the performing media when it comes to funds, apparatus, and size of audience. But though it is vastly richer than radio in those properties, it is also poorer in elements that exercise the imagination. A modest measure of this claim is that nobody ever wrote to a television program requesting that a fairy or any other creature, gratis or paid for, be sent through the mail.

Television is too young and active to have generated much in the way of genial recollection, but the theatre of radio, having been forced into early retirement, bathes in nostalgia. Proof lies in John Dunning's *Tune in Yesterday,* a stout and formidable compendium of old-time radio, and in addition there exists in the libraries of the land a substantial and growing shelf of reminiscences of this latest of bygone golden ages.

Of all these memoirs, Arthur Anderson's partly autobiographical account is in my view the warmest and most affectionate. Arthur was one of a group of children recruited by the resolute Nila Mack, and forged by her into an acting company which quickly established itself as the outstanding children's theatre on the air. Thanks to the benign dictatorship of Madam Mack the program enjoyed a run of 24 years, during which it scooped up almost half a hundred national awards, and also during which the adapter-director-producer smoked two and a half packs of cigarettes daily.

Throughout most of the volume, the presence of Nila Mack (originally Mac, but she thought that sounded too much like a nickname and so added the k), is in every way indomitable. Anderson alludes to her as "a wise-cracking surrogate mother [who] chose 'children who seemed simple,

1

unaffected and eager to pretend along with me.'" Her credo was bold and clear: "You don't need to explain happenings. You simple believe or you don't."

There were millions of believers. To this day, nearly half a century after the death of Nila Mack, veteran believers recall their enchantment with the series, recollections so vivid that Anderson does not exaggerate when he writes, "She could have had no idea how strong would be their childhood memories of it."

The Pretenders, as they were called, successfully pretended to be dragons, talking horses, kings, queens, gnomes, dwarfs, princes, princesses, witches, beauteous maidens, assorted knaves, varlets, cats, dogs, nightingales, and various flora and fauna. Anderson himself filled a good many of those roles, once even playing "a pitiful mewing kitten." When the principals traveled in "Let's Pretend," it was always first class, in golden coaches, wearing purple robes, and as often as not they traversed enchanted forests or lived in castles with emerald halls, rooms of jade, and groaning boards furbished with golden goblets. Not only the lives of rich and famous characters were told but also those of wicked and infamous ones. The villains, we are reminded in this memoir, were completely evil and were invariably punished or eliminated by the time each program ended. Virtue was rewarded, and there would be a moral lesson to be learned, "but it always came out naturally."

This book is handsomely researched, with copious data on the subsequent careers of the actors and actresses who performed Nila's stories (133 of them written or adapted by Nila herself), and enriched by anecdotes of great charm. The reader is also indebted to Anderson for discovering and memorializing children's letters that properly should decorate the walls of Nila's chambers in Valhalla. These would include the imperious demand of a determined young listener: "If you do not play 'Snow White and the Seven Dwarfs' again . . . I will tell everyone not to tune in again. I have a lot of friends, and they do everything I tell them." And a joint message from a caucus of eight little girls: "We like all the stories except the stories we don't like, but you make them so good that we like them."

Since, as the author relates, I once had an office at CBS just a few doors down the hall from Nila Mack, I may possibly be permitted to confirm and endorse what is written in the following pages, and, further, be licensed to propose three old-fashioned cheers for Arthur Anderson in recognition of his multiple services as historian, biographer, archivist, and anecdotalist.

Norman Corwin became well known on the pioneering CBS series "Columbia Workshop" and for his special broadcasts at the outset and at the end of World War II. He has written many screenplays, including Lust for Life, *and in 1980 began serving as a visiting professor at the University of Southern California.*

Introduction

Once upon a time there was a magical land beyond the Big Dipper. It was a country of both beauty and peril. In it lived brave heroes who faced impossible adversaries, like wicked witches and fire-breathing dragons, but who always found victory in the end, and usually the true love of beautiful princesses whom they had rescued. It was a land where animals could sometimes talk after midnight, and where, if you were lucky, your wishes would be granted by a fearsome genie who materialized out of an old brass lamp. In this kingdom the good people triumphed and the evil ones were always vanquished. This was the Land of "Let's Pretend," which for nearly 25 years came to life every Saturday morning on the CBS radio network. It was truly the "Theatre of the Imagination" that radio seemed made for.

Though the so-called "Golden Age of Radio" is long past, it is occasionally recalled in recordings of some of the classic shows played on present-day radio and in the memories of those who are delighted to recite these verbal cues: "Amos 'n' Andy": "I'se regusted!" "The Lone Ranger": "Hiyo Silllver!" "The Joe Penner Show": "Wanna buy a duck?" Any reference to "Let's Pretend" is sure to bring a smile and an attempt to remember the words and music of our Cream of Wheat theme song:

> Cream of Wheat is so good to eat,
> Da da da, da da, da da.

The main reason for this great affection for the vivid memories of the show that seem to remain with a large cross-section of the American public in a certain age group is that the nine years it was sponsored by Cream of Wheat were part of their most impressionable years: those of childhood, when young imaginations were developing and were open to the stimulus of our magical fairy tales. "Let's Pretend" in its time was an American institution, just as important a part of Saturday morning as Jack Benny was an important part of Sunday night.

The biggest reason for the success of this phenomenon was its creator, writer, and director, Nila Mack – a short, blonde fairy godmother who held in her right hand not a magic wand but a stopwatch and in her left a cigarette. Miss Mack's clever, entertaining radio adaptations of the classic fairy tales were performed by the group of child actors she chose to populate this land of fantasy.

What was it like to be a child actor in radio? If you were on "Let's Pretend" it was like playing the imaginative games that most children 6 to 12 years old enjoyed: "Okay, you be the mommy, and I'll be the daddy, and he'll be the horrible ogre." But there was a difference. This was show business, and we were expected to obey grown-ups' rules – in this case Nila Mack's rules – and those who did not would sooner or later be off the show. Though none of us realized it, we were making radio history. It was an exciting time.

The story of Nila Mack and her child actors of "Let's Pretend" parallels almost exactly the period when radio was king among the entertainment media. From 1929, when it started growing explosively and television wasn't even a gleam in David Sarnoff's eye, through 1954, when that one-eyed monster had crept up on it and devoured much of its entertainment audience and its advertising revenue, the creative programming of radio brought information, entertainment, and joy to a whole generation of Americans. "Let's Pretend" gave fun, excitement, and inspiration to their children, and let them believe that things like honesty, courage, and idealism did matter and that they too could live happily ever after.

Chapter 1

Cold Hands

In an essay she entitled "Report from a Notion," Nila Mack wrote that at 12 noon on Saturday, August 18, 1930, with "two cubes of ice in place of hands, I, Nila Mack speaking, started the notion that radio was an ideal medium for dramatized Fairy Tales. It's worked pretty well." With one of those frigid hands, the newest member of the Columbia Broadcasting System directorial staff had given a cue from the control room of Studio 3 at 485 Madison Avenue, the network's New York headquarters. Thus began her first children's broadcast. But it was not "Let's Pretend."

Nila Mack had inherited a children's radio program which was already on the air. "The Adventures of Helen and Mary," a 30-minute weekly show, broadcast since September 7, 1929, was written and directed by Yolanda Langworthy. The format was this: two little girls named Helen and Mary, played by eight-year-olds Patricia Ryan and Estelle Levy, play together and imagine all sorts of tales of romance and adventure, which are then performed by a cast of adult actors, with sound effects, and music provided by a six-piece string ensemble. The scripts were from standard works of fiction, adapted for radio by Langworthy, who was Columbia's director of children's programming. She also directed adult programs for the network, including "Arabesque," which had dramatic segments, poetry readings by David Ross, and music by Emery Deutsch and His Gypsy Violins. These programs were only a small part of the daily output of the expanding Columbia Broadcasting System network – and every program was live.* In 1930 radio was almost the only growth industry in a country which was in the throes of a serious depression. It was the ideal medium for people who didn't have much money and needed a shot of optimism, and that included a very large segment of the population. If you could afford $10 for a little five-tube Emerson or a Fada, the world was yours, and it

---

*A live program is one that is actually taking place at the moment the listener is hearing it. The networks in the 1930s had strict policies forbidding recordings on their airwaves. Anyone who wanted to hear a record could play it on their Victrola. The present-day term "live on tape" is a contradiction.

Helen (left), Patricia Ryan; Memory, Harry Swan; and Mary, Estelle Levy. © 1931 CBS Inc. Used by permission.

was free. William S. Paley, son of a Philadelphia cigar manufacturer (La Palinas – 10 cents each) had bought a small group of radio stations, starting with WCAU, Philadelphia, which in 1927 became the Columbia Broadcasting System. In the broadcast industry, where nothing was or is immune from criticism or satire, the second word in the title was sometimes changed to "Broadchasing."

Paley presided over his creation in a paternalistic, hands-on fashion at the network's headquarters in four rooms in the Paramount Building at 1501 Broadway. At that time CBS did not even have a New York outlet, and used to buy time on stations WOR and WABC. (WABC is not to be confused with the present stations WABC-AM, FM, and TV, owned by the American Broadcasting Company, which in 1930 did not even exist. The old Station WABC is now WCBS, New York – AM, FM, and TV.)

In December 1928 the network bought WABC, which became its New York flagship station, and in July 1929 proudly dedicated its new studios and offices in a just completed 25-story building at 485 Madison Avenue, corner of Fifty-Second Street.

Children's programs were just as important on radio in the early 1930s as they are on television today, and the usual broadcast times were early mornings, late afternoons, and Saturday mornings. At that time they were all produced by the networks themselves (and on a less elaborate scale by many local and independent stations throughout the country). "The Adventures of Helen and Mary" was meant to be Columbia's premier children's show. The consensus of the CBS executives, however, and that pretty much meant Bill Paley in this case, was that the program was rather dull, and that a change had to be made. Yolanda Langworthy was apparently not working out as a writer and director of children's programming. Then someone thought of Nila Mack.

Nila Mack was not new to radio, a point in her favor. She had performed on CBS in New York the previous year in a comedy program called "Nit Wits" and on a dramatic series "Radio Guild of the Air." She has also written a series for the network called "Night Club Romances," in which she also narrated each week's story as a slightly cynical Texas Guinan–type nightclub owner. She was short (5 feet 3 inches), blonde, blue-eyed, and full of energy, enthusiasm, and good humor. Moreover, she had an extensive background in show business.

She was born Nila Mac, on October 24, 1891, in Arkansas (pronounced Ar*kan*sas) City, Kansas, the only child of Don Carlos and Margaret Bowen Mac. She had been a precocious child performer, singing, playing the piano, and dancing. In fact, she had won 208 cakewalk contests before she reached her teens. (A cakewalk was a promenade or march of African American origin. Contestants who devised the most intricate or eccentric steps won cakes as prizes.)

In 1907 her father, a Santa Fe Railroad engineer, died a hero by reversing the throttle when his engine derailed at 60 miles an hour and kept his hand on it instead of jumping. Though the engine and four of the train's five cars tumbled down an embankment, the last car stayed on the track. There were some injuries, but Don Carlos Mac was the only one killed, scalded to death by live steam. (Another well-known CBS employee whose father was a railroad engineer was Edward R. Murrow.)

After this tragedy, Nila's mother sent her to a girls' finishing school in Lake Forrest, Illinois, where she earned some money acting, probably with visiting touring companies, when not in class. The next year her mother took her to Boston for training in dramatics, French, and elocution, and it was there that she obtained her first full-time acting job, as an ingenue with the Western Repertory Company, doing split weeks and one-night stands for $25 a week. Her mother went along on the tour as her daughter's chaperone.

After two years of touring, the company finally went broke, leaving the actors stranded in the small town of Metropolis, Illinois. Nila, her mother, and the repertory company's leading man, Roy Briant, instead of accepting this fate, decided to strike out on their own, and they opened a movie theatre in Metropolis. Roy was the manager (and probably projectionist), her mother manned the box office, and Nila was pianist for the silent films. This lasted about a year, until another touring rep company was passing through, and Roy and Nila joined it. They were married in St. Anthony, Idaho, on March 20, 1913. Nila Mac was 21.

Nila and her husband performed extensively in vaudeville in sketches he wrote, and later in song-and-dance numbers they wrote together. Later, based in Chicago, her reputation grew, first as an ingenue then as a leading lady, in both comedy and dramatic roles. She was seen there in 1915 by the famous Russian actress Alla Nazimova, with whom she later developed a close friendship. She played the second female lead with Nazimova in the highly popular and dramatic antiwar play *War Brides*, in which they toured the vaudeville circuit. She later repeated the role when it was made into a highly acclaimed silent film. Now based in New York, she and her husband continued to work as actors both together and separately on Broadway, on tour, and in stock companies. Meanwhile, Roy Briant had several of his plays produced in New York, and earned extra money by writing vaudeville sketches and scenarios for silent films.

Nila toured in this country and in Canada for two years with the well-known comedian Tom Wise, sometimes in plays written for her by Roy. She later played on Broadway in a successful revival of the earlier hit play *Fair and Warmer*. By then she had added a "k" to her name, because she said that "Mac" sounded like a nickname. Her husband moved to Hollywood to write scenarios for Paramount, and died there in 1927.

It was soon after that time began to catch up with Nila Mack's career. She was no longer the winsome, blonde ingenue, or the striking young leading lady. Moreover, the American theatre was changing. In 1927, a banner year, 268 productions had opened on Broadway, a number never equaled before or since, but from then on the total declined every year, and Nila's various sources of income began to dry up. The rise of the film industry was causing a serious drop in the number of legitimate theatres. Vaudeville was declining, permanent stock companies were no longer able to survive, and the number of touring shows was greatly reduced. Her husband had died. She was alone, and it was time to do some serious thinking.

There was only spotty acting work available in New York. She subsisted by writing film scenarios, including a short for Fanny Brice. Then there was a vaudeville sketch she wrote for Nydia Westman; but a living in show business, for Nila Mack at least, was no longer easy to come by. That was when radio entered her life twice, and both times unexpectedly.

Late in 1929 Miss Mack had applied for a permanent writing berth at Columbia Broadcasting. While working in a stock company she had met Georgia Backus, an actress who was also a writer, evidently with connections at the network, who recommended her. In the meantime, after a long dry spell she got a part in a Broadway play, and things were evidently beginning to look up for her. But this suddenly became unimportant when in February she received word that her mother was seriously ill in Arkansas City. She left the cast immediately, and took the first train back home to care for her.

The problem now was how to support them both since, as one might say jokingly, casting was nonexistent in Arkansas City. Ah, but that changed. Almost at the time of her arrival back home, radio came to Arkansas City with the opening of station WEEB, and a major part of the operation became Nila Mack. "Mrs. Nila Mac Briant (still using the old spelling), New York actress, playwright and moving picture star, has accepted the position as announcer for the local studio," reported the *Arkansas City Tribune*. "She will be known on the air as Nila," the paper continued, adding that "she possesses a beautiful contralto voice, [and] has broadcast in many sketches over the national chain out of New York City."

Besides being the station's chief announcer, Nila was also producer and director of almost all of its programming. She wrote scripts, she wrote advertising copy, she manned the telephone to sell advertising time, and she persuaded many nervous local musicians and vocalists to face a microphone for the first time. Nila Mack's boundless energy and resourcefulness was proving a godsend, not only to her ailing mother but to the new little radio station as well.

The Arkansas City radio adventure lasted six months. Then Nila

Nila Mack as a young leading lady, ca. 1918. Billy Rose Theatre Collection: the New York Public Library for the Performing Arts Astor, Lenox, and Tilden Foundations.

received a response to her application of the year before – a telegram from CBS in New York offering her a permanent writing and directing berth. It was an exciting offer – a chance to get back into the mainstream of show business. Now that she had been a theatre professional for over 20 years, it is doubtful that she would have been satisfied for long as a big frog in the smallish puddle of Station WEEB.

   She was reluctant to leave her mother, and there was also one aspect of the CBS offer which to her must have been a shocker. The network was replacing Yolanda Langworthy, and what they wanted was someone to write and direct children's programs. Nila Mack was experienced in show business. She had trouped all over the United States, had endured hardships on the road unknown to actors of today, and had written material ranging from vaudeville sketches, snappy one-liners, and songs to dramatic motion picture scenarios, but had never done anything in any medium specifically aimed at children.

Nevertheless, here was steady employment being offered, in her own line of work, in New York, at a time when the country was in the midst of a major economic depression. Nila's beloved aunt Mrs. P. B. Hanway, whom she called Aunt Potie, was willing to look after her mother. So, despite serious misgivings about the children's aspect of the job, she decided to take it. In August 1930, at slightly less than age 39, Nila Mack made an abrupt change in her career and in her life. She ceased performing and writing for the stage, vaudeville, or films and began what was to be her work for the rest of her life – writing, casting, producing, and directing children's radio programs for the Columbia Broadcasting System.

None of the Yolanda Langworthy scripts of "The Adventures of Helen and Mary" survive, but we do know that Miss Mack did not like them, and neither apparently did the CBS executives. Something had to be done with the show, and acting on her previous radio credentials and their faith in her, they were giving her complete freedom to revamp the program. It was a gamble on their part, and surely Nila Mack knew that it might not pay off. No wonder her hands were freezing that hot August morning.

The first show she directed was "Sinbad the Sailor," one of Yolanda Langworthy's adaptations from *The Arabian Nights*. She was distinctly uncomfortable with it, and with the actors' performances. To her, the whole tone of the show was too heavy-handed for the 6-to-12-year-old audience for whom it was intended. Obviously, the whole program could not be completely reshaped overnight, but the new director moved fast. Two broadcasts later the first and most drastic change had been made. The grownup actors had disappeared, and the cast now consisted entirely of children.

The first thing she had done upon returning to New York was to listen to "The Adventures of Helen and Mary" very carefully. She wrote later, "I hoped I could think of something better. I thought back to my own childhood," she continued. "The thing that had given me the greatest happiness was hearing or reading fairy tales and pretending that I was a beautiful princess. And so I had my idea. While I was working it out, I began interviewing and auditioning children. I chose children who seemed simple, unaffected and eager to pretend along with me." She added years later in the preface to her book of "Let's Pretend" stories in narrative form what was probably her basic philosophy in writing and casting the show.

"One of the nicest things about happenings in the Land of Let's Pretend is the fact that you don't need to explain them. You simply believe or you don't. Personally, I enjoy being with those who do."

Surveying "The Adventures of Helen and Mary," which CBS wanted changed and pronto, Nila Mack had made two determinations: First, how ideally suited to radio would be the classic fairy stories, with their built-in fantasy, mystery, adventure, and fun. Second, how much better would be a cast of child actors, who could convey much more than grownups the openness, innocence, and simplicity she wanted for the show. The cast changes came first; the story adaptations would take a bit more time.

Miss Mack's wise judgment and her resolve to carry through this new approach to children's radio programming was to have an effect on the lives of thousands of children in America. She was about to make a gift to them, and to the network, which was to gather kudos for the next 24 years for the program which evolved as "Let's Pretend," and became the most popular of its kind on the air.

Chapter 2

The Earliest Pretenders

There were many radio programs which stayed on the air for years, during which the participants formed close bonds and friendships, but "Let's Pretend" was unique in this respect. Nila Mack remained the show's writer, producer, and director for almost 23 years, counting from the time she took over its predecessor "The Adventures of Helen and Mary." Though there was some turnover in our repertory company every year, a basic group of us eventually formed, who stayed with the program for almost its entire life, and who Miss Mack called upon week after week until her death.

CBS director Earle McGill had this to say in his excellent book *Radio Directing*:

> The professional child actor is frequently an amazing, sensitive and pliable artist. Billy Halop, the twin Mauch boys [Billy and Bobby], Walter Tetley, Junior O'Day, Estelle Levy, Vivian Block, the Donnelly boys [Andy, Jimmy and Tommy], Arthur Anderson, Jackie Kelk, Jackie Jordan, Joyce Gates, Kingsley Colton, Sybil Trent, Jackie Grimes and Betty Philson are boys and girls who have received most of their training in radio, and every one of them can carry the burden of an entire broadcast and do it complete justice.

Every one of the children he mentions were Let's Pretenders, and probably the only reason more are not included is that he had not yet had the chance to work with them.

The children Miss Mack selected and built into a solid repertory company were a diverse group. We were from many ethnic and economic backgrounds. Some of us had brothers and sisters, some did not. But there were certain things we had in common: almost all of us were born in New York City, and we all had mothers who ranged from mildly to desperately ambitious for us to get into radio. They were able to help us because mothers in general did not have jobs in those days. *Fathers* had jobs, if they were lucky, the early 1930s still being Depression years. The most important trait we shared, though, was a childish naïveté and openness, combined with acting talent and intelligence. Not that we were all Quiz Kids with

13

high IQ's, any more than was Miss Mack herself. She never claimed to be an intellectual, and was slightly suspicious of those who were. It is important to relate something of our backgrounds and who we were, because we were the privileged ones, this group of child actors whom Nila Mack selected, taught, loved, scolded, cajoled, manipulated, helped, and directed, both on and off the air. These biographical notes on those who were long-term Let's Pretenders, and others who were important on the show for shorter periods, should give an idea of what kind of people we were, and what it was like to be a child actor in radio.

To begin with, there were some very good child actors already in the cast of "The Adventures of Helen and Mary" when its new director came on the scene. Besides Estelle Levy and Pat Ryan, they included Don Hughes, Ronald Liss, Walter Tetley, Howard Merrill, Roslyn Silber, Madeline Lee, Jackie Kelk, Julian and Elmer Altman, Phyllis Chalzell, Amy Sydell, and Ethel Blume. Estelle (now Gwen Davies) and Don were the only ones still on the show when we went off the air. By 1934, when our title became "Let's Pretend," the others had all been replaced for one reason or another.

Howard Merrill was the son of Fanny Merrill, long-time associate of Gertrude Berg, who created "The Goldbergs." He later became a radio writer. Ethel Blume continued as a busy actress, and stayed in radio into adulthood. She later married singer Felix Knight. Madeline Lee grew up as a radio actress, also doing baby cries and cartoon voices. She later became a casting director, then a Broadway producer, and married actor Jack Gilford. Julian Altman became a violinist and his brother Elmer Altman a cellist, and they both played with the National Symphony in Washington, D.C., as adults.

Nila possibly felt these children were losing their childish charm as their voices changed, or she may have replaced them because she found others in her auditions better suited to the program.

Then there were youngsters who left "Let's Pretend" because they had transferred their loyalty to Madge Tucker, who produced "The Lady Next Door" at NBC. Little curly haired Ronald Liss, who also played the violin and had absolute pitch, was one. He remained busy in radio well into adulthood, and eventually became a producer of television programs. Then there was Walter Tetley, who was a great comedian, and who at the age of eight did imitations of Sir Harry Lauder, with kilt, bagpipes, and Scottish burr.

Opposite: **The cast of "The Adventures of Helen and Mary," ca. 1933, in the CBS studio at 485 Madison Avenue. Standing, left to right: Amy Sydell, Roslyn Silber, Howard Merrill, Lester Jay, Elmer Altman, Florence Halop, Julian Altman, Nila Mack, Donald Hughes, Betty Philson (with ukulele), Billy Halop, and Ethel Blume. Seated: Patricia Ryan, Harry Swan, and Estelle Levy, (unidentified). ©1933 CBS Inc. Used by permission.**

Walter's voice never changed, and before he died in 1975 in California at the age of 60, he had gained lasting fame in radio annals as 12-year-old Leroy, wise-cracking nephew of "The Great Gildersleeve." Another of Nila's youngsters who later crossed over to Madge Tucker was Jack Kelk (then Jackie), who auditioned for her at age nine, playing his ukulele and singing "Would You Like to Take a Walk?" He became very successful in radio in running parts* which included Junior in "Dick Tracy" and Junior in "The Gumps," later becoming well known as Homer, Henry's best friend, in "The Aldrich Family." He eventually went into the production end of television as an advertising agency casting director.

Each child chosen by Nila Mack had to have the versatility to play many types of roles in her growing library of radio fairy-tale adaptations, although as she got to know each of us better she cast us more often in those in which she saw we were especially good. During our director's first four years at CBS these eight child actors – Estelle Levy, Patricia Ryan, Don Hughes, Vivian Block, Albert Aley, Mickey O'Day, Miriam Wolfe and Daisy Aldan – became the basic members of the juvenile "Let's Pretend" repertory company.

Gwen Davies

In the beginning there was Estelle Levy. Gwen Davies was not "born" until 11 years later. Nila found little Estelle, age eight, in 1930 playing Mary on "The Adventures of Helen and Mary," the show she was to take over. She had great vivacity and great flexibility as a child actress. She was small, had black hair in long curls, and a voice which she could change from a tinkly, giggling fairy to an aged grandmother. She and Patricia Ryan were the show's framework, and I am sure Miss Mack never considered replacing either of them.

Estelle's father was Greek and her mother Romanian. She was born in Manhattan, an only child. At the age of five she was taken to dancing school, then to a piano teacher. A year later she and many other children were being taken by anxious parents to audition for the broadcasting companies. It was Depression time. The parents saw not only fame for their children but also money to feed the family.

Once established on the show, Estelle's versatility was tested more and more. She would occasionally have a singing part on "Let's Pretend," and

---

*A running part was one which "ran with" the story of a daytime radio serial or a nightime weekly dramatic program. It was an actor's "consummation devoutly to be wished." Anyone landing a running part could expect a steady income from it for a week, a month, or even years, even though there might never be a written contract. There were no running parts on "Let's Pretend," as we did a different story on each broadcast.

Estelle Levy (later Gwen Davies), age 9, ca. 1931.

would play fanfares on her saxophone in scenes where royalty was being announced. "I was so embarrassed to be doing this," she said, "that I would have Pat Ryan carry the saxophone case when we left the studio." Estelle was always used in the lead-in, but frustrated at not getting to play the beautiful princess parts. "I felt like a garbage pail. If Nila had a strange voice to be done, I was stuck with it." She was later glad of this experience when she started to get calls for character voices in radio and TV commercials. For years she was the cartoon voice of Casper the Friendly Ghost.

During the Depression Estelle supported her parents by radio acting when her father was out of work, put herself through school, and later Columbia University. She had running parts on "Hilltop House," "Mrs. Wiggs of the Cabbage Patch," and other daytime serials, and did nighttime shows, including "The Kate Smith Hour" and "The Aldrich Family." She was Little Cosette with Orson Welles when he did *Les Miserables*, first as a serial on the Mutual Network, and later on "The Mercury Theatre on the Air." She also had her own show, singing with an orchestra weekly on station WEVD in New York, and also working with Molly Picon in dramatic programs on that station.

In the early part of 1937 Aaron Copland was casting his new opera *Second Hurricane*, and, assisted by Hiram Sherman, was auditioning children at the Professional Children's School. (PCS is a private school for children who are performers. It was then in an office building at Broadway and Sixty-First Street. In 1937 the tuition was $100 a year.) The chorus and some small parts were to be done by students of the Henry Street Music School and Seward Park High School, but professionals were needed for the leads. Estelle was dying to audition, but for some reason the principal, Mrs. Ethel Nesbitt, did not want her to. Estelle, making believe she had to go to the lavatory, went down to the tiny auditorium on the fourth floor, and stood in the back. The auditions were over. Finally Copland noticed her and said, "Can you sing?" "Well, I don't know what you call it, but I call it singing," said Gwen, which she admits was sort of cocky. Copland said, "Well, come up and sing," and with no music and no accompanist, she sang what we PCSers had learned during our Friday assemblies, the Negro spiritual "Let My People Go." "That's my Gwen," said Copland, and she was cast in the role of Gwen in the opera's world premiere, which took place at the tiny Henry Street Playhouse on Grand Street, on April 27, 1937. I sang the role of Gyp; Vivian Block, another Pretender, was Queenie; and Joseph Cotten played the small role of an aviator. The opera was directed by Orson Welles and conducted by Lehman Engel – quite a thrilling and historic premiere, and "Let's Pretend" was well represented.

In 1941 Estelle, now 19, heard that CBS was to do a new summer musical show. Dozens of singers had been auditioned, and she had not been called. She tried to convince Perry Lafferty, who was holding the auditions, by continually dropping into the control room. "Come on, Estelle," Lafferty would say. "We know you're a good actress. Can't you leave it at that?" One day when he had lost count of the control room visits and the door opened on Estelle's smiling face, Lafferty said, "Now what do you want?" well knowing the answer. "Perry, please let me sing." "Oh, all right," said

Lafferty, as much to get rid of her as anything else. Again, there was no music and no accompanist, but she did know some chords on the piano. What Lafferty and the others in the control room heard was a warm, sensuous delivery of "Embraceable You," a little reminiscent of Judy Garland, and a world removed from the twinkly elves and doddering old ladies she did on "Let's Pretend."

After the song, Lafferty said, "Stay there," and went downstairs and got CBS Music Director Lyn Murray. The result was that Estelle got a year's contract with CBS, starting with a show called "The Class of '41," with the orchestra conducted by Walter Gross, guest stars such as Jim Backus and Arnold Stang, and scripts written by Abe Burrows.

There was only one problem: the network said she would have to have a new name. They asked her to come up with one. The first name was easy, taken from the character of Gwen she had played in *Second Hurricane*. The last she took from her mother's Romanian family name Davidescu, which translated to Davidson in English, and she turned that into Davies. And so Estelle Levy became Gwen Davies, and Nila decided to have an official name-changing during a "Let's Pretend" broadcast. After it she took the new Gwen aside and said with mock severity, "Now listen, Toots – you may be a famous singer, but here you're still Estelle Levy, and you'd better behave yourself." Nila had already become much more than a radio director to many of us. She was a wisecracking surrogate mother, and to a few, including Gwen, her mother and later her husband, a close friend.

Gwen also had a brief career as a band vocalist, leaving "Let's Pretend" for six months in 1943 while she toured with Bobby Sherwood. One day Gwen's mother got a phone call from Miss Mack telling her that "Let's Pretend" was going commercial, and that she wanted Gwen to sing the theme song. The money, of course, would be many times what we children had been getting on "Let's Pretend" all those years. Gwen left Bobby Sherwood. Touring with a band was a rough life, and the salary was only $75 a week, out of which she had to pay her own hotel bills and expenses. Though she later did some recording with other bands, namely Artie Shaw and Jan Garber, Gwen stayed with "Let's Pretend" after that until its last broadcast.

Patricia (Pat) Ryan

Patricia Ryan, whom everyone called Pat, was born in London, England in 1921. As a small child she was brought to New York by her father John Ryan, who was Irish, and her mother, who was English and spoke with a slight Cockney accent. And it was there at the age of four that Pat got her first taste of audience response. At the Park Lane Hotel, where an afternoon social and entertainment was being held, her mother begged and pleaded with those in charge that her little girl be allowed to perform. She sang, she danced, and did a little recitation, as follows:

> If no one ever marries me I shan't mind very much;
> I'll buy a squirrel in a cage, and a little rabbit hutch.
> And when I'm getting really old, about twenty-eight or nine,
> I'll buy a little orphan girl, and bring her up as mine.

The applause was enthusiastic, and Pat was given vanilla ice cream, a piece of cake, and $5. That was the beginning of her career, which at first included photography modeling and one-shot theatrical appearances, some paid and some not. At the age of eight she was cast by Yolanda Langworthy in the role of Helen in "The Adventures of Helen and Mary," a radio association which for Pat was to last almost 20 years.

The Ryans lived in an aging six-story apartment house on the upper West Side of Manhattan. Mr. Ryan was a steward at the exclusive Metropolitan Club in Midtown New York. Pat had two sisters, Peggy, who was older, and June, younger. She attended Catholic grammar school and later Wadleigh High School, meanwhile being a faithful member of the St. Cecelia Choir at St. Michael's Church. Her most prized possession was a pin given to her for seven years' perfect attendance in the choir, and for general excellence.

In addition to her radio acting Pat became interested in writing, and next to the choir pin she was proudest of having had her original story "The Silver Knight" broadcast on "Let's Pretend" in 1935.

Pat had blonde hair and grey-blue eyes. To judge from childhood photographs she seems to have been rather plain, but in her teens she blossomed in poise and attractiveness, leading various feature writers to gush: "A fact to which she is happily oblivious is that she is by the way of becoming Columbia's glamour girl," and, "She is also a figuresome find for radio photographers."

There was some truth in the part about being oblivious. The dream world in which Pat lived was expressed partly in her short stories and the radio script she wrote, but also resulted in a slight reserve which no one could ever completely penetrate – even Gwen Davies, who had known Pat since they were small children. Pat was always friendly and completely honest in the showbiz world in which we were growing up, which had so much affectedness and false glamour. This honesty and sincerity, in addition to a natural talent, probably made her a better actress too. During all of her career she never had any professional training.

Once Pat began doing radio, and learned the knack (not easy) of combining a professional career with schooling, many other shows followed, including "We the People," "American School of the Air," and the running parts of Myra Lee on "Joyce Jordan, Girl Interne," Elly on "The Parker Family," and Henry Aldrich's friend Geraldine on "The Aldrich Family." As she reached maturity she was also starred in what sounds like a more-maudlin-than-most daytime serial called "Girl Alone" on the NBC network. For masochist readers, a synopsis follows: "No matter how huge a fortune a girl may have, money cannot guarantee her future against heartbreak – against the fact that many men will propose marriage just to get possession of her money, while the one man who may really love her will shy away rather than have his friends say he married his wife for her money. Patricia Ryan in "Girl Alone" faces that problem." Evidently, Pat did not face it for long, because no record shows that the show was renewed, or that it ever obtained a sponsor.

Things did get better, though. A wonderful break for Pat, indeed one of the high spots of her career, was landing the lead in "Claudia and David," the serialized radio version of Rose Franken's hit Broadway play of 1941. Publicity blurbs claimed that over 200 actresses were auditioned for the role, to play opposite Richard Kollmar. The show, sponsored by Grape Nuts Cereal, started as a summer replacement for "The Kate Smith Show" on Fridays at 8:00 P.M. Pat Ryan's naïve quality, plus a slightly breathless vocal delivery, at once ingenuous and sensuous and rather reminiscent of Margaret Sullavan, plus the complete honesty and sincerity I have mentioned, all made her ideal for the role of the child bride in a woman's body, whom her husband David, and the audience, found so appealing.

Pat's photo, in color, was on the cover of the October 1941 *Radio and Television Mirror*, and the following excerpt from the feature article, by one Adele Whitely Fletcher, though it will admittedly not shed much light on Pat Ryan's career, does provide a good example of fan magazine writing at the time.

It starts out describing gentlemen playing bridge at New York's fine Metropolitan Club, reading the evening papers, and watching the New York panorama through the large plate glass windows. The faithful steward Ryan, who has served there many years, brings a scotch and soda to a millionaire shipbuilder, then hurries to switch on the radio, and . . .

"Into that room came a girl's voice – young and breathless as dawn. Ryan straightened, and the lamplight shown full upon his silvery hair. 'That's my daughter Pat Ryan, Sir,' he said. 'She's making her debut tonight in a new program called Claudia and David.' Slowly, as these rich and powerful men listened, they realized that there were other things in this world besides Stuka bombers and vassal people and war and hatred." Adele Whitely Fletcher – where are you tonight?

Nila had for some years predicted great things for Pat, and she was delighted with her success, as she was when any of us made a splash in

some other venture. And Pat Ryan kept on turning in excellent performances every Saturday morning on "Let's Pretend."

Don Hughes

Don Hughes was one of the earliest Pretenders. Born in 1918, he was
12 years old and already a cast member of "The Adventures of Helen and
Mary" when Nila took over the show. He had an elfin face, expressive blue
eyes, and a cute grin. He was born of theatrical parents. His mother Beth
Stone was an acrobatic toe dancer in vaudeville and also in Broadway
musicals. She married her vaudeville partner Frank Hughes (Stone and
Hughes). They separated before Don was born and divorced when he was
three. As a small child he traveled with his mother on the vaudeville circuit,
then was put into Professional Children's School so that he could do his
work by correspondence when they were on the road. Being in PCS also
meant that he and his mother heard about all sorts of casting calls, which
eventually resulted in his doing Broadway plays – *The Enemy*, an antiwar
play presented by Channing Pollock in 1925, and *Mima*, done by David
Belasco, in which Don was an imp, costumed in green oilcloth.

Don took to radio easily and especially to "Let's Pretend." Acting, after
all, was fun, and Don was clever and talented. He also had a prominent role
in a radio show called "Daddy and Rollo," playing opposite Nick Dawson.
As later on "The Baby Snooks Show" starring Fanny Brice, the kid had all
the gags, and Daddy was mostly a straight man. "Daddy and Rollo" was
sponsored by La Palina Cigars, owned by William Paley's father. It was on
15 minutes, three times a week, in 1931–32. The sponsor liked the show so
much that performances were increased to six a week, then to nine. But
"Daddy and Rollo" disappeared abruptly when the writer, J. P. McAvoy,
asked for a hefty salary increase.

Don's busiest time as an actor was in early childhood. Once into
adolescence his work tapered off, and as he matured he developed a strong
antipathy to "making the rounds," as it was called, of casting directors. It
was not laziness. Over the years he and I became close friends, and from
time to time he would express the opinion that promoting oneself, in effect
saying, hey, I'm good, hire me, was somehow immoral, or at least unprin-
cipled. To be successful, said Don, an actor has to have a combination of
overweening ego and abject humility. And, to remain true to his own code
of ethics Don sometimes antagonized people in an effort to avoid at all costs
the impression that he was trying to curry favor with an eye to getting
work.

"I liked acting," Don once said, long after having retired. "I like it to
this day. I liked the companionship." Don was also a much better actor than

he would admit to himself or anyone else. Jack Grimes would observe Don's performances, especially when he was playing a lead, such as Faithful John or Rumpelstiltskin, and claimed that you could see Don begin to do a truly brilliant piece of work, then suddenly seem to say, "Oh dammit – it's showing," and pull back.

Don went on hiatus from "Let's Pretend" at about age 17, when his mother and a friend decided to open a dancing school in West Palm Beach, Florida. Don taught ballroom dancing there and helped his mother in many other ways, including cleaning the studio and keeping it free of scorpions and palmetto bugs. The venture failed, and when they returned north and settled in Elizabeth, New Jersey, Don was welcomed back on the show by Nila.

It was after Don's return from Florida that we began noticing his writing talents. A young man named Austin Beardsley, an heir to the then considerable Beardsley Codfish empire, hired a studio at Broadway and Fifty-Sixth Street and formed a group called the Young Professionals. All of us were indeed young. After a production of A. A. Milne's *Mr. Pim Passes By*, we did a revue titled *And Be Merry*, to which Don contributed music, lyrics, and several sketches. I was involved, as were Albert Aley (by then also a good friend of Don's) and Jack Kelk, among other Pretenders.

He was also good at light verse. In the summer of 1941 he composed a set of epitaphs for some of the "Let's Pretend" cast. Unfortunately, most of them are unprintable, leaving only the following as a slight example of Don Hughes's wit:

A. A.
Kind friend, A. Anderson lies here;
His life was good, though somewhat queer:
With just one interest in his heart
He didn't care for sports or art
Or business, food or drink or sex,
But only vocal sound effects.
A legend says that he was born
Making a noise like an auto horn;
And this we know: he met his end
With a sound like a steamboat 'round the bend.
D. H.
Here's what's left of poor Don Hughes
Beneath this cold, cold earth.
He knew not ballads, babes nor booze;
Hell, he was dead at birth!

Don was away from "Let's Pretend," beginning in May 1942, for over three years, serving in the Signal Corps attached to the Army Air Corps in England, France, and Belgium. As soon as he got home Nila put him right back to work playing wise counselors, talking animals, and evil dwarfs.

Don's was a complex personality. He had a brilliantly creative mind, an unusual acting talent, and a warm heart. He was able to use only a fraction of his gifts on "Let's Pretend," but Don, with his distinctive style and sometimes strident voice, was for over two decades one of the show's most important assets.

Vivian Block

Vivian came back to Nila Mack's attention in 1931 when she was about nine years old. She had already auditioned at station WOV, and after having been referred by the pianist there to Madge Tucker, at NBC, she started being called for Miss Tucker's children's show "Coast to Coast on a Bus." Meanwhile, Nila Mack discovered that Vivian was not only a good actress but had a beautiful soprano singing voice. This was especially effective when we did "Rapunzel." The prince hears the girl who is held captive by the witch in the stone tower singing (it was "Solvejg's Song" by Grieg), and is determined to rescue her. Somewhere along the line, Vivian does not remember when, she began doing less and less of the Madge Tucker show, and more and more of "Let's Pretend," becoming another permanent addition to our juvenile repertory company.

Vivian also became a busy actress on other shows, including Nila's own "Sunday Morning at Aunt Susan's," "Showboat" with Charles Winninger, one of Henry's girlfriends on "The Aldrich Family," and an early series with Bobby Jordan called "Peter and Pan in Wheatenaville." She had a running part on the CBS series "Wilderness Road," with Ray Collins, Bill Johnstone, Anne Elstner, and Jimmy Donnelly, and also found time to do baby cries on "The Life and Loves of Dr. Susan." She was one of the three Pretenders in the world premiere of Aaron Copland's opera *Second Hurricane*. Meanwhile, she graduated from the Professional Children's School and kept up her musical studies as well.

American family life was different in the 1930s. If you were young and had a job you automatically brought your salary home to your parents. At one time Vivian made over $300 a week – a considerable sum at that time. And so she was surprised, but not at all resentful, when she found that it had all gone into her father's business. Vivian once put her head on her mother's lap and cried during the period when the work wasn't coming, and she could not bring home as much as she had been making.

There was a solution, though, and it wasn't in radio. At the age of 17 Vivian came to the attention of a Mrs. Kelly, who was the proprietor of an exclusive gentleman's private club, in a brownstone on East Sixty-Fifth

Street. The membership consisted entirely of wealthy male business executives. Delicious gourmet meals were served in softly lit, luxurious surroundings. The place was immaculate. For musical entertainment there was a pianist and two singers – Vivian and another girl – on Saturday nights. Their repertoire ranged from jazz and pop to classical and operetta. They would also do requests, and the members would tip generously. Vivian remembers returning home from work one night, making her mother spread out her apron, and filling it with ten-dollar gold pieces, ten-dollar bills, and a few twenties.

There were also at least three other attractive young women always on duty at the club – a blonde, a brunette, and a redhead. They would talk, eat, and drink with the members, and sometimes leave with them. Indeed, these gentlemen would often book suites at the Plaza Hotel for mutual entertainment. Vivian describes Mrs. Kelly as "a real pro." The working conditions were pleasant, and nobody ever bothered her for any reason other than to request another song. The club could not be described as anything but high class – but one would have to admit that in certain respects it was far removed from the Land of Let's Pretend.

Vivian Block was the first of the Pretenders to marry. In 1942 she chose Dr. Irving Marsh, a dentist whose practice was in Bridgeport, Connecticut. She continued to commute to New York to do the show as long as possible, until she was six months pregnant, which was by then very obvious.

Jackson Wheeler, our CBS announcer assigned at the time, was rather too smarmy for my taste. During the warmup for the studio audience he would introduce everyone on the program, finishing up with, "And there in the control room is our director, Nila Mack. . . . She's a schweet-heart!" On the occasion of Vivian's last broadcast before becoming a mother, he apparently felt like indulging in a bit of wit. As the cast entered, including Vivian, who was having some difficulty mounting the stairs onto the platform stage, Jackson said delightedly: "And here come the kiddies now!" I am sure Nila could have killed him.

Although family had taken precedence over career for Vivian, she retained a strong sentimental attachment to "Let's Pretend" and its director. When she and her husband built their new house, they had it designed with a round stone tower in classic fairy-tale style, or at least as close to that as you could get on the suburban streets of Bridgeport.

When Vivian Block Marsh returned to "Let's Pretend" on July 8, 1944, for a farewell performance before retiring from the show permanently, she once again did her favorite (singing) role of Rapunzel. Her husband was there, and after the broadcast they introduced the Pretenders to their little one-year-old daughter, Nila.

Vivian Block's "Let's Pretend" castle. Photo by the author.

Albert Aley

Albert, born in 1919, joined "Let's Pretend" at the age of 13, in 1932. His father was Spanish, his mother Swiss. His parents had owned their own photography studio, but lost it in the Depression, and they went to work for another photographer. Their little boy Albert was a handsome child with a sensitive face, and light brown hair which always seemed to end in a cowlick at the top.

Albert's first ambition had been to be an athlete, but rheumatic fever in his childhood caused a heart murmur, so he started doing photographic

Albert Aley, child model, age 12, ca. 1931.

modeling, first for his father's employer then for others, and his income helped pay family expenses, plus his tuition at the Professional Children's School. The principal, Mrs. Ethel Nesbitt, helped him write a letter to Miss Mack saying why he would like to be on "Let's Pretend," which so impressed her that she called him for an audition.

Albert was not a character actor, and did not "do voices." He always sounded like Albert Aley, and on our show he was most often cast as either the handsome prince, or the youngest son who goes out into the world to seek his fortune. These so-called straight emotional parts in our tales of fantasy and adventure could have been ridiculous, but Albert played them with complete honesty and sincerity. Nila used him as one of the two children (the other was Vivian Block) on her "Sunday Morning at Aunt Susan's," and on the Thursday "Tales from Far and Near" segment of "The American School of the Air." Later he auditioned successfully for Frances von Bernhardi at Air Features, producers of many of radio's daytime serials, and landed the role of Bob James on the long-running "Stella Dallas."

As Albert grew into his teens he became rather lanky and bony, and stayed that way until old age. He certainly did not have a "leading man" face or body, but that did not matter on radio, which as far as acting was concerned was Albert's medium for his entire career. His voice was most sympathetic, with attractive "lows." Nila knew that she could depend on him to carry an entire show. She also noticed that as he matured, many letters in feminine handwriting arrived asking for his picture.

By 1937, before he was 18, he was helping Miss Mack in the office, reading fan mail, and making calls to the other actors for the coming Saturday broadcast. When Albert would give Jack Grimes his "Pretend" call at home he at first mistook him for his mother and addressed him as "Mrs. Grimes." Jack hated this. He was seven years younger than Albert, and his voice hadn't changed yet. He eventually forgave him, and it became a standing joke between them.

Albert was one of our most precocious Pretenders. In 1938 he was billed as "Radio's Youngest Director" when at age 19 he directed our broadcast of "Babes in the Wood" while Nila was on her annual vacation. His writing talents were starting to bud too. An April 1938 article in the *Jersey Journal* said that he had had scripts produced on radio, and that another would be done soon on New York's station WNEW. His most important early credit was when a script he submitted was broadcast coast to coast on "The First Nighter." When he was 21 he had his only stage experience in the Young Professionals with Don Hughes, myself, and other Pretenders, and Albert directed several of their productions.

Albert's important writing, directing, and producing accomplishments were still in the future, but for the time being, though cast sizes varied and Nila could not use all of her "regulars" every week, I cannot remember a broadcast on which he did not appear. The roles he played, though never spectacular or flashy, were an essential part of the believability of our program.

Michael O'Day

"Junior" was a popular nickname for little boys in the 1930s, and Michael D'Addario, born in 1920, adopted Junior O'Day as his professional name when he did his first acting at the age of 12 in films made in Fort Lee, New Jersey. The D'Addarios lived in Bloomfield. His father was a supervisor with the Prudential Insurance Company. He changed his name to Mickey as he got older, then finally back to Michael as an adult. By whatever name, he was one of the most versatile and talented actors we on "Let's Pretend" had ever encountered.

He may have inherited some of his talent from an aunt who had been in silent pictures, and from a great-uncle who it was said had been a Shakespearean actor and a Jesuit priest – an intriguing combination.

Bloomfield was not that far from New York and the radio studios, and Mickey soon became busy in all of them. He joined "Let's Pretend" in 1933. One of the earliest of his other shows was the lead in "Robinson Crusoe Jr.," on CBS in 1934. He was soon a regular on Madge Tucker's NBC children's hour known as "The Lady Next Door," which later became "Coast to Coast on a Bus." Like "Let's Pretend," that show called for his versatility in character voices. But he was just as clever at playing the mostly stereotyped children's parts on radio we all played: the mean kid, the spunky kid, the sensitive kid, the crying kid, not to mention the foreign or regional kid (he was good at dialects too).

As network radio grew, and Mickey's reputation with it, he began to do important nighttime shows – early comedy programs with Bob Hope, Al Jolson, and Fred Allen. When he was 16 he began a long run as Ruth Wayne's little brother Neddie on "Big Sister," one of the most durable of the daytime serials. It lasted from 1936 through 1952, with Mickey on most of that time. He outlasted five leading ladies (Alice Frost, Nancy Marshall, Marjorie Anderson, Mercedes McCambridge, and Grace Matthews) and two sponsors (first Rinso, made by Lever Brothers, then various products made by their competitor, Proctor & Gamble.) And for years he was the newsboy who opened "Big Town" with: "Get yer Illustrated Press." To give more of Mickey O'Day's credits would be simply to reel off a list of most of the important dramatic shows on radio.

Nila often cast Mickey and myself in the same parts in successive broadcasts of the same story. But one part Mickey retained over all the years that we performed it was Santa Claus in her original script "The Night Before Christmas." When Mickey played this part, you could sense the warmth and love the old man exuded, and you could almost see his fat belly. Nila did experiment with the casting of Santa on one occasion, during our pre–Cream of Wheat days. She had Burl Ives play it instead. (This was before Ives had become a star, so there was no problem with our budget.) But it did not work out. Though even in his thirties Ives did look like Santa Claus, this was no help in radio. His voice at that time was rather high, and his acting experience limited. At about the same time – no one knows for sure, but we can assume it was before 1937 – Nila was approached by Orson

Welles, who also wanted to play Santa Claus. Orson had not yet become a director, and was still a very busy radio actor. Nila told Orson she was sorry, but that "Let's Pretend" only used children in its cast. The mind truly boggles trying to visualize Welles's overpowering presence in our rather low-key, charming Christmas story – not to mention what it would have been like if he had ever become a regular "Let's Pretend" cast member. In any case, as long as we remained on the air after the Burl Ives experiment, Santa Claus belonged to Mickey.

His career had only one drawback, and that was his height. All the D'Addarios were short people, and Mickey never grew to be more than 4 feet 6 inches. He was neither a dwarf nor a midget. His body was perfectly formed. Special shoes partly compensated, and his suits were custom-made. He had good Italian features – black hair, dark eyes, and heavy eyebrows. He was always impeccably groomed, and I hardly ever saw him remove his jacket, even on the hottest days. Furthermore, he was always good-natured, though his life surely could not have always been easy. One positive thing he must have realized, however, as he reached adulthood and the show headed into its long-term sponsorship by Cream of Wheat: there would always be a place for him on radio and on "Let's Pretend," as long as both of them existed.

Miriam Wolfe

Miriam was born in Brooklyn in 1922. She did her first radio performance at age four, on "The Uncle Gee Bee Kiddie Hour" on station WGBS (the call letters stood for its owner, Gimbel Brothers' Store). Almost from childhood she played older parts on radio. "I never had a child's voice," she says. Before she reached her teens she was playing ingenues and leading women on "Five Star Final" on station WMCA, and doubling as the newsboy signature of the show.

Nila, when Miriam was introduced to her, asked if she could play witches. Miss Mack had decided it was time to replace Ethel Blume and Amy Sydell, who had both reached the advanced age of 16. She was also looking for someone to play the Voice in the Wind in "Beauty and the Beast," which she herself had always done previously. As for witches, the answer was definitely yes. Miriam had already played Hecate in a Hecksher Foundation production of *Macbeth*, with an otherwise adult cast. And so in 1934 she became a Let's Pretender.

Her best-known witch role in radio, besides the many she played on "Let's Pretend" over the years, was Old Nancy on "The Witch's Tale" on the Mutual Network. This show was written, produced, and directed by Alonzo Dean Cole. The original Nancy, Adelaide Fitz-Allen, had died at age

80, and apparently her replacement was not working out. In 1934 Miriam went to audition for Cole in the WOR studios at 1440 Broadway at midnight, after one of his broadcasts was over.

Cole thought it a great joke when he first saw her – a 12-year-old girl with a straw hat and Buster Brown haircut, carrying her school bag. But when he heard the aged, toothless vocal delivery, and the spine-chilling, cackling laugh she produced, his mouth fell open. Miriam was hired. The fee was $10 a broadcast, for which she not only played Old Nancy in the prologue and epilogue, but also doubled in other character and leading woman parts in the story.

Meanwhile, Miriam was becoming an attractive teenager, and like many performers on radio, her looks gave no hint of her vocal talents. Besides the Alonzo Dean Cole episode, there were many other instances in later years in which people, especially casting directors, expected her voice to match her appearance. The most embarrassing (not for Miriam but for the director) happened on "Popeye," a new radio version of the well-known comic strip. The director, Walter Craig, who had never met Miriam but knew of her reputation for doing older voices, cast her as the Sea Hag. Miriam and the rest of the cast gathered in the studio at the appointed time, but the rehearsal did not begin. The director fidgeted, fumed, lit cigarettes, and paced, then finally, exasperated, announced, "I'm sorry, ladies and gentlemen. As soon as that bitch Miriam Wolfe arrives, we'll start." "But I'm here!" said Miriam. Once that misunderstanding was ironed out she became a regular on the show, also doubling as Olive Oyl.

She had a four-year run on "The Witch's Tale" until it went off the air. Her other radio work at that time included weekly stints on "The Bob and Ray Show," and daytime serials such as "Portia Faces Life," and "Aunt Jenny's Real Life Stories."

Miriam, after Albert Aley, was the next of the Pretenders to branch out into work other than acting, producing and directing dramatic shows for New York City's municipal station WNYC in 1940, when she was 18. Then, recommended by the CBS casting director Marge Morrow, she went to Buffalo to play the lead in a new network serial that would originate there, "I'll Find My Way." Her salary at Station WGR/WKBW was $50 a week. A year later she had become an actress-DJ-producer-writer there, all for the same $50. Meanwhile, as she had promised Miss Mack, Miriam returned weekly as needed to perform on "Let's Pretend."

Back in New York in 1942, she landed a job on the staff of the Office of War Information, assigning studios and directing overseas multilingual broadcasts. Meanwhile, Miriam continued as a successful radio actress, and a permanent member of the cast of "Let's Pretend."

Miriam Wolfe as Old Nancy on "The Witch's Tale," age 13, ca. 1935.

Daisy Aldan

Theatre was the subject Daisy heard at home on East Ninety-First Street from infancy. Her father was in the costuming business. Her mother Estelle Edel was an actress in silent films and in the then very active Yiddish theatres in New York. Together with Daisy's two uncles she organized the Yiddishe Folksbiene, which still exists. So it was only natural that by age ten Daisy was doing imitations of Maurice Chevalier in amateur programs at local movie theatres, and tap dancing on roller skates. She was also writing letters to radio directors asking for auditions. One of them was Nila Mack.

Nila thought Daisy's audition was excellent. There was just one problem. Her voice was too similar to that of Miriam Wolfe, who was already on the show. Miriam and Daisy were good friends, having worked together in a huge pageant done at Madison Square Garden called "The Romance of a People." And so when a year after the audition Daisy had not been called for the show, Miriam went to Miss Mack and said, "Don't call me for a while—use Daisy." As a result, Nila did call Daisy, and from then on had increased respect for Miriam for her unselfish gesture. Eventually, she found that there were enough witches, mothers, stepsisters, and enchanted talking animal roles for both of them, and Daisy became a regular on our program in 1934.

The problem of the vocal similarity disappeared as Daisy grew into her teens and developed a drier, more clipped vocal pattern, while Miriam's voice became more resonant and her speech pattern more legato. Like Miriam, Daisy had an air of maturity beyond her real age, and though she had a secret yen at times to play the beautiful princess roles on "Let's Pretend," that ambition was never realized. Nila found Daisy had become much too valuable as quaint old ladies and mysterious voices.

As her mother was too busy in her own acting career to be a stage mother, Daisy did her own promotion. As a small child she appeared at the Heckscher Children's Theatre. She did monologues at union halls for $5 a performance. She became involved in school dramatics, first at Public School 151 in Manhattan, later at Herman Ritter Junior High School when the family moved to the Bronx. She would act, for pay or no pay, wherever there was a stage and an audience. Daisy was hopelessly stage-struck.

In addition to "Let's Pretend," her other radio shows included "The Columbia Workshop," "Big Sister," and "American School of the Air"; but except for our show, radio was not as important to Daisy as it was to the rest of us. Some of her great energy was going in a quite different direction. She had started writing poetry at the age of five, and her first published poem, "In the Dark Hour," appeared in Chicago's magazine *Poetry* when she was 12. At Hunter College she became poetry editor of *Echo*, the school's literary magazine.

Daisy had always been precocious, graduating from high school before she was 15. This caused a brief problem when she began to attend Hunter College in bobby socks and with her hair in ribbons. The dean sent for her and said, "You are now a college woman, and you must wear stockings, a hat and gloves."

In 1943, as "Let's Pretend" acquired a sponsor and was about to enter its tenth year under that name, Daisy was already a veteran of nine of them, and long ago had been established as an important member of our now no longer juvenile repertory company.

In a traditional stock or repertory company, which today no longer exists in our theatre, the actors were hired according to the guidelines provided by the plays they would be doing: leading man, leading lady, second leads (male and female), juvenile, ingenue, character man, and character woman. "Let's Pretend" was a radio repertory company, but in the sometimes fantastical stories we did these categories did not always fit.

Who would Nila Mack cast for a talking horse, for instance? Or a messenger bee? Or the West Wind? With the eight child actors just mentioned, plus many more who will be introduced later, she developed a company of players who could handle any of these roles and many others, as we gained experience and became more and more versatile. Without the instant hit or flop pressures which exist today in network television and in the theatre, Nila Mack was free to experiment with casting, as she expanded, developed, and improved the "Let's Pretend" company.

Chapter 3

The Scripts

Although Nila Mack was convinced that her dramatizations of the classic fairy tales would be an improvement over Yolanda Langworthy's scripts, she could not instantly create a whole new story repertoire out of thin air, and felt that for the time being she had to live with Langworthy's material – a year's worth – which could be repeated, with improvements she hoped, by herself. Luckily, we have Nila's own log of most of the scripts, and their broadcast dates, from the beginning of her presence with the show through 1950, and I am counting those titles which Langworthy probably wrote as Nila's, because she did from slight to extensive rewrites on every one of them.

For "Sinbad the Sailor," her first broadcast, a laconic margin notation reads "First script, yet." The second broadcast was "Gulnare of the Sea," and was the last one to use an all-adult cast. There is no record of the story on the third show, her first with an all-juvenile cast, but we know that at least into October 1930 all of the "Helen and Mary" scripts were drawn from *The Arabian Nights*, and several were broadcast in two parts.

There was a special Christmas broadcast Nila logged as "Christmas Story – Portrait – Sick Girl," which could have been either an original by herself or adapted from her predecessor. It was done on the show during the following two Christmas seasons, and afterward was never heard of again.

It was not until early in 1931 that Nila Mack hit her stride as a writer of radio fairy-tale scripts. Her friend Dorothy Stickney had given her the book of *Grimm's Fairy Tales* which she had had as a child, and before the new year was a month old Nila had started to phase in her own adaptations from the works of not only Grimm but also, among others, Andrew Lang, Charles Perrault, and Hans Christian Andersen. She also turned out an original story in time for St. Patrick's Day, "The Leprechaun," which was charming and touching, and it was repeated every year afterward for the entire life of the program. Before 1931 was half over, the stories from *The Arabian Nights* were now only less than six among what was now a rich mixture of fairy tales from many sources, and all of them now had Nila Mack's special touch.

The period setting of most of the "Let's Pretend" scripts was from medieval times up to the eighteenth century, because most of the folk tales upon which they were based had originated then. The language used was present-day, but never slang. People were always courtly and respectful when addressing royalty. When characters spoke roughly or threateningly, you "knew" they were up to no good.

People in our stories traveled on horseback, or in carriages if they were royalty or of the nobility. People who were poor but honest lived in humble cottages. There were noble kings (and an occasional evil one) and gallant knights. There were beautiful ladies who wore fine gowns. There were ancient magicians in long robes, who had grey beards. There were fierce giants. There were scheming dwarfs. And very often there were wicked witches who would point their skinny fingers (obligatory: you never heard of a fat witch, did you?) at beautiful princesses and cast terrible spells upon them.

The colorful aura of the historical period in which the stories took place, plus the nature of these tales of magic and fantasy were both ideally suited to what came to be called the "Theatre of the Imagination" – dramatic radio.

One reason parents were pleased that their children enjoyed "Let's Pretend" was its high moral tone. However, the stories were never "throwing goodness at you," as Alfred P. Doolittle put it. It just happened that way. The good people, whether royalty or paupers, were completely and uncompromisingly good. And villains were completely evil, and so had to be and indeed were either punished or in some way eliminated by the time each program ended. There was a moral lesson to be learned in each of our stories, even the light comedies, but it always came out naturally and in the context of the plot, and it did not detract from the excitement and adventure.

I do not believe Nila set out primarily to teach and uplift her young audiences. She was savvy enough to know that if you're going to do that, you have to entertain them first. Though we in the cast never heard her express any denominational preference, the religious atmosphere in the Arkansas City of her childhood was strictly fundamentalist. Her own family were Christian Scientists. Certainly, the locomotive engineer's house at 306 South C Street was a place where there was not only order but love, and Nila, though she once said that she did not "buy" all of the fundamentalist values, obviously had developed her own set of religious and moral convictions. This could be seen in her scripts.

Why, we even mentioned God on "Let's Pretend" – imagine that. In "Childe Roland to the Dark Tower Came," Roland with his magic sword Excalibur faces the evil King of Elfland:

KING: Who dares to enter the tower without my permission?
ROLAND: I do, you monster. Release my sister.
KING: Oh, no! She belongs to me.
ROLAND: She belongs only to her God. Release her!!

And, of course, the King does, with Excalibur at his throat. In another story, "The Nuremberg Stove," the little boy August hides inside his beloved Hirschvogel, the beautifully enameled German stove, because he cannot bear to part with it when it is sold by his poverty-stricken father. During a long journey inside the stove, the child falls asleep. When its door is opened, he stumbles out and sees that it is the king of Bavaria who has purchased it. The child kneels before royalty. "Rise, my child," says the kindly king. "Kneel only to your God."

Not that the deity was dragged into "Let's Pretend" scripts. Nila was not a moralist – she was just a good radio writer. If such mentions were included in a national network program today, would their headquarters be picketed by atheist organizations demanding equal time?

In dramatizing "Let's Pretend" for radio, Nila Mack had a rich heritage to draw upon. These folk tales from many countries – mostly European – had been handed down for many generations. Most of them, luckily for Nila and for CBS, were in the public domain, meaning that no royalties had to be paid.

The earliest chronologically were *The Tales from the Arabian Nights*, otherwise known as *The Thousand and One Nights*, authors unknown, but considered classics in world literature. They were thought to have originated in Persia. The first European edition was printed in 1704. The best known, "Ali Baba and the Forty Thieves," "Bluebeard," "Aladdin and the Wonderful Lamp," and "Sinbad the Sailor" were all included in our repertoire.

Charles Perrault (1628–1703), a French poet, adapted and retold eight traditional stories, including "Bluebeard," "Sleeping Beauty," "Cinderella," "Puss in Boots" (originally called "The Master Cat"), "Beauty and the Beast," "Hop o' My Thumb," and "Little Red Riding Hood." According to Nila's notes, this last we did as a vaudeville show – an example of how experimental you could be when so much of radio was sustaining.

Jakob Grimm (1785–1863), a German philologist and folklorist, came next. He and his brother Wilhelm collected and rewrote a great number and variety of folk tales, published between 1812 and 1815 as the celebrated *Grimm's Fairy Tales*.

Jakob also published a German grammar and a work on German mythology, and the brothers Grimm together produced a 16-volume dictionary, which, though it must have been a monumental work of scholarship, is today all but forgotten, while their fairy tales have become lasting classics.

Hans Christian Andersen (Danish, 1805–75) was a prolific writer of children's stories. From his works we used "The Emperor's New Clothes," "The Flying Trunk," "The Little Mermaid," and "The Tinderbox."

Richard von Volkmann (1830–89), born in Leipzig, Germany, became a surgeon, and wrote scholarly medical treatises on his earliest interest, anesthesia. Forced to wait outside Paris for five months during the siege of that city in the Franco-Prussian War (1870–71), he began to write fairy tales, which he mailed home to his wife a page at a time. They were published later under his pen name of Richard Leander. Those we used on "Let's Pretend" included "The Rusted Knight," "The Invisible Kingdom," and "The Queen Who Couldn't Make Spice Nuts."

Andrew Lang (1844–1912), an English scholar and man of letters was born in Scotland. He was a poet, interested in myth and folklore, and known for his prose translations of Homer's *Iliad* and *Odyssey*. But he is remembered now mostly for his many translations and adaptations of children's stories, done with his wife Leonora Blanche Lang. *The Blue Fairy Book* was published in 1899, and after that came *The Red Fairy Book*, *The Yellow Fairy Book*, and several others. Some of the tales were from the same sources used by the Brothers Grimm and by Perrault, but most were from sources not touched by those authors.

"Let's Pretend" also broadcast some scripts by living authors, and from unexpected sources. The first was our own Patricia Ryan, who at the age of 12 authored a radio play called "The Silver Knight," a well-written adventure story, done on our program April 27, 1935. A 7-year-old girl named Jean Barhydt, of New Hartford, Connecticut, sent in her story, "The Little Black Pot." Its length was 150 words, and it involved a dispute between a little girl and a witch over the ownership of the pot. It was a charming story, and the CBS publicity department made the most of it. The broadcast, on May 15, 1937, was filmed by Paramount News.

Flora Spiegelberg, an 80-year-old great-grandmother, was the author of three stories done on our program, "Princess Goldenhair and the Wonderful Flower," "The Flower Queen's Daughter," and "The Enchanted Toystore of Fairyland." For the broadcast of the second part of that story Grandma Spiegelberg, as she called herself, brought along from Connecticut representatives of four generations of her family.

Nila Mack wrote and adapted no less than 133 stories for the program, though several CBS press releases have blown the total up to 200.

Some of the most popular and well-known stories we did every year, or more often. These included "Beauty and the Beast," "Cinderella," "Hansel and Gretel," "Jack and the Beanstalk," "Puss in Boots," "Rumpelstiltskin," "Snow Drop and the Seven Dwarfs" (the original title, which Nila always insisted upon using), and "Sleeping Beauty."

Certain stories, all originals by Nila, were repeated at the same times every year. These included "The Night Before Christmas," always broadcast on the Saturday nearest to Christmas. In dramatizing the beloved Clement C. Moore poem, she integrated a subplot telling how the Mouse family, which lives inside the wall right next to a beautiful Christmas tree, is getting ready to celebrate the holiday in its own way. The very next week we always did another Nila Mack original, "The House of the World," an allegorical story in which a Little Child meets Good Will, and together they topple the four terrible walls of Selfishness, Greed, Poverty, and Intolerance.

Near St. Patrick's Day we would always do another of Nila's original works, "The Leprechaun," the story of Paudeen, the lad who thinks that if only he can catch the wily Leprechaun, the fairies' shoemaker, he will get his wish to have his homely face and twisted back made whole, and win the love of the fair lass Eileen.

Our annual Halloween observance was always "Fairer Than a Fairy," in which the witch Lagrima, in a jealous rage, lays a curse on the little princess, because her parents have dared to name her Fairer Than a Fairy. She also has to put up with an annoyingly fun-loving Assistant Fairy (always Gwen Davies) who is constantly fouling up the witch's orders to put curses on mortals.

For a number of years, beginning in 1942, we would always present the classic story "The Little Lame Prince," as a tie-in with the annual March of Dimes President's Birthday Ball polio fund drive. In Nila's dramatization the little Prince (always played by Kingsley Colton) has ruled wisely as king for 60 years, but now it is time for him to fly to the Beautiful Mountains, leaving his faithful aging Councillor in charge, and the Councillor now speaks to the people in the voice of President Franklin D. Roosevelt, who himself had been crippled by polio for years. It was done by Bill Adams (first hired for this before he was Uncle Bill), chosen by Nila Mack because of the faultless imitations of FDR he had done so many times in the dramatized news stories on "The March of Time." Special permission was granted by Stephen Early, Roosevelt's press secretary, with the proviso that the actor's name must be mentioned. It would have been highly unsuitable and confusing for people to think that the president of the United States was on "Let's Pretend." On a later broadcast of "The Little Lame Prince" Bill Adams was unavailable, and the voice was done by Art Carney, which is why he appears in Appendix B as a Let's Pretender.

One of Nila's best original stories, "The Castle of Hatred," was written in 1935 in response to a listener's letter protesting that stepmothers in fairy tales were always mean, and usually turned out to be witches. In Nila's script a father confesses to his children that he is lonely after the death of his wife, and would like to remarry. The children are very much against this. They've heard what stepmothers can be. Their only friend is a lovely neighbor lady who helps them and their father in many ways. It is only after they have learned to love her that their father reveals that he has married her, and she is indeed their stepmother.

Being limited only by the pattern of doing special stories appropriate to the season, Nila was otherwise completely free to choose whatever script she wished for each broadcast. And if there was a scary tale one week, or one of the few "Let's Pretend" stories which did not have a completely happy ending, such as "The Little Mermaid" or "The Juniper Tree" you might be sure that the following week the story would be light-hearted, or even a wacky comedy such as "The Flying Trunk," or "The Queen Who Couldn't Make Spice Nuts."

Since we now have a generation, already adults, which often has not been exposed to children's fairy tales (except in their modernized, sometimes overwhelming Disney versions), a little more explanation of what these tales were like—at least on our radio program—might be appropriate. To illustrate the kind of atmosphere which was created every Saturday morning on the Columbia network, here is a synopsis of one story, "Beauty and the Beast" as it was done on our show.

For the nine years of our Cream of Wheat sponsorship and until our last broadcast, the story opened with narration by the warm, friendly voice of Bill Adams.

> UNCLE BILL: Once upon a time, there was a rich shipowner, who had two daughters...

The spell was cast. Whether Mom was drying the dishes or the kids were playing in their rooms or outside, they would all get closer to the radio.

In the dialogue we learn that the father, who had lost most of his fortune, is off to the seaport where, he has heard, his last remaining ship has been sighted. If he regains some of his wealth he promises to bring back a gift for each daughter when he returns. Ethelinda, the eldest, rattles off a list of jewels and perfumes, while his youngest daughter Beauty asks only for her father's safe return—and one perfect rose. "Traveling on horseback" music, followed by sounds of seagulls and many voices, telling us that we are now at a busy seaport. An old codger (usually played by me) tells the father that the ship's dishonest crew have already sold the vessel and divided up the cargo.

Shaken with the bad news, the father starts home, but is overtaken by darkness, and a fierce storm (rain, thunder, horse's hooves, and whinny of the frightened horse). He glimpses lights from the tower of a castle. A mysterious butler conducts him into a beautiful moonlit garden, where the storm has magically disappeared (bird sounds).

After a sumptuous meal and a refreshing sleep, the father asks to thank his host, but is told by the butler, "My master sees no one." As he leaves the castle through the beautiful garden, he remembers Beauty's request, and picks a rose. A fearsome roar is heard, and a horrible Beast appears (you, the listener, could, of course, make that Beast look any way you wanted – tusks, matted fur, yellow eyes, or whatever). The Beast will kill the father for picking the rose, unless he goes home and returns with one of his daughters. The father is borne home on the wings of the wind (wind sound, transition music).

Beauty, to spare her father's life, insists on returning with him to the Beast's castle. She agrees to stay, and the Beast promises that no harm will come to her. After a tearful farewell, the Beast turns a ring on his finger, and the father is magically whisked back to his home. "It's almost as if he were really kind, for all his fearsome looks," says Beauty when she is alone. "I'm not as frightened as I thought."

As beauty sleeps that night, she has a strange dream (Mysterioso music, clock strikes):

> *VOICE*: Beauty ... Beauty.
> *BEAUTY*: Who are you? Where are you? I see nothing but the moon.
> *VOICE*: I am in the moonlight. I am in the mists and the wind. I am in the perfume of all flowers, but you cannot see me.
> *BEAUTY*: What would you have of me?
> *VOICE*: Do not be misled by appearances. Do not judge by what you see on the surface. Be true to your heart. Be gentle. Don't be afraid.

(When Nila Mack first dramatized the story in 1931 she played the Voice in the Wind herself, but was glad to relinquish the part when Miriam Wolfe joined the cast. Miriam, even at age 12, had the maturity to do it, and as long as she was in New York no other actress played it from then on.)

After a year alone, with no one but her maid Clotilde and occasional visits from the Beast, Beauty is terribly lonely and asks to go home for a visit. The Beast reluctantly agrees, but warns her that if she does not return by the dark of the moon it will be too late. At home, Beauty is awakened one night by the same mysterious Voice, which warns her:

> *VOICE*: (Mysterioso music behind) The moon is on the wane. The Beast is dying.

Beauty is taken on the wings of the wind to the castle. She now realizes that in spite of his fearsome appearance, she has come to be very fond of the Beast.

She finds him in the garden, half dead. With a gasping breath, he asks,

"Beauty . . . will you . . . marry me?" "Yes, dear Beast," replies Beauty. "I will marry you whenever you wish." "Oh, my dear!" And in an instant the horrible Beast is changed into a handsome Prince (sound of a small mouth siren, which Nila called a "whiz bang," used on "Let's Pretend" for all instantaneous magic transformations). The Voice now appears in human form as a beautiful Fairy Godmother, and explains that the Prince was the Beast, and had been placed under a wicked witch's spell, which could only be broken by a maiden who would truly love him for himself, in spite of his outward form. "Bless you both," says the Godmother, "and may you live happily ever after" (a few notes of triumphal wedding music, which segues into the "Let's Pretend" theme playoff).

This synopsis might make the story seem terribly amusing and naïve, but on the actual broadcasts it worked for 23 years. Children were moved and excited, as were their parents (and, incidentally, "Let's Pretend," though supposedly a children's program, had a loyal adult following). Synopsizing all of our stories would probably not serve any useful purpose, but their titles, listed in Appendix C, will give the reader an idea of the richness and variety of our "Let's Pretend" repertoire.

In a chapter from *Off Mike – Radio Writing by the Nation's Top Writers* (Jerome Lawrence, editor) Nila Mack herself tells how she writes for children: "I don't! When I write it's for people of all ages who enjoy fun and fantasy. No picture comes to mind of pigtails, tow-heads and hair ribbons, but rather the whole family listening and each one finding something in the story for his own personal enjoyment." She went on to say that clarity was uppermost in her mind. The listener must be informed either in dialogue or in narration where the scene was taking place, the identity of the people in it, and their relationship to each other. And in radio she learned the value of simplicity – in the action and in the words.

For fantasy, which had become her specialty, she found out how valuable sound effects could be, to help tell the story in ways that dialogue alone could not, though she resisted the temptation to add sounds just for their own sake. Our director once said, "I am not of the school who feels there is great drama in 'footsteps are heard.'" (Her CBS colleague, director Earle McGill, once wrote that there were so many unnecessary footstep sounds in radio that you'd think no American home could afford a carpet.) She took care not to let the sounds become overwhelming, and gave extra clues in the dialogue so that there would be no doubt as to what we were hearing. "If the scene demands a crackling fire in the fireplace," she wrote, "the cellophane sequence isn't quite enough for me.* I quickly throw another log on with the first line of the scene."

---

*For a fire sound effect, cellophane or other stiff plastic wrap or paper being slowly crushed still sounds very convincing on the microphone.

Good radio writing can form just as clear a picture in the listener's mind as if he were witnessing the event. As Bill Adams once said in an interview, "Your imagination was part of the cast." It brings to mind the little seven-year-old boy who was asked which he liked better – plays on the radio or on television (that was when both were still available). "On the radio," he said. When asked why, he replied, "Because I can see the pictures better." On television, of course, everything is supplied, and there is only one way a viewer can look at it. Perhaps that is what Fred Allen was thinking of when he defined that medium as "the chewing gum of the mind."

Miss Mack had two problems in transforming fairy tales into playable radio scripts. First, the original stories were often bare scenarios. There was plenty of action, but the people in them had almost no individual characteristics. Second, they were written in rather stilted, archaic language. The Brothers Grimm, by the way, said that they did not write their stories for children in the first place. They were merely compilations of old folk tales from many sources, and some were full of violence and highly unsuitable for young people. For instance, in one there appeared a witch who had made a fence around her house from the bones of her former lovers. (No – we didn't do that one on "Let's Pretend.")

A good example of the technique which Nila learned by doing it was the script for "Rumpelstiltskin," barely four pages long in the original Grimm version. The characters are as follows: the miller, who to make himself look important, tells the King that his daughter can spin flax into gold. There is the King, who is avaricious, and jumps at the chance – the royal treasury is rather low. The poor, unfortunate girl Winifred, threatened with death if she does not spin the gold before morning, appeals to Rumpelstiltskin, the little man who magically appears, and he agrees to do it in exchange for her necklace. Pleased with the gold, the King orders the girl to spin a second time, also on pain of death. This time Rumpelstiltskin demands her ring. The King and the girl are married, and after a year, insolvency rears its head again, and the King makes the request a third time. (It is remarkable how in almost all fairy stories things comes in threes – three beautiful daughters, three wishes, or three impossible tasks for the hero to perform.)

This time the little imp demands the queen's first-born child, and tells her that her only chance to keep the baby is that she guess his name in three days' time. The fourth character in the original story is the messenger whom the desperate girl sends to try to find unusual names. Through a lucky chance the messenger happens upon the little man dancing around a fire in the forest, gleefully cackling that his name is Rumpelstiltskin. Happy ending. Period.

To open up the story for radio, Nila invented extra scenes, and gave the characters more human dimensions. First, the miller, with a few snide remarks to his daughter, is established as a less than caring father before he disappears from the story. The King, more importantly, loses his menace and becomes a cheerful, lovable bumbler, impossibly absentminded, who can't even remember the name of his own kingdom (it was Yaltoria). There are the many giggling maidens who assemble for the King to pick a wife (a new scene created by Nila). There is the patient Councillor ("No, Sire, you haven't grown a beard overnight. That's not the mirror you're holding – it's your hairbrush.") There is the girl herself, who is terrified but courageous. Then there is the baby's nurse, who sends out not one, but two messengers to scour the kingdom for names – two, so that they can have dialogue together in the exciting scene in which they discover Rumpelstiltskin's name, then race on horseback to beat the midnight deadline to save the queen's child. There was now a full cast of characters to interact with each other, and plenty of excitement, adventure, and suspense, with a little comedy thrown in. Nila gave her script a short coda at the end, after the evil elf has angrily stamped a hole in the floor and disappeared, no doubt to oblivion. It went thus:

> KING: (*Fade on*) What's happened here? What's wrong, Winifred?
> WINIFRED: Oh my husband, we had a caller, and he was so angry when he found you were not at home that he stamped on the floor until it collapsed and he disappeared into the earth.
> KING: Who was it?
> WINIFRED: His name was – Rumpelstiltskin.
> KING: Rumpel ... Oh, it's just as well. I never could have remembered it anyhow.
>
> (*Music playoff.*)

Chapter 4

"Helen and Mary" Becomes "Let's Pretend"

As Nila Mack began the task of completely reconstructing the program, scriptwise and castwise in 1930, it was still her responsibility to get "The Adventures of Helen and Mary" on the air every Saturday morning, no matter what changes were taking place. This was not easy, conditions at CBS being what today would be called somewhat primitive. In 1930 there were many dramatic programs originating from 485 Madison Avenue every week, but the sound department consisted of only 3 people (15 years later there were 40 on staff). So Nila called on her friends Georgia Backus, her original mentor when she applied for work at CBS, and Don Clark to pinch-hit.

There were other problems, as Nila recounted many years later:

> As for music – we had to be a little resourceful there too. Emery Deutsch and his ensemble were available – but only for the air show, since they were doing programs like crazy all over the place. In order to get them, Emery, in Studio 5, would sign off the ensemble program while Sidney Raphael, the pianist, would tear into Studio 3 and whip up the opening for our show. About the third musical bridge we were a complete unit.
>
> Of course I never had a dress rehearsal and had to devise some quaint way of timing strictly by ear. It was almost disconcerting, come the day CBS expanded to the extent of assigning production men to programs – men who could add and subtract – an art I have not learned to this day.

Nila Mack had gone out on a limb with an audacious idea – that of a network dramatic program with all of the parts played by child actors. Now she had to make it work. Nila had confided to friends that she didn't really like children, but she was gregarious, outgoing, and made friends easily, and, despite her original reservations in dealing with what *Variety* would call moppet thesps, it did not take her long to realize that she had been wrong. She found over time that she not only began to like children but grew to love them, and the exquisite patience she eventually developed in working with juvenile performers proved to be one of the most important qualities Miss Mack brought to "Let's Pretend" and all the other children's programs she directed.

However, she was a professional, and expected her cast members to be the same. The program was not like the many radio kiddie talent shows of that time, on which you would do a little song or dance for which you had been carefully coached by your mother at home. Our cast members had to be able to sight-read from a script, which, unless they were very young, they had not been given until first rehearsal. They had to take direction and to observe discipline, which meant, among other things, pick up your cues, read exactly what is in the script without stumbling, and do not hog the microphone.

Any coaching by mothers between rehearsals was frowned upon by our director. ("Frowned upon" is too mild a term. She told them: "Don't do it!") Occasionally, of course, she might ask a parent to go over the words with a very young child who was having trouble with them. I once saw a mother smack her small child in the face in a hallway during a "Let's Pretend" rehearsal break; having the script in advance, she had coached the little boy at home. At rehearsal, Nila, being the director, worked with the child and got him to do it her way, but he was then punished for disobeying his mother.

Having made her decision to create a company of child actors, it was our director's job to get to know the children she had inherited from Yolanda Langworthy and to quickly recruit others; and so she started auditioning children for the show, a process she would repeat every few months for the next 20 years, as the talent pool was always changing.

When she auditioned a new child she would always have some "Let's Pretend" scripts to be read from, but about 1934 she developed a new one just for audition purposes. It was a monologue we called the "dog script." A little newsboy (it worked just as well for a girl) is happily walking along the street with his dog named Tubby. The dog runs in front of a car and is hit. The child holds the limp animal and sobs: "Oh, please, God – don't let Tubby die. He's such a good dog, and he's all I got. Oh, please . . . don't let him die!" If the tears were real, Nila knew she had probably found new material for her cast, and would often hire the child on the spot. But if the sobs sounded faked, Nila would probably say, "Thank you very much, dear – that was lovely. We'll let you know."

Sybil Trent remembers doing this audition scene under particularly trying circumstances. When nine-year-old Sybil walked into the audition studio it was pitch dark, and she stumbled over several bodies on the floor. It seemed that Nila had scheduled the audition during a rehearsal break in the show, and the children in the cast were in the middle of a game called "Murder."

The stodginess of "The Adventures of Helen and Mary" as a children's program probably came from the fact that the two little girls of the title were strictly incidental; the rest of the cast were almost all adults. As Nila Mack later wrote, "It had nothing to do with fairy tales. . . . I went to work, changed the format but kept the title." The new format was one with which children could identify.

Helen and Mary are playing in their attic. Their little friends come up and join them, and they start playing a game of make-believe. They want to hear a story, so they call upon a new character Nila had created named Memory, and this was written for the one adult actor allowed on the program – Harry Swan.

Nila remembered the happy tomfoolery of *Eva the Fifth*, a backstage comedy in which she had played two and a half years before at the Little Theatre (now the Helen Hayes), and that Harry, besides playing a drum in his character of a railroad flagman and being able to sing, was also adept at many voices and animal sounds. He would be very useful on the show. There was never any description of what Memory looked like, but he was obviously small and pixie-like, and rather shy.

On one occasion, in one of the last of the "Helen and Mary" scripts, which Gwen Davies recently found in a musty trunk in her basement, the children coax Memory to come out of his box and take them to the Land of Let's Pretend. He magically changes a bench into a sightseeing bus, and they all ride off happily. At the end of the broadcast the announcer says, "So ends another adventure in the Land of Let's Pretend. Was "Melilot" your favorite story? If not, write to Helen and Mary in care of this station, and they will try to have your story come true."

Helen and Mary had been traveling to that magical country for almost five years when, on March 24, 1934, Nila changed the title of the show to "Let's Pretend." By then we had long been on the 10:35–11:00 A.M. time period after a 5-minute newscast, so it was no longer necessary for the musicians to frantically tiptoe in from their previous show.

Along with the title change, the format was changed as well. Helen and Mary no longer existed. Estelle, Pat, and the others were now simply themselves, in the studio. Memory had disappeared too, and Harry Swan became a benevolent straight man (no more pixie voice) known as Captain Bob. In the hundreds of children's programs then existing, both network and local, you would find countless uncles, aunts, captains (probably a few majors), and other titles, all used to denote friendly, nonthreatening authority figures.

Harry still appeared in the program's lead-in, and continued to do animal sounds, and an occasional "Make way for the king!" At the program's opening, having been introduced by the CBS staff announcer, he would start by discussing with the children in the cast the fan mail that had come in asking for favorite stories. Occasionally, there would be a misunderstanding, such as the letter Nila received which began: "Dear Niles and Max," and another which started "Dear Nylon Max."

Once the story had been decided upon, there began the ritual of deciding how to travel to the Land of Let's Pretend, which became the program's trademark, and never varied for the next 20 years:

> CAPT. BOB: How shall we travel to the Land of Let's Pretend?
> PAT: Walter Tetley – why don't you tell us?
> WALTER: Well, the weather's pretty warm – why don't we all go on a cool, breezy ocean liner?
> CAPT. BOB: An ocean liner it is. A-one, and a-two, and a-three!
> SOUND: Whiz Bang

A ship's whistle could be heard and a gong, and someone would call out: "All ashore that's going ashore! This liner now sailing for Let's Pretend, the Topaz Islands and the story of 'King Midas and the Golden Touch!'" Everybody would ad lib "Goodbye, goodbye" (and I would stick in, "Don't forget to feed the goldfish!" Ah, what innocent days). The ship's bell and the huge whistle would be heard over the ad-libs, then the orchestra would play the bridge music into the first scene of the story.

In those early years, as Nila later wrote, "Listeners would sit up with a snap when the announcer would say [as the program ended], 'The Queen Mother played by eight-year-old Patricia Ryan. The Wicked King played by nine-year-old Billy Halop.'" That was part of the program's unique appeal – all of the parts, from children to adults to doddering geriatrics being played by children. Nila's pioneering idea was a success: so much so, in fact, that as we child actors became better and more sure of ourselves under her direction, she did not replace us when we grew into our teens, as she had most of the original children on "Helen and Mary." The device of announcing our ages was dropped in 1937. They were no longer that remarkable.

The casting had now come full circle, and as we grew it had gradually changed back into what it was when Nila took over in 1930 – basically adult actors. As before, the child actors used were those playing children's roles. However, there was now a vast difference. These adult actors had been hand-picked, brought along, trained by Nila Mack, and we had a unified acting style uniquely suited to fairy tales and to fantasy. We had also developed a great ease and facility in working with her and with each other, which Daisy Aldan later referred to as a group karma. In any case, by 1940, Nila's tenth anniversary with CBS and with the program, the Let's Pretenders had become a smoothly running repertory company of some of the best young actors in radio.

It is not difficult to work up a pretty good estimate of what it cost to put on a "Let's Pretend" broadcast in the early days. Nila Mack, as the show's writer, producer, and director, was on salary as a regular staff member, and so were the musicians and sound effects people. The classic fairy tales the scripts were based upon were in the public domain, so that the only net fees payable were those to the actors. When she first went to work at CBS Nila had been given a metal cash box out of which to pay the cast. Harry Swan, being an adult, probably got $10. Henry Boyd, our bird whistler, was told by Nila one week that she had $8 for him in the box, and for his next engagement she had only $7. But all of the children got the same fee: $3.50 for two and a half hours of rehearsal and a half-hour performance on a national network.

This fee was no doubt based on the proposition that "Let's Pretend" was just like any other kiddie talent show, and since you were a child getting to broadcast on the radio and it was so much fun and all, you didn't really expect to get *paid*, did you? (Our $3.50 checks remained the same until 1938.) And so the net cost to CBS for a typical "Let's Pretend" broadcast in those early days, with a cast consisting of Harry Swan and 12 children, was about $52: a bargain.

When the first contracts were negotiated with the American Federation of Radio Artists in 1938, the regular rate for a half-hour sustaining show such as ours was $21, but the networks were able to convince the union to waive this fee when more than 75 percent of the cast were children – the kiddie talent show syndrome.

Though the children on "Let's Pretend" were miserably paid, even by 1930's standards, it was for many of us our first professional performing experience, and the training and confidence we gained enabled us to go on to other shows, some of us eventually earning hundreds of dollars weekly. Nila Mack was once heard to remark, I am sure without bitterness, that some of the kids she had trained were currently earning several times her own salary in their busy radio careers.

During those first few hectic, almost desperate weeks of August and September 1930, Miss Mack was also given additional writing and directing chores, not to mention an occasional acting job, such as the continuing role of Mrs. Webb on a program called "The Magic Voice," all, no doubt, included in her weekly salary as a CBS staff member. She directed several other children's shows early on, including "You Decide," a children's discussion program, and "The Junior Bugle – The Child's Newspaper of the Air." That was replaced by "Sunday Morning at Aunt Susan's," presented on Sundays for an hour at 9:00 A.M. Nila chose Elaine Ivans, another friend with whom she had worked in *Eva the Fifth*, for the title role.

There were two children, Teddy and Jean, played by Albert Aley and Vivian Block. It was a family oriented show, with the same string ensemble as on "Let's Pretend." It would always open with the family singing a hymn and conversing. Then guests would drop in – a well-known author, the curator of the aquarium, an arctic explorer, or some of the actors Nila Mack knew, with made-up names, such as Henry Boyd, who would be called Mr. Robin. He would talk about birds, and do some of his bird calls. The program was folksy and informative. It went on the air in 1931 and lasted until 1937.

Nila directed several performances of "The Columbia Workshop," which started in 1936. Two of her earliest offerings were "A Letter from Home," written by her friend Charles Jackson, and "The Ghost of Benjamin Sweet," both done in March 1938 and preserved on tape at the Museum of Television and Radio.

In 1940 she directed two Dr. Seuss stories: *To Think That I Saw It on Mulberry Street*, with Jack Grimes, House Jameson, and Ted DeCorsia, and *The 500 Hats of Bartholomew Cubbins*, featuring Jack again, with Howard Lindsay as King Derwin. Nila did not have much opportunity to use her friends the Lindsays in radio – they were always busy in the theatre. She did use Dorothy Stickney (Mrs. Lindsay) on "Let's Pretend" once; but there is no record of the part she played. Also in 1940 Miss Mack directed the much-anthologized "Inside a Kid's Head," by CBS staff writer Jerome Lawrence. Nine-year-old Pretender Skip Homeier played the lead.

"The American School of the Air," which had been broadcast since 1930, assigned Nila to adapt the stories for and direct their Thursday program "Tales from Far and Near." Many of us Let's Pretenders worked on that. She also directed the children's quiz program "The March of Games," starring our own Sybil Trent, and another program for young people, "So You Want to Be," aired on Fridays at 5:45 P.M., beginning in July 1938, in which some person outstanding in his or her field was interviewed by a youngster, who would ask questions from the viewpoint of someone just becoming interested in choosing a career.

There were only two continuous programs assigned to Nila Mack which were not for children or did not involve fantasy. They were "Let Freedom Ring," a 13-week series for the Department of the Interior, and "Mrs. Miniver," a series based on the Jan Struther novel, and one has to wonder whether, being a woman, she would have received either of them if it were not for the wartime manpower shortage.

Nila Mack had a deep sense of patriotism, and doing these programs must have given her a great deal of satisfaction. They were one direct contribution she could make to the war effort. Another was a book she wrote as a result of a suggestion made by one of the secretaries at CBS, *Animal Allies*. It was a short book for children, designed to answer questions they might have about why we were in the war and why we had to win it. All the countries involved in World War II were represented by animals. The book showed how Chief Sam Eagle came to the aid of Stoutheart the Lion, Shaggy Sovietsky the Bear, Chang the Dragon, and Kid Aussie the Kangaroo to prevent Greedy Gruber the Vulture from destroying Pleasant Forest, where they all lived. Mussolini was depicted as a big monkey telling the vulture how strong he was. Emperor Hirohito was a snake who attacked Sam the Eagle's nest, while the Mugwump in Sam's country cried: "Quick! Somebody should *not* do something about it!"

In addition to all Nila's directing and writing assignments at CBS, it was also expected that she would fill in for other directors during vacations or illness (though no research has indicated how she found the time). However, whatever difficulties she met at the network, Nila Mack was now firmly established at CBS, and well liked by all those she worked with. She had proved that she was a versatile writer and director, able to capably handle any of the assignments she was given.

But the star in her crown – the program she created and which through the years brought so much honor and recognition to CBS – would always be "Let's Pretend."

Chapter 5

Sounds, Animals, and Music

As Nila Mack became more skilled at writing and directing "Let's Pretend," she became more and more aware of how wonderfully sound effects could contribute to her tales of fantasy and magic. As her CBS colleague Earle McGill wrote, "Sounds effects are to radio what scenery is to the theatre." And sound helped immensely in our now familiar device of "How shall we travel to the Land of Let's Pretend?" When we had all decided to ride on a fire engine, and you heard those sirens and clanging bells and the delighted shouts of all the Pretenders, you were already part of the make-believe, and your imagination was open for anything, before the story had even begun. With sound effects it was easy to believe that you were under the water with Andersen's Little Mermaid, or at the side of the brave Prince who is given the task of climbing a glass mountain on horseback to rescue the beautiful maiden on top. How do you do the sound of a horse climbing a glass mountain?* Our sound men did it with those well-known coconut halves, clopping, sliding, and squeaking on a thick pane of glass covered with wet sand. In order to show just how difficult it was for the Prince and the horse to climb the mountain (they made it, naturally, to the cheers of the crowd of villagers below), the sound men had to be performers. They were not called "sound effects artists" facetiously.

Nila wrote that with some trepidation she asked first for such hitherto unimagined sounds as talking wings, angry dragons, shimmering moonbeams, and King Midas's flower garden being changed into solid gold. The sound department received the scripts several days in advance, so there was time for them to experiment in their own laboratory if necessary, and sometimes Nila would be there working with them and making suggestions.

Though complete libraries of sound effects are now available on compact discs, which can be cued very accurately, horses' hooves are still one sound which is best when it is done manually, so that the horse can react instantly to the situation in the script. Two half coconut shells are used, with small leather straps on each for hand holds. Rubber drain plungers are also used. A talented sound effects artist can simulate the horse pawing the ground impatiently, walking, trotting, or at a full gallop (also done on the chest with open palms), perhaps with a few snorts interspersed vocally. The hooves can be done on loose dirt or sand (in a shallow wooden box), on wood, gravel, or whatever surface the action calls for.

If an effect was too complicated to do live, they would occasionally cut an acetate recording to be used on the broadcast.* But one way or another, when Saturday morning came, everything that our director had asked for was ready.

Admitting some prejudice, I will say that the CBS sound people were the best in the business. When I joined the cast in 1936 there was Walter Pierson (head of the sound department), Ora Nichols, Ray Kremer, Jim Rogan, Henry Gautier, and George O'Donnell. Walter Pierson looked like a scholarly scientist who worked in a laboratory, which is exactly what he was, experimenting with a new or difficult effect in the sound workshop on the third floor at 485 Madison, or perhaps building some sound apparatus from scratch. Ora Nichols, known as radio's only woman sound technician, was rather short, had wire-rimmed glasses, and wore her hair gathered in a bun at the back, making her look like the stereotype of a New England schoolmarm. She had once played piano in a Massachusetts movie theatre, while her husband Arthur played drums, and gradually they began to improvise sound effects in the pit for the silent movies being shown. This led to having their own vaudeville act and eventually doing sound effects for CBS. Ora took over her husband's job there when he died. Ray Kremer was tall, thin, and laid back. Jim Rogan looked like his Irish ancestry. He was stocky and he had a black mustache; he had an extensive music education, and played violin and cello; and coauthored, with our conductor Emery Deutsch, the popular songs "When a Gypsy Makes His Violin Cry," and also "Stardust on the Moon," which was for six weeks on "Your Hit Parade." Henry Gautier was small, capable, and very good-natured. George O'Donnell was humorless, but very conscientious and competent. All of them were unflappable, and at times could be very creative.

Even after having been with the show for some time, I was still fascinated by watching our sound men who, wearing earphones and watching both the script and Nila for cues, might simultaneously be cueing up one or more sound effects records,† opening doors, rustling straw, breaking

---

*Phonograph records were made (and still are) by a needle cutting grooves in a heavy wax disc, those grooves then being molded into a matrix or "mother," from which an unlimited number of shellac (later vinyl) records could be pressed. With acetates, however, grooves were cut in an acetate coating on an aluminum disc, and that same disc could be played back immediately, though only a limited number of plays were possible before it started to show wear. Until tape recording was perfected, acetates were widely used to record auditions, special sound effects, and entire programs for later rebroadcast. The use of acetates became a bit chancy, however, during World War II. Aluminum was needed for the military. Glass-base records were used for acetates, and woe be to the dolt who dropped one.
† Cueing up sound records was an art. The discs were all 10-inch 78 r.p.m. records – much easier to find the right groove in a hurry than on a slow-turning LP. The sound man would mark the approximate groove of the cue he wanted with a yellow crayon, play the record up to that spot silently, heard only on his earphones, then stop the record by holding his thumb on it lightly, while the turntable continued to revolve. When the cue came he would

berry boxes to simulate splintering timbers, or maybe running up and down a short flight of prop stairs.

Some of the most important sounds on "Let's Pretend" were those of animals. Though every animal in creation had become available on records, they were far better when done live. The animals, after all, were characters in our stories and had to react to the situation, just as did the humans. Their sounds could never be just thrown in at random. However, our sound effects people did not claim to be adept at wolf howls or kitten mews. For those a different kind of specialist was needed, and over the years, "Let's Pretend" had some of the best.

First came Harry Swan, a fixture on "The Adventures of Helen and Mary" and on "Let's Pretend" until his retirement. I remember him in 1936 as being in his mid-forties, with thinning hair, watery blue eyes, and a sallow complexion. I found him rather morose. He was not a great actor but his animal sounds were excellent. It was said that he had been shell-shocked during World War I. We were all occasionally mortified by some of his bitter remarks. Once, when he thought he was underpaid for some animal sounds on a commercial program, he sent the check back to the ad agency with the words *"Please don't call me again"* written across the front. He left our program and the business before we became sponsored in 1943, and went to live alone in a small house in Hudson, New York, which I believe had been his home town. Every year Gwen Davies would take up a collection to send Harry a Christmas package – we knew he would not take money. In the late 1940s his mental condition had apparently deteriorated, and when officials came to take him to either a VA hospital or some other institution, they found that Harry had blown his brains out and left a note with wording to the effect that "I beat you to it."

Henry Boyd came on the scene not long after Harry Swan. Henry as a boy in East Orange, New Jersey, had always been fascinated by birds, and taught himself to imitate them. In 1923 at the age of 15 he walked into the studios of WOR (then located above Bamberger's department store in Newark), announced that he could imitate birds, and asked, could he be on the radio? Their reply was, of course – you can do a 30-minute broadcast. Henry wrote a little narration called "A Walk in the Woods" with all the appropriate bird calls, which he did on the air the following week. There was no audition – but no mention of pay, either.

Henry's next radio try was in the early 1930s, at CBS. Luckily, Nila Mack was assigned to listen to his audition. By now he had refined his routine into something called "The Bird Opera." Nila not only had him do this on "Sunday Morning at Aunt Susan's" but also called him for "Let's

(continued) *release his thumb and simultaneously turn up the speaker volume, and there was the sound, right on the button – if you knew how to do it right.*

Ora Nichols, the industry's only woman sound technician, ca. 1938 (from an old newspaper clipping). Note berry box for sound of splintering timbers, branches, telegraph key, pulley and belt, and compressed air tank. Courtesy Anthony Tollin.

Pretend" whenever there were stories involving bird songs. These included "The Chinese Nightingale," "Jorinda and Joringel," and "Thumbelina."

Henry, who was slightly built, prematurely balding, and not really trained as an actor, made his living for 13 years in the 1930s and early 1940s jerking sodas at Whelan's Drug Store at Eighth Street and Sixth Avenue in Manhattan, and later at Bigelow's, a block uptown. In the early days when Nila still lived on West Tenth Street next to her friends the Howard Lindsays, she would come up to the soda fountain on her way home from work and say, "I need you this Saturday, Henry."

Henry Boyd started to get other radio work involving bird songs. He

was the whistle of Aunt Jenny's canary, occasionally heard in her kitchen while she told her "Aunt Jenny's Real Life Stories" to her announcer and straight man Dan Seymour ("sponsored by Spry, the all-vegetable shortening"). His biggest success in the business, though, was doing the Rinso White bobwhite bird whistle. This being before the age of recorded commercials, he was called to the studio to do it live every time the singing duo did the Rinso jingle. Beginning in 1940, he did this every week for 14 years.

Brad Barker came next. He had originally been a good-looking young leading man in silent films made in the East. With the advent of sound, he was on the set one day when a sound effect of frying eggs was needed. The electric frying pan had gone dead, and Brad offered to do the sound vocally. It was a spectacular success. From there it was just a step to doing the sounds of animals, which Brad had always loved. Coincidentally, he was getting on a bit for his young romantic roles, and here was radio – a young, exciting industry. A new career was born.

When he started doing "Let's Pretend" Brad was already busy on many other radio shows. His wolf howl was a regular part of the signature of "Renfrew of the Mounted." He was the original "Arf!" of Sandy in "Little Orphan Annie." And it is Brad Barker's lion's roar that you will hear introducing literally hundreds of the earlier MGM motion pictures.

The only time I ever saw Brad accept help with any of his sounds was when he first did a horse whinny on our show. As Brad did the lower, gutteral part of the sound, Jack Grimes chimed in with the high part, whistled through his teeth. Our first reaction was to laugh, but this combination two-man horse was so real that from then on our director insisted that it be done by both Brad and Jack.

We all knew Brad as a serious-looking, soft-spoken man with a pencil-thin mustache and horn-rimmed glasses, who wore double-breasted suits and a homburg hat. One might think he was a bank loan officer as he entered the studio with a brown leather portfolio under his arm – until he unzipped it, removed a small wooden box, and used it to make more resonant the frightening snarl of a leopard.

He also had a lively if corny sense of humor. I remember his once asking me if I knew the difference between a cocktail lounge and an elephant's fart. Since I didn't, he supplied the answer: "Well, a cocktail lounge is just an ordinary barroom. ... But an elephant's fart is a BARRR-ROOOM!!"

One reason Brad's sounds were so authentic was that he frequented

Opposite: **Ca. 1937. Studio 1. Nila Mack instructs her cast; Patricia Ryan, Estelle Levy, Vivian Block, Arthur Anderson, Donald Hughes, Florence Halop, and Nila Mack. Note door sound effect in background. ©1937 CBS Inc. Used by permission.**

Ringling Brothers' Circus whenever it was in town, and had many friends there, including, I am sure, the animals.

If anyone doubts an animal imitator is also an actor, the following should prove it. Homer Fickett, director of "The March of Time" put in an emergency call to Brad. There was a fast-breaking news story to dramatize on the air that night involving a tiger. Brad got there just before air time, and asked for a script. "You don't need a script – there isn't time," said Fickett. "Just roar when I give you the cue." Brad still insisted that he must have a script. "What for?" said Fickett. "Because," said Brad, "I have to know what the tiger is thinking."

Brad Barker's career in radio lasted almost 20 years, and he was with "Let's Pretend" until he died in 1951.

Brad Barker had an appropriate name, as dogs were his specialty. Harry Swan (and Henry Boyd, if you stretched it a little) both had bird names. All three were gifted and talented artists, and over the years their contributions to radio and to "Let's Pretend" were invaluable.

From the first, music was an essential part of "Let's Pretend." For the program's entire life, starting with the "Helen and Mary" days, there was always a six-piece string ensemble consisting of first violin, second violin, cello, viola, bass, and piano. (The only exception was during a short period in 1938 when a 20-piece orchestra, led by Alexander Semmler, provided the music. They were probably all on salary, and assigned by CBS to our show because they had little or nothing else to do at the time. The orchestra's size was rather overwhelming, though, and it detracted greatly from the program's charm.)

The music chosen for the theme and for bridges between scenes was light classical, or what was termed slightly contemptuously "parlor music" by serious musicians. However, these pieces were ideal for a children's radio program. They were simple and bright, and a definite melodic theme was established within their opening bars, or 15 or 20 seconds, which was all the time there was for each music cue. They included such delightful melodies as "The Flatterer," by Chaminade, "Solvejg's Song" by Grieg, "Dark Eyes," "Song of the Volga Boatman," and Kreisler's "Liebesfreud."

Our theme music was "Fairy Tale," originally played in the key of D, written by Karel Komzak (1850–1905) of Czechoslovakia, the second to bear that name. Like his father he was a musician, a bandmaster, and a composer. He wrote no less than 80 polkas, 20 waltzes, and 60 marches, and also like his father he introduced Czech folk songs into his arrangements. The first thirteen bars of "Fairy Tale" (never heard on our program) are marked "Andante (with gloomy expression)," but the part used for our "Let's Pretend" theme is marked "Allegretto (very delicately and in march tempo)." If one hums the melody of "Fairy Tale," the "oompah" of a small Czechoslovak band can readily be imagined, with happy couples in a little mountain village, stepping and twirling to this bright, lilting tune.

As Nila Mack became more and more confident as the writer and director of "Let's Pretend" she also took over the selection of its music. She was well qualified, having learned much of the kind of music required when, as a child, she had played piano for her mother's dancing classes in Arkansas City. In the vaudeville and legitimate theatres where she performed later there was always a small orchestra which played an overture including some of the same kinds of pieces. Thus in her 39 years she had acquired an extensive knowledge of musical repertoire, and all she had to do each week was to send a list of the music she wanted to Emery Deutsch, our conductor and first violinist, and it would be rehearsed and ready for Saturday's broadcast.

Emery Deutsch called himself a gypsy violinist. He was indeed Hungarian, by parentage and background, having been born in Budapest. He was a member of the legendary A & P Gypsies, the first radio musical ensemble to gain a national reputation. He also wrote two hit songs of that genre, "Play, Fiddle, Play" and "When a Gypsy Makes His Violin Cry." When he left after 12 years with CBS to lead his own orchestra, Leon Goldman took over as conductor and first violinist, and he stayed with us to the end.

Another long-term "Let's Pretend" musical survivor was Sidney Raphael, who doubled on piano and celeste. His daughter Gerriane Raphael was a child actress on our show and several others, who later developed a successful adult career acting and singing in the theatre and in commercials. Our cellist Maurice Brown later became our conductor and composer of original music for the program when Cream of Wheat took over as sponsor. Other long-term members of the ensemble were Isaac Klaas, violin, Howard Kay, cello, and Elias Tenzer, bass. Another of our cellists, Bernard Greenhouse, studied with Pablo Casals and later became well known in the classical music field.

Though she had acted on radio shows before, Miss Mack did not truly learn the importance of the engineering department until she began to direct "Let's Pretend." Anyone who was uninformed might think that the engineer was merely someone who plugged in the microphones, then just sat there in the control room.* But she found that the engineer was the

---

*A control room is a soundproof room where the program's engineer, director, and other production personnel sit. There the engineer mixes and regulates the sounds from the various microphones or other sound sources, which are heard on large loudspeakers. Meanwhile, the director can see the performers through a double-paned, plate-glass window, and communicate with them by hand signals during the broadcast.

Orson Welles, who always performed in the programs he directed, would stand on a podium in the studio, wearing earphones, but other radio directors preferred being in the control room, so as to hear the broadcast exactly as it would sound to the radio audience.

master of the sound mechanics of a radio program, and that his skill was just as instrumental in creating a good show as were all the other elements – cast, music, and sound effects.

"You Are There" was a radio program, first broadcast in 1947, in which CBS news correspondents described famous historical events as if radio had existed then. But all of radio drama could have been subtitled "You Are There." You were there in "Jack and the Beanstalk" when Jack started climbing that magical plant, and described to his mother the wonders he saw as he rose higher and higher, up into the sky. Jack Grimes always played the title role. One memorable performance of that story took place when we were broadcasting in 1942 before a packed house in one of the Broadway theatres CBS had leased. The dialogue went thus:

> JACK: (*Going off mike, on echo*) Mother, I can see the top of the church steeple. . . . Now I can see   the next village. . . . There's the river. . . (Even farther off) Now I can see the who-o-o-le wo-o-o-rld!

It was very effective radio, with the help of the echo chamber* to give the effect of distance, Jack slowly backing away from the microphone as he spoke. But as Jack said "Who-o-o-le w-o-o-o-rld!" he fell backward off the stage of the theatre. Luckily, he wasn't badly hurt, and scrambled back on stage in time for his cue in the next scene.

Nila Mack learned a lot early on from the engineers with whom she worked, both as a writer and as a director. The first lesson was that the script had to be written so that the listener would always know who the characters were, and where they were. The next was you couldn't just put a bunch of people in a studio, turn on the mikes, and expect a believable radio show. The microphones had to be placed correctly for the right sound balance in that particular studio, and each actor, musician, and sound effect had to be the right distance from the microphones, in order to carry out the

---

(continued) *Anyone during radio's golden age seeing a photograph showing a radio director standing next to the performers in the studio and throwing cues would always know that it was a staged publicity shot.*

Echo chambers were often used, and very effectively, in radio drama for portentous voices, for instance, such as Aladdin's Genie of the Lamp on our program, or for effects of great distance, as in the "Jack and the Beanstalk" scene.

Originally, echo chambers were long, narrow, concrete-lined rooms. The speaker's voice came out of a loudspeaker at one end and was received by a microphone at the other, with wonderful reverberations in between. The whole effect was mixed with the other voices, music, or sound effects in the studio engineer's console. (Some orchestra leaders liked to have a little echo mixed with their music as well.) Every network had echo chambers at its studios in each major city, and the director of each show needing one had to reserve it in advance.

A present-day echo chamber can be as small as a wardrobe trunk, and may be lined with steel springs or loosely hanging steel plates for the reverberation effect. Other devices, some no bigger than an attaché case, achieve the effect completely electronically.

writer's intent. Anyone in the studio could be faded in or out, either by moving toward or away from their microphone, or by the engineer changing his volume control on that mike, but obviously none of this could happen unless the engineer knew how to achieve these things, and the director knew what to ask for.

Nila Mack once wrote a preface to a published version of her radio adaptation of "Rapunzel," in which she said that this story was a definite challenge to the engineer and to the sound department, as well as to the cast. She added, "Only a fine gradation of sound volume as well as voice will make the action of the scenes quite clear to the listener." What she meant was that as the Witch climbs up the tower on Rapunzel's hair, the director must decide which of them the microphone "goes with." As Rapunzel leans out of the tower to call to the Witch, the echo chamber is used to give the effect of height. Then as the Witch, later the Prince, climbs closer, the echo volume is slowly turned down, then killed. This particular effect was beautiful, and the listener was indeed there.

Nila could never be sure which engineer she would be assigned. Those I remember include John Dietz, who later became a CBS radio director, and Fred Hendrickson, who later became the producer of "The Arthur Godfrey Show" on radio. A good audio engineer could be, just as much as the others I have mentioned, essential to the success of any radio show.

Under Nila Mack, with the help of her child actors and the many other talented experts she learned to rely on – the sound technicians, the animal imitators, the musicians, and the engineering department – a true repertory company was created, in which all of us worked with each other in a spirit of mutual respect, and took pleasure in our work. American radio broadcasting when at its best was a superb combination of artistic creativity and technical expertise, and there was no better example of this than "Let's Pretend."

Chapter 6

Working with Children

It had been Nila Mack's idea to convert the cast of "Helen and Mary" to one entirely made up of children, but now she had to learn to work with them. And so over the months and years she developed ways of dealing with her youthful cast. Her first instinct, she said, was "to make the children see that I was not their teacher nor yet their mother. I was one of them. We were going to have a grand time – a thrilling time – bringing fairy tales to life." In a later interview she said that after having been with the show for ten years, "children have taught me that talking down to them is fatal. It gets me in trouble fast. But an eye-to-eye conversation, using words and expressions they can understand, gives the same response that adults give. The same? I mean better."

Another time she said,

> There's only one difference between children and adults anyway. Children are more honest. . . . Encouragement is far better than criticism. . . . Confidence draws out better performances. Children accept direction eagerly when given as a means of improving their performances, rather than criticizing their first approach. When a rehearsal begins on "Let's Pretend," the youngsters sit around a table. The cast is assigned. Then we read the whole script straight through without stopping, so that each gets a clear idea of the story first, along with a clearer picture of his relationship to the other members of the cast. After that is over, and before I "put it on the mike," I discuss, in an impersonal and businesslike way, the characterizations they have given me. I listen to their ideas, and try to learn just why they read as they did. If they are wrong, my answer will be something like, "I see what you mean. But I believe in this instance, you can get more out of the part if you tackle it like this."
>
> I may read one line. But rather than have a group of parrots, I much prefer to recall a certain movie, or a story, or even another script wherein there was a character something like this one being discussed. The response is instantaneous, and we start to build it along the lines I want. In the meantime, the child has not been humiliated, and, while he plays it differently than he originally did, he doesn't feel that his first reading was unintelligent, or that his ability was questioned.
>
> Scolding is no good when there is a broadcast in the offing. . . . It brings two definite reactions. To single out one child and scold or punish him

62

creates a "gang" feeling. The child knows he mustn't come back with an argument and the others are embarrassed with and for him, with the result that they hang together in self-defense. The second reaction is an unsteady air performance wherein the child will very likely "fluff" his lines or miss cues because he's thinking of the hurt he had.

At times when Nila felt direct criticism was necessary, and that could include our personal conduct not just our "Let's Pretend" performances, she always had the consideration to do it in private. None of us was ever humiliated in front of the others.

Contrary to many newspaper articles and CBS press releases of the 1930s and 1940s, our director did not give us acting lessons or teach theory. That was not her job. She had a show to put on and very little rehearsal time in which to do it. She gave us directions on how to be a better princess, giant, enchanted frog, or wicked witch. We learned by doing, and any child who proved incapable of learning was eventually not called any more. She would work patiently with a new child – start the newcomer in small parts (Third Fairy, Second Goblin), and gradually nurture the child's talent until he or she was able to emote as confidently as the rest of us and was, incidentally, often launched on a lucrative career as a juvenile heartthrob on other programs. Nila made real actors out of many of us who would otherwise have been doomed to quick fadeouts after brief careers as "cute kiddies."

In spite of her patience with the youngest children, Nila's sense of humor could occasionally get the better of her. Once, for the sake of a yock, she cautioned a new snippet playing a lady-in-waiting: "No, dear – it's not *Mad*ame. It's Ma*dame*. Just remember – *dame*, as in God."

There were also certain technical things to learn, of course; for example, "hold your script up and speak directly into the microphone, and don't be a mike hog – that is, we should stand aside a little when someone else on the same side of the mike had a speech. Then we needed to know which was the live side of the mike and which was the dead side, and what was the difference between a physical fade (turning or backing away from the microphone while speaking) and a board fade (done by the engineer in the control room). And we all had to learn to be constantly alert for the director's hand signals. Pointing to you meant that was your cue to start a speech or a scene. Moving the index finger in a circle meant speed up – the performance was a little behind. Stretching an imaginary thread as the two hands slowly separated meant slow down, or literally, stretch it out. A cupped hand to the ear meant "I can't hear you – speak up." All of us, no matter how small, had to learn these radio protocols.

Another thing that had to be known, seemingly simple, was ad-libbing.*

*Ad-lib is short for "ad libitum," which means literally "in accordance with one's wishes." Ad-lib directions in scripts, radio, or otherwise are seldom more specific than (Crowd murmurs) or (Sailors protest).

Neither Nila nor any other good radio director was satisfied with a bunch of actors saying "Walla, walla, walla," the accepted cliché for ad-libs. You were expected to improvise words appropriate to the situation. For instance, if a crowd were in the king's throne room waiting for an announcement, and the script read simply "Crowd murmurs," it might be something like: "Well, I certainly hope they start pretty soon. I'm tired of standing around. Doesn't the Princess look beautiful today? Oh, here comes the king now – maybe we'll find out what's going on" until directed to fade down (the director's hand held out and slowly lowered) as the king speaks.

If you happened to be eight years old at the time, and had to remember all these things, meanwhile being careful not to fall off the little two-foot-square platform you were standing on to be in range of the mike, it could be rather scary. All of Nila's patience, directorial ability, and knowledge of radio were needed for it to come together successfully.

There was, even for the most experienced radio actors, always the risk of fluffing a line – saying the wrong word inadvertently. After a broadcast when this had happened to one Pretender, Nila's advice to all was: "If you make a fluff, don't call attention to it by going back and correcting yourself. Most listeners will not notice, and most of those who do will think they heard wrong."

In live radio a fluff was always a possibility, no matter how many rehearsals you had gone through. On "Let's Pretend," if a child had trouble with a word or a phrase in rehearsal, Nila would change it to something more simple. But the chance always remained. The annals of radio are full of famous fluffs, some obscene, some just goofy, but always unplanned. Here are the few that I recall on our show over the years:

Daisy Aldan (intoning mysteriously on the well-known story of "The Juniper Tree"): "I . . . am the the voice . . . of the Jupiner Tree."

Bill Lipton (on the story of "How Six Traveled Through the World," as the slightly slow-witted Stack the Strong, who discovers that the room in which the Witch has locked them all is an airtight oven with a fire beneath it): "Why, it's . . . it's an onion!"

Jack Grimes (showing Kingsley Colton through a magical underground garden): "And here, Your Majesty, is the Avenue of the Golden Freet Trues."

Our most spectacular fluff also belongs to Jack Grimes. In the original New Year's allegory written by Nila, "The House of the World," the Spirit of Good Will is attempting to break down the walls of Selfishness, Greed, Poverty, and Intolerance, and Jack, who lives behind the wall of Intolerance, seems to remember this not being their first meeting. Jack (to Good Will): "Haven't we wet somewhere before?"

Though this might seem to the reader like an insignificant bobble, amidst the tension of a live coast to coast broadcast it could well have caused temporary hysteria. In any case both Jack and Albert Aley, who played Good Will, got through the rest of the broadcast with real difficulty. Rolling on the floor with laughter was not allowed. (The next year when the story was done again, we found that our director had changed the wording and the rhythm of the line to an innocuous: "I've seen you before, haven't I?")

From the first broadcast of "Let's Pretend" until Cream of Wheat came aboard in 1943, rehearsal and performance took place in one continuous session. When I started with the show our rehearsal began at 8:30 A.M. in Studio 1. After we'd kissed Miss Mack hello we would sit in a semicircle, boys on one side and girls on the other (our choice, not hers) and study our scripts. All of us would be dressed neatly, the boys in shorts or knickers, with knee-length stockings (no one wore "longies" until they were in their teens), wearing neckties and jackets, even in summer. The girls would always be in dresses, or "middie" blouses and skirts, also with knee-length stockings ("bobby socks" did not appear until 1943) and often with bows in their hair, which might be bobbed (in the early 1930s), or worn long, in curls or in pigtails if they were very young.

Meanwhile, Miss Mack sat at a small table in the center with her script, her cigarettes, and her stopwatch. She smoked two and a half packs of Kool Menthols a day, and all of us Pretenders have vivid memories of our director coming into the studio with her bustling walk, holding a lighted cigarette, the pack, matches, and the stopwatch in her right hand, and a bundle of scripts and a pencil in her left.

After the first reading of the script there would often be cuts for time purposes, but if a story had been done before there was often no need. Then she would go into the control room, and we would get on our feet and start working through the story scene by scene, as she gave the actors and sound men directions, speaking patiently and deliberately to the small children who might be newcomers, and in grown-up terms to the more experienced Pretenders. This was a serious work situation, but also a fascinating game. We children were very fortunate, though we did not realize it at the time. We were enjoying the magic of make-believe and the glamour of show business simultaneously – and getting paid for it.

As we grew older, if there was too much clowning during rehearsal, the talk-back* would carry the director's admonition: "Now cut that out, or I'll come out there and sock you! And you know I can do it, too!" But all of us knew she wouldn't.

After this work-through and before the dress rehearsal there would be a short break. You could go to the restroom or report to your mother in the reception room outside, if you were still young enough for your mother

*The talk-back is an amplifying system used during rehearsal that enables performers to hear the director's instructions from the control room over a studio loudspeaker.

to be there. Meanwhile, our string ensemble was rehearsing in another studio.

The dress rehearsal was meant to be exactly what the broadcast would be – no stops, no hesitations. After the dress, the tension increased as Miss Mack gave us last-minute notes, and possibly cuts. An audience of about 30 or 40 children and their parents filed in. Then at 10:30, after the opening bars of Komzak's "Fairy Tale," the announcer said, "The Columbia Broadcasting System presents Nila Mack's 'Let's Pretend'!" (Enthusiastic applause.)

The longer Nila Mack worked for CBS and directed "Let's Pretend" the more she became devoted to the show and the children on it. Both were in a sense her creations. But because of her insistence on keeping a tight rein on her young performers, many of us were afraid of her at the same time we grew to love her. The proportion of love and fear was different for each of us. As for myself, I distinctly remember feeling a pang in the pit of my stomach when, during a rehearsal break in Playhouse 3 (I was then in my mid-twenties), Nila pressed the talk-back button and said, "Arthur – will you come into the control room please?" (The memory of whatever minor foible, professional or personal, I had been indulging in is mercifully blotted out by the passage of many years.)

Her concerns also extended to the personal lives of some of us. My mother once received a phone call from Miss Mack, probably about some obstreperous behavior of mine, in which she said, without criticizing Mrs. Anderson directly: "He's been encouraged in these whimsies." Exactly what that meant I never figured out. There were other instances of Nila calling parents about their children's behavior in the studio. Kingsley Colton, a most polite and well-behaved child, was horsing around, as he phrased it, in the corner of the studio one day when our director entered, and he didn't go over and greet her. "Next day," said Kingsley, "she called my father and said, in effect, that I'd better shape up."

We were all in varying degrees precocious, which means in the original Latin "precooked," or "cooked ahead of time." We could and did act up. We were, after all, children. We could be mischievous, noisy, and playful at the wrong times. In general, I suppose, some of us were rather pleased with ourselves. This was evidenced one day during an "American School of the Air" rehearsal when one of my contemporaries (we were both 12 or so) was starting to get obnoxious. Our director was out of the room. George O'Donnell the sound man dealt with the child by saying, "Yes, you're a very clever little boy – now shut up!" Nila could have gotten off a much better zinger, I am sure, but the point is, if she had been there the child wouldn't have acted up in the first place. She was pretty good at keeping the lid on our precooked behavior.

Though Nila had said early on that she was neither a teacher nor a

mother to her cast of children, a mother was what she eventually became –
a sometimes strict and even unreasonable mother, but always a loving one.
I believe the pattern was formed by her own mother, Margaret Bowen
Mac, back in Arkansas City. Her daughter Nila had inherited her humor,
determination, and drive. Both of them had carved out new careers for
themselves after the death of their husbands. Margaret Mac's at first was
managing her daughter's early career. She then eventually returned home
to Arkansas City to reestablish her former dancing school. As for Nila, her
talent, determination, and some good luck had combined to provide her
with a new career, and the closeness, leadership, and care that she had
received from her mother she now bestowed on her own "children."

Her own need to be loved, however, was insistent, and, as will be seen,
it sometimes caused a neurotic possessiveness. Another throwback to
Nila's relationship with her mother was the loyalty and devotion she expected and received from us. This increased as we regulars on the show
grew to be adults. She was indeed our surrogate mother, and an exacting
one.

Nila had said in many interviews that it was her policy not to let any
of us get inflated ideas of our own importance. This was unlikely to happen
anyway because we were a repertory company – a different play and a
different cast every week. If you played the lead one week you would just
as likely have a small part with two lines the next, or you might not be called
at all. There were no stars on "Let's Pretend."

This system accomplished several things. It kept egos in check, and it
made us a better, more versatile company of actors. It also meant that
there were no jealousies between us. We were a family, and every one of
us who survives still has warm memories of that family feeling and of Nila
Mack.

In the 1980s and into the 1990s there have been news stories of the
psychological and sometimes legal problems of former child stars in
Hollywood – alumni either of the golden age of films, or the television age
of sitcoms. All of these children had once been highly paid and led quite unnatural lives, and all the rewards and attention of stardom were showered
on them – sometimes at a very early age – then suddenly taken away when
they reached adolescence. This rarely happened in radio, because child actors were not starred, and especially not on "Let's Pretend."

In radio during the Depression and post–Depression years a cute and
clever child could sometimes earn a lot of money, and since in those days
every member of the family was expected to contribute, the child's radio
earnings, if Pop was out of work, might be the entire week's bankroll for
the family. The child did not feel exploited, and the family did not feel
guilty.

There were cases in which the parents simply took advantage of their high-earning child, but those were rare. It was just such exploitation, involving the famous child actor Jackie Coogan in Hollywood, which led to California's Child Actors' Bill, better known as the Coogan Act, designed to protect the earnings of future child actors in that state.

What became of a child's earnings depended on each family's financial situation and their code of values. With my first radio money, while I still lived on Staten Island, I was allowed to buy a bicycle, then my own dog (a Boston terrier pup I named Gus, after the Swedish prize fighter, played by George Frame Brown, in my first paid radio job "Tony and Gus," in 1935). Later, living in Manhattan, I paid for my own school tuition and clothing. I learned to put almost everything else in the bank. But we were one of the lucky families: my father was always employed.

As Depression financial pressures eased, child actors' families were more likely to put their earnings aside for education. The father of one successful child actor I knew put the boy's earnings into investments, which paid off handsomely when he was grown. Usually, children in radio were aware of their families' financial problems, which put unbearable pressures on them. When I was about 13, I once saw another child actor, a boy who was going through the adolescent voice change and was not working much, sitting on one of the leather-covered benches on the eighth floor at NBC, looking forlorn and desolate. I asked him what was the matter. "My father told me not to come home until I have a job," he said.

In spite of the casting on "Let's Pretend" being very democratic – what you might call a democracy with a very strong president – Nila did like to boast about her kids who had achieved prominence elsewhere: Patricia Peardon who starred on Broadway in *Junior Miss*; Patricia Ryan who costarred on radio in "Claudia and David; the Mauch Twins, Billy and Bobby, who went to Hollywood to play in *The Prince and the Pauper*; Billy Halop who went to Hollywood to repeat his Broadway role in *Dead End*; and Eddie Ryan, who went the same route to play in the wartime film *The Sullivans*. All of them had benefitted from the acting experience and the values instilled in them by Nila. She had a right to be proud.

As Bill Lipton says, "She demanded strict loyalty and personal dedication. But she gave a lot to us, too – in attention, and interest in our personal lives, especially when later on some of us married, and had children." Jack Grimes remembers, "Most of us were very happy to be on 'Let's Pretend.' We had a training ground in radio acting – in voice – in diction – and also in personal behavior."

I have been referring to our director, mentor, and surrogate mother mostly as Nila, but we Pretenders as children always addressed her as Miss Mack. For one thing, said Sybil Trent, "The director was God." And children in the 1930s were taught to respect elders more than nowadays. I do not know when she became Nila to each of us, but for me, at least, it did not happen until after I had returned in early 1946 after three years in uniform, and ten years after I had started as a Let's Pretender.

Nila's insistence on complete loyalty occasionally became unreasonable. She did not take kindly to our accepting other shows which conflicted with "Let's Pretend." She wanted the right to choose which actors to call each week, but did not want to hear that someone was unavailable.

There was also a bit of trouble about Pretenders who worked on Madge Tucker's "Coast to Coast on a Bus" over at NBC, even though it aired on Sunday and there was no time conflict. The show, which Tucker had started as "The Lady Next Door," was more or less a kiddie variety show, but with a connecting story line of everybody riding a bus on the White Rabbit Line. There was some tension between Nila and Tucker, after that lady had said that anyone who did "Let's Pretend" could not be on her program. Some of those who left "Pretend" for that reason included Billy Halop, his sister Florence Halop, and Jimmy McCallion. Billy and Florence later returned.

Besides total commitment and constant availability, another thing our director expected from all her actors, no matter how young, was good speech. This did not mean affected or cultured pear-shaped tones, just clear and correct pronunciation of the words; and from occasional players to those of us who were on every week, she never let us forget it. To Albert Aley, who usually played romantic leads: "Don't say, 'Lovely Princess, forgimme.' It's two words – forgive – me. And it's not buh-loved – it's BE-loved." She admonished Jack Grimes: "Strength has a 'g' in it – don't say 'strenth'." And to Sybil Trent: "Say, 'I'll wait for you at the castle' – not 'I'll wait FER you at the castle.' This isn't a commercial for the I. J. Fox Fur Company." Sybil learned well these lessons in good speech from Nila, but this once got her into trouble on a daytime serial when the director said, "Don't be so cultured. Why don't you speak like normal people?"

Nila's own speech was exactly what she expected from us – clearly and correctly articulated but never exaggerated. Her voice was low-pitched, but never weak. (It later became lower and huskier, and punctuated with coughing, because of her constant smoking.) She would look at you directly with her large, blue eyes, which bulged slightly because of a thyroid condition, and would speak from the front of her mouth, without pushing, except for emphasis. Her speech pattern no doubt came from a strong background of training from her mother, at school, and her years of performing in vaudeville and in the theatre, where your voice had to be audible at the rear of the balcony of any size theatre, without benefit of microphones or amplifiers.

As with any mother, surrogate or not, there was the matter of discipline. Besides the verbal criticism we sometimes got (but always in private),

Nila's only disciplinary measure – and it was a powerful one – was simply not calling us. This applied to adult actors as well. Back in the 1930s Nila did not approve of the continuity Henry Boyd had written to go with his bird songs on a "Sunday Morning at Aunt Susan's" broadcast, so she changed it. She was not there for the air show, possibly due to illness, and Henry reinstated his own script. Nila must have heard this on her radio at home, and Henry did not get called for a long time. Finally, he went to her office with a large bunch of lilacs, which he knew she loved.

"Are you trying to bribe me, Henry?" asked Nila. "Yes," said Henry. He apologized, and Nila told him that you really couldn't get away with saying whatever you felt like on the radio, and all was forgiven.

On another occasion, in the "Helen and Mary" days, Madeline Lee, then a little girl and new on the show, was cast by Nila in a leading role on that week's program. She came down from the Bronx on the subway Saturday morning with her mother, but they took the wrong train and were five minutes late. When she arrived, Madeline found that her part had been given to another child, and so she had just a couple of lines. She burst into tears. But Nila's point had been made – don't be late for my rehearsals.

Our director found that in dealing with the children on "Let's Pretend," and those who aspired to be on it, there were inevitably . . . *their* mothers. Of course, every small child who performs must have a parent or guardian for the guidance of his or her career and for an escort to and from performances and rehearsals. But when a mother intrudes in rehearsals and other business sessions, or demands special or star treatment for her child, she becomes a *Stage Mother* – a form of life universally detested by all those who have to deal with them.

One of the best-organized and most aggressive stage mothers was Walter Tetley's. For years, until Walter finally moved to the West Coast, any director getting off the elevator on NBC's third floor knew that he would probably have to run a one-woman gauntlet with flaming red frizzy hair and steel-rimmed glasses consisting of Mrs. Tetley, who would accost him with, "Don't you have anything for Walter today?"

Nila Mack did not suffer stage mothers gladly. First, she did not like them present when she interviewed their children. When the parent did all the talking or put words in the child's mouth in response to questions, that to her was bad news, and she would usually pass that child up when selecting new cast members.

Eddie Ryan remembers being allowed to sit in when our director was auditioning a very young girl. "Her mother was primping her and giving her last-minute instructions, when Nila asked her to leave the room," he writes. "The mother didn't want to go. Nila said, 'I'm auditioning your daughter only. If you prefer, we can just call it off.' Suffice it to say, mother left."

The children who came without their mothers, Miss Mack said, had a better chance of pleasing her. It was easier for her to get to know the child's personality and talent. Stage mothers, she found, usually spoiled the children, made them nervous, and, she said, "they get in our hair." (Please note that *Stage Fathers* were practically unknown.)

To quote an early story in the *New York Sun*,

> While training the children requires a lot of patience, training the parents is quite a different matter. There are mothers, it appears, who believe that their young hopefuls should be given the lead in each performance, and, quick to grab a battle-axe at the slightest suggestion of what they term discrimination or favoritism, they soon would have the whole cast in a temperamental uproar were it not for the iron rod with which the directress rules her clan. Too much temperament on the part of a fond parent will result in her offspring's involuntary absence from the next program listing, and no more dire punishment can be meted out.

Dire punishment indeed. It was not so much the $3.50 that the mothers were interested in as being able to list "Let's Pretend" on their child's credits, printed on the 3×5 cards which all radio actors sent to casting directors for their files.

Most of the mothers of "Let's Pretend" children were no problem. They handled their children's calls and business affairs. They brought the youngsters to rehearsals and broadcasts and were there to pick them up afterward. Otherwise, they were invisible. For the most part Nila got along with them very well. She formed a close friendship with Sandra Levy, Gwen Davies's mother, when Gwen was in her late teens. But this did not change her opinion of stage mothers in general, which she expressed in an article written in 1945: "These grey hairs were never caused by the kids but by some of those horrible, incredibly ambitious *stage mothers* who shall be nameless and, I'm afraid, with us forever."

Beginning with the necessity of keeping her job in 1930 and continuing through her years of experience at CBS, Nila had learned to deal with, work with, and love the children on "Let's Pretend." She possibly had not really articulated her feelings about them until approached by an interviewer in 1947. "Do you think that's why you put fairy stories on the air? . . . Because you are a widow without any children?" Nila replied, "As a matter of fact, I think it's because I just love fairy stories. I've loved them since childhood."

"And of course you love children too?" Nila flared at this. "I don't do any such thing. I love people – provided they are nice people. If some of those people happen to be children, fine. Children are just as much individuals as grown-ups are, and you can like or dislike them just as much." And in spite of her own insecurities and personal eccentricities, this feeling towards her child actors was apparent to everyone who met her.

Besides Nila Mack's scripts, her genius for choosing and working with her juvenile cast was the main reason the show survived longer than any other dramatic program on American radio (unless one counts "One Man's Family," which was a continuing serial). In its time "Let's Pretend" won dozens of awards and audience polls as the best children's program on the air. Nila cherished these honors and the high regard in which she was held on the executive floor at 485 Madison. But more valuable to her was the loyalty and affection of her "kids." Her work was her life, and we were her family.

Chapter 7

Nila

Nila Mack's personal life as well as her professional life were now very different from the years when she had lived in hotels and rooming houses. Mr. and Mrs. Howard Lindsay (Dorothy Stickney) had become her closest friends. She and her husband Roy had met them while summering at Lakewood, Maine, where the Skowhegan Playhouse was located. Lindsay was director there, and Dorothy Stickney was the ingenue, and they fell in love and were married in 1927. The Briants, Roy and Nila, had also been part of the happy theatrical community on the shores of Lake Wesserunsett.

When Nila returned to New York from her radio venture in Arkansas City and began her new life working for CBS, she leased an apartment directly down the hall from the Lindsays, in a brownstone row house at 41 West Tenth Street in Greenwich Village. From then on she was never without a piano, pianos having been an important part of her childhood. One night when there was a party at the Lindsays the piano was wheeled down the hall from her apartment into theirs.

In 1934 when Howard Lindsay and Russel Crouse were writing the new musical *Anything Goes*, Howard told Nila that Cole Porter was coming down to let them hear the score for the first time. The ancient upright was wheeled in again, and so the first performance of those now classic hits "Anything Goes," "You're the Top," and "I Get a Kick Out of You" was on Nila Mack's piano. The instrument did have problems, though. Not only was it somewhat out of tune but when Porter launched into the first number, "You're the Top," the ivory top of one of the keys flew off (characteristically, in the version of the story from the CBS publicity department, it was *two* key tops).

Meanwhile, Nila kept up with other friends she had met during her days in the theatre. Two of them were Georgia Backus, whom she had met in a stock company, and who had helped start her career with CBS, and also Elaine Ivans, whom she had met in the brief vaudeville tour of *Eva the Fifth*, and as we have seen, she used both of them in radio.

As Nila got into the swing of things at CBS, being gregarious and outgoing, she soon formed friendships with others in the production department on the fourteenth floor. Jerome Lawrence, later a celebrated American playwright (best remembered as coauthor, with Robert Lee, of the Broadway hits *Inherit the Wind, Auntie Mame,* and *Dear World*) had his office down the hall from Nila. So did Norman Corwin, who became famous for his series "26 by Corwin," which he wrote, directed, and produced, along with many other brilliant radio plays, on the network's pioneering series "The Columbia Workshop." Edward R. Murrow (no doubt with cigarette in hand) would poke his head into Nila's office to say hello. And, of course, William Paley, whom everyone called Bill, and who kept in personal touch with all of the network's workings, including program production, was never far away.

Her closest friend at Columbia, though, was Charles Jackson, whose scripts for the network never attained any fame even remotely approaching his best-seller novel *Lost Weekend,* later made into a film starring Ray Milland.

As I got to know Miss Mack better, I became increasingly impressed by the contrasting sides of her nature. She had the ability to be sentimental – even reverent, when human values were in question, a feeling expressed so well in her scripts – then the ability to instantly show her other side in a hearty, ribald laugh at someone's joke, or by a quick on the uptake gag of her own. It was her humor especially that endeared her to the many adults she worked with at CBS – actors, production people and executives.

Once when Nila entered a crowded elevator on the fourteenth floor, she saw at the back one of her dear friends, a CBS vice president. Between them stood the Deep River Boys, a black vocal quartet under contract to the network, and just leaving rehearsal. Without hesitation she greeted her friend: "Doctor Livingstone, I presume."

Then there was Frank Readick's urine. Frank (the father of Bob Readick), whose distinctive, slightly rasping voice was heard regularly on "The March of Time" and many other network shows, had just come from his yearly physical, and was boasting to his fellow actors at Colbee's Restaurant downstairs that the doctor had said his urine was as clear as a bell. "Nila ought to know about this," one of them said. Frank went right over to a pay phone, dropped a nickel in it, and called her office. "Nila, this is Frank. Guess what? I just had my physical, and my urine is as clear as a bell!" "Good," snapped Nila. "I'll take two cases." And hung up.

Of course, none of this is to say that Nila Mack did not have a temper or wasn't hard to get along with at times. She did have what Jerry Lawrence called a dark side, which could be attributed at least partly to the executive pressure cooker in which she was now sealed. Though Douglas Coulter, her immediate supervisor, was a friend and protector, Nila Mack was nevertheless pretty much a lone woman in a man's world.

The only other women on the staff in the mid–1930s were Nila's close friend Dorothy Gordon, who produced educational and public service programs; Margaret Lewerth, a writer who probably did not have any executive input; Marge Morrow, the casting director; and Lucile Singleton, who auditioned vocalists and staff singers. Otherwise, the executive and production floors were all male, except for secretaries and receptionists. Nila was intelligent, resourceful, and high-spirited. She could match any of the men, idea for idea, joke for joke, and drink for drink. But it could not have been easy. During all of her career at CBS, she was always conscious of being a woman, and thus a member of a very small minority.

In 1936 the Lindsays moved from West Tenth Street into a house they had bought on West Eleventh, and Nila had already moved uptown, to be nearer her work. CBS was at Fifty-Second Street and Madison Avenue, and she found a floor-through apartment with a large terrace, two flights up, in a brownstone at 55 West Fifty-Third Street, less than four blocks away. This was to be her home for the rest of her life, and it was a place many of us got to know, since we were all invited there for Christmas parties and other special occasions. Besides the apartment itself, one of the most permanent and dependable parts of her existence from then on was her maid Maud Wilson, who loyally stuck with her for 18 years.

Nila, much too busy to long nostalgically for the good old days in the theatre or in vaudeville, was using her talents to the fullest. In a 1937 newspaper "thumbnail biography" she was described thus:

> She'd like to look like Miriam Hopkins, and have Dorothy Parker's brains.
> Current hobby: Trying to understand 50,000,000 children.
> Likes very feminine clothes, large show hankies and turkey dinners. Is unusually mechanically inclined. [Nila often wore dark-colored dresses with polka dots and wide collars, and a bow in her hair. As for her being mechanically inclined, I never saw any evidence of that.]
> Favorite star: Charlie Chaplin.
> Attracted to sincere, honest he-men and regular, feet-on-the-ground women. [She was definitely still attracted to the opposite sex. Some surviving Pretenders have vague memories of a romance with a man who worked for CBS, but there is nothing to indicate that, if it existed, it was very serious or of more than brief duration.]
> Has never had enough dancing, congenial companionship or seen enough mountains.
> Weighs 130 lbs., is 5'3" tall, has curly blonde hair and blue eyes. [I would describe her hair as ash blonde, and as for her weight, she did gain a few pounds in the years following this interview.]
> Programs: "Let's Pretend" and "Sunday Morning at Aunt Susan's."

Elsa Maxwell, in her newspaper column "Party Line" described Nila in 1943 as "plump and soft. She laughs constantly. She has hair the color of wheat, a pink skin and a tough mind." *Newsweek* the same year saw Nila as

"large, plump, hard-boiled and shrewd." All of these writers, on very short acquaintance, were trying to sum up Nila by describing her as the Texas Guinan–type New York nightclub proprietor she had once played on radio in 1929, an image no doubt reinforced by her constant smoking. They failed to see, or at least completely left out, her warmth and sincerity, qualities that were also present in abundance in her scripts.

In 1940 *Time* magazine, on the occasion of Nila's tenth anniversary with CBS, also mentioned, only incidentally, one of her chief interests: "Scripteuse for 'Let's Pretend,' ... is blonde, broad-beamed Nila Mack, who used to be an actress, now lives with a cat in Manhattan." The cat referred to was a grey Persian named Cloudy. Nila had several cats over the years in New York. Another was Mr. Pinney, a white Persian who was called that, she said, because no one knew him well enough to call him by his first name.

A newspaper article described Pinney as liking water in a big way. "He drinks directly from the water faucet, ... and likes to curl up in the wash bowl to take a siesta. A guest in the Mack menage knows he is welcome when Pinney leaps up to the broad brim of the bowl and supervises ablutions."

One of Nila's friends, CBS engineer Jack Mason, once went to her apartment to repair her radio. "She used to have at least one cat there," he remembers. "They clawed the devil out of the sofa – the furniture. When I first saw them doing it I got upset. She said, 'Let them alone – they get so much fun out of it.'"

In Nila's later years, at one of the Christmas parties she gave for the Pretenders Sybil Trent's husband Andrew Nieporent, who had never been in her apartment, was admiring a pair of perfectly matched life-sized statues of fawn-colored Siamese cats, placed on opposite ends of the fireplace mantel in Nila's living room. As he came nearer to examine them, the two statues leaped off the mantel in perfect unison and scampered away, almost giving him a heart attack, as he later described it. The leaping felines were her two Siamese, Sapphire and Tsing-Fooey, who had been posing as cats do, and inspecting the crowd from a safe vantage point.

Nila may have preferred dogs originally. There had always been dogs in the Mac household from her early childhood, but now, living alone and with a busy professional life, cats were just the thing. She later started a collection of cats made of porcelain and crystal.

Like Dorothy Stickney, she also collected music boxes. At the time of

Opposite: **Ca. 1938. A party at Nila Mack's apartment. Maud Wilson, Arthur Anderson, Kingsley Colton, Jack Kelk, Jack Grimes, Patricia Peardon, Vivian Block, Harry Swan, Estelle Levy, Arthur Ross, Betty Jane Tyler, Nila Mack, Miriam Wolfe, Patricia Ryan, Daisy Aldan, Sybil Trent, Michael O'Day, Albert Aley, Eddie Ryan, and Sidney Lumet. ©1938 CBS Inc. Used by permission.**

her death she had dozens. Other than the cats and the music boxes, she liked reading, mostly historical novels, eating well, and going to the theatre. Those of us who survive do not believe she was particularly happy when alone. Her chief satisfactions in life were her work and the people she worked with – mostly her family of young actors on "Let's Pretend."

As we regulars on the show formed closer bonds over the years with our director (early newspaper accounts always referred to her as a "directress") we learned more of the things that amused or pleased her and the things she could not abide. Among other things she had always been strongly patriotic. She once stopped a rehearsal of "The March of Games" during World War II to read from the control room a communiqué that had just come in (she was so excited that she pronounced it "comuneek") to the effect that our navy had just sunk 23 Japanese ships.

From time to time we would catch glimpses of the things she had been exposed to in her years in vaudeville, such as the dialogue (possibly from Weber and Fields) that went like this:

> Say! Vot's de difference between ah cynic and ah stoic?
> I couldn't even emegine.
> It's simple. Ah stoic is vot brings de babies, and ah cynic is vere you vash dem.

As was often said back then, that's what killed vaudeville.

For several years before our Cream of Wheat sponsorship there were annual "Let's Pretend" Christmas parties at the New Weston Hotel, at Madison Avenue and Fiftieth Street. There would be a long table in the oak-paneled dining room and a large Christmas tree. The menu was pretty much the same every year: Chicken croquettes with gravy on mashed potatoes and Holland rusk, with green peas, rolls and butter, and ice cream for dessert. Each of the boys would get the same present, and each of the girls another. (I still have the binoculars from one year, which have weak lenses but immense sentimental value.)

There was always a piano there, and Nila would do one of two acts. The first consisted of some of the thumping revivalist songs she had heard as a girl in Arkansas City, which she would sing in her throaty voice. One of

Opposite: Ca. 1936: A "Let's Pretend" Christmas party at the New Weston. Standing, rear: Elaine Engler, Albert Aley, Arthur Anderson, Jack Jordan, Don Hughes, unidentified, Vivian Block, Milton Kamen, unidentified, Patricia Ryan, Estelle Levy, Patricia Patterson, Patricia Goodwin, Joyce Gates, and Miriam Wolfe. Extreme rear, against wall: Andy Donnelly, and Eddie Ryan. Seated, far side of table: Margaret McKee, Harry Swan, unidentified, and Ronald Liss. Near side of table: Florence Halop, Lester Jay (note cigarette), Lloyd Barry (the boys that year were given Burgess flashlights), Betty Philson, Nila Mack, and unidentified. ©1936 CBS Inc. Used by permission.

them was titled "I'm H-A-P-P-Y Cause I Am S-A-V-E-D," and another was "The Bells of Hell Go Ting-a-Ling-a-Ling, for You But Not for Me."

More familiar, because she did it at almost every "Pretend" cast gathering, was Nila's rendition of the silent film music she had played back in 1912 in Metropolis, Illinois. As she played the cues for "Danger," "Romance," or "Chase," you could see reflected in her large, expressive eyes exactly what was happening on the imaginary screen.

The Christmas parties at the New Weston are for me a marvelous memory of my childhood, and the Yuletide season. Needless to say, parents were not invited. At one of them, someone (we are pretty sure it was Lester Jay) crawled under the entire length of the long, white-clothed table to give another boy a hotfoot. (And if you, dear reader, do not know what a hotfoot is, you may congratulate yourself on your youth.)

Chapter 8

The Cast Grows

Nila Mack once said that when she found one child during each of her semiannual talent auditions who showed promise of fitting into the "Let's Pretend" cast, she considered herself fortunate. They were either too self-conscious, too brash, or, more usually, just did not have any feeling for how to read lines or relate to a script or to other actors. But the need was there, for children were constantly either dropping out or were being eliminated by Nila as it became obvious to her that they were not integrating well into the Land of Let's Pretend.

Gradually, Miss Mack did find more child actors who were versatile and talented. There were eight more long-term Let's Pretenders, who, starting in 1935, stayed with the show and became part of its identity. They were, in the order of joining the cast, Sybil Trent, Arthur Anderson, Jack Grimes, Kingsley Colton, Betty Jane Tyler, Bill Lipton, Bob Readick, and Rita Lloyd, the last to join us, in 1948, whose career will be outlined in a later chapter.

Sybil Trent

Sybil Trent, together with Gwen Davies, is even today more closely identified with "Let's Pretend" than any of us, first because during our sponsored years she and Gwen Davies would open every show with the Cream of Wheat theme song, and also because very often she would have the female lead in the story.

Sybil was an only child. During the Depression her father went to work for the Swee-Touch-Nee Tea Company. The family originally lived in Brooklyn, moving to midtown Manhattan when Sybil got a part in a Broadway show. For many years they lived at the Whitby, an apartment hotel on West Forty-Fifth Street, just down the block from the Martin Beck Theatre, and where most of the tenants were show people.

Sybil was three and a half years old when her mother took her to Warner Brothers studios in Brooklyn to audition for the *Our Gang* comedies. Though nothing came of that audition, she was called within a week to do a short subject with Fatty Arbuckle. She then became a member of the Warner Brothers stock company, doing singing, dancing, or dramatic roles in more than 25 shorts, as well as features, for RKO. These included *The People's Enemy* with Lila Lee and Melvyn Douglas, *Keep 'Em Rolling* with Walter Huston, and short subjects with Ruth Etting and Sammy Davis, Jr. (New York in the 1920s and early 1930s was still a major studio production center.) By the time "Let's Pretend" entered her life, Sybil was, at the age of nine, already a show business veteran.

When Sybil did her first "Let's Pretend" broadcast in late 1935 she was fresh from a more spectacular triumph, having opened November 16 in Billy Rose's extravaganza *Jumbo*, at the huge Hippodrome, which occupied the entire block on Sixth Avenue between Forth-Third and Forty-Fourth streets.

(The Hippodrome probably hit its high point during the run of *Jumbo*, which played 233 performances, closing in June 1936. The huge house was only 30 years old at the time, but had been closed for 5 years previously, no doubt due to the Depression and the high costs of producing any show big enough to fill its 5,200 seats. It later had a few desultory bookings of lesser-known opera companies, then wrestling matches, then nothing, until it was pulled down in 1939. The site stood empty until 1952, and now only the name remains at that location: the Hippodrome Parking Garage.)

The score of *Jumbo* was by Rodgers and Hart, conducted by Paul Whiteman, and directed by George Abbott (book) and John Murray Anderson (musical numbers), and starred Jimmy Durante, Donald Novis, and Gloria Grafton. Grafton dreams of being in the circus, whereupon little Sybil Elaine, as she was then known, enters in a silver and crystal coach with grey satin seat, drawn by two white ponies. She tells Grafton the circus isn't under canvas but in your heart. This was known as the spangled dream scene. The classic song "Little Girl Blue" was later sung to Sybil, after which she made her exit riding on an elephant.

Another major part of Sybil's early background, shared by several other Pretenders, and many other child performers of the 1930s, was the influence of Mabel Horsey, a large, black lady who, assisted by her husband Leonard, ran a performing school at 155 West Forty-Sixth Street. Children sang, danced, did monologues and imitations, and under Horsey's tutelage performed in benefits at the Town Hall and many other places in the New York area. Her pianist was Hazel Scott.

By the age of six Sybil was emceeing her own radio show on station WHN, "Baby Sybil Elaine and Her Kiddie Revue," sponsored by a Brooklyn furniture store. She would imitate Joe Penner (with cigar) and the Block and Sully comedy team, finishing her act with a tap dance, and closing each show by singing "Thank You for a Lovely Evening." Another of

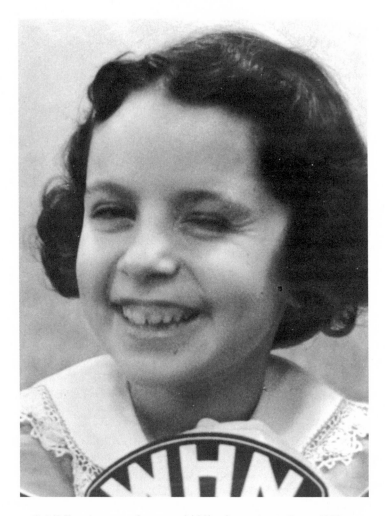

Sybil Trent emcees her own kiddie show at age 6, ca. 1932.

her performances was the sure-fire crowd pleaser "I Wish There Were a Radio Up in Heaven So Mother Dear Could Listen In to Me." The culmination of Sybil's musical career was later, when she sang "I Love You from Coast to Coast" on "The Kate Smith Show" on the CBS network.

In 1935 Sybil was attending public school 17 on West Forty-Seventh Street when Nila Mack and Dorothy Gordon went there to interview children for "The Children's Forum of the Air." Sybil was not chosen for this, but Miss Mack said, "Why don't you come and audition for 'Let's Pretend'?"

Nila found she liked everything about Sybil but her name. "No one can go through life with two first names," she said, and after a conference with

Sybil's mother, Sybil Elaine became Sybil Trent. Not only was it short and easy to remember, said Miss Mack, but the initials were the same as those of Shirley Temple, who hadn't done so badly herself.

Sybil had black hair, lively brown eyes, a ready smile and was very good-natured, but most important for radio was the fact that she had great emotional range, could read lines and follow directions easily, and also had (and still has) a remarkably warm and sympathetic vocal quality. In one interview Nila called Sybil her future Claudette Colbert.

The radio production industry in New York in the mid–1930s was a comparatively small group, and word about Sybil Trent got around quickly. Once she had been auditioned by Air Features, that most prolific producer of daytime serials, she started being busy on shows for them and for many others. She remembers playing a little blind girl on "David Harum" early on, and doing a running part on "Front Page Farrell." She was also on two of the five a week segments on the CBS-produced "American School of the Air."

For two years Sybil was the Drum Major on a children's quiz program, "The March of Games," which was on two weekday afternoons a week in 1939, and later shifted to half an hour on Sundays. There were questions to test vocabulary and general knowledge; and there were tongue twisters and musical questions as well. Master of ceremonies was another Pretender, Arthur Ross, who billed himself as the youngest MC in radio. Sybil appeared in full costume, with visored hat, white satin dress, white cape lined with red, and carrying a baton. How she was able to also hold her script I do not remember.

As Sybil grew into her teens her two occupations were acting on radio and completing her schooling. Her mature vocal quality won her emotional adult roles on several daytime serials, including Thelma, the lead, on "We Love and Learn," as well as on night-time shows, including "Gangbusters," "The March of Time," and "Famous Jury Trials."

Though Sybil became one of the mainstays of "Let's Pretend," she was not called steadily until 1943 when we were sponsored, and she and Gwen Davies became the show's musical signature, as well as usually appearing in the story and in the commercials as well. However, neither of the girls, or for that matter any of us, ever received written contracts in advance. None of us could assume we would be on that week's show until called the previous Tuesday. Nila had said many times she did not want any of us to get swelled heads. It is most unlikely that Sybil ever would have anyway, but a rule was a rule, with no exceptions. Our director was taking no chances.

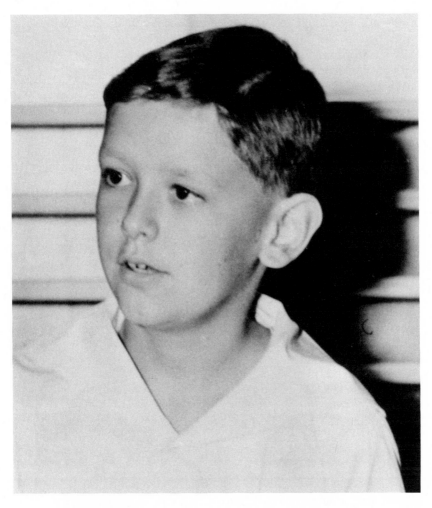

Arthur Anderson, age 12, on NBC's "Tony and Gus," 1935.

Arthur Anderson

I came on the "Let's Pretend" scene May 6, 1936, and from then on until our last broadcast, except for military service, I was on consistently almost every week. My father was Danish. He was an engineer with the Mack Truck Company. My mother was English, born Violet Elizabeth Brookfield. My great-uncle Charles Brookfield, born in 1857, was a British actor in plays and in vaudeville, a well-known wit, and later a play-wright.

I was born on Staten Island, New York, in 1922 and had two elder brothers, Edward and George. I came to radio indirectly through my first drama teacher Cecyl Grimes, who ran the Children's Playhouse in Dongan Hills in a little barn in her front yard. My first role there, at age seven, was Rip Van Winkle in a Christmas pageant, and it included a song to my dog Schneider. A character man already! I started appearing regularly in 1934 on a kiddie hour on station WMCA, emceed by the *New York Daily Mirror* columnist Nick Kenny who, with his brother Charles, Miss Cecyl's friend, formed one of the foremost songwriting teams of the 1930s (for example, "Love Letters in the Sand," "There's a Gold Mine in the Sky," "While a Cigarette Was Burning"). Charles Kenny also wrote songs independently of his brother, songs of a more fanciful nature. Some of his titles were: "I Wear My Glasses to Bed Every Night (So I Can See You in My Dreams)," "Every Street Is Canal Street in Venice," and "I'm Planting Little Onions (So I Can Cry Over You")."

On Uncle Nick's program I did little two-minute sketches written by my mother and myself, doing all the voices, plus dog barks.

It was through a friend of my mother's that I got my first paying radio job in August 1935 as an orphan boy named Buddy who cried a lot, on a show called "Tony and Gus" on the NBC Red Network, sponsored by Post Toasties. Once I had done a general audition and had been put in NBC's talent file, I was cast in many of their programs, including the lead in a series called "Peter Absolute," about the adventures of an orphan boy in the Erie Canal days of the nineteenth century. And it was the writer of "Peter Absolute," David Belasco Howard – later to become my good friend and mentor – who introduced me to Nila Mack.

From the first, at age 13, I was an all-around character man on "Let's Pretend." I was good at doing voices. If there was a mysterious old man sitting by the side of the road who warned the prince of danger ahead and gave him a magic charm to protect himself, that was me. I was always one of the three talking crows on "Faithful John." I was a crooked innkeeper who stole the magic gifts that had been given to the innocent young hero in "The Donkey, the Table and the Stick," and innumerable others over the years.

All of the juvenile actors on the show could "get into" or assume the characters we were playing, but I was one of the few who could do a complete voice change, using different inflections, rhythms, or age characteristics – sometimes a dialect – whatever I thought was called for when I saw the script. It was great fun. Miss Mack saw at once where my talents lay, and thanks to her I used them to the fullest. I do not believe that what I or any of us did on "Let's Pretend" was hokey or exaggerated – she would not have allowed it. We were dealing in fantasy, but our director insisted that it be played legitimately.

Because of the great variety of roles I played on the show, people were sometimes confused when I told them I was a Let's Pretender. They could never identify me with any particular part or even any kind of part. I did not mind. Not only did I get what I thought were the juiciest roles but I was on almost every week. It is often said that some people become actors to escape reality, and, if this was or is true of me, nowhere did I have the chance to do that more completely in my career than on "Let's Pretend."

My mother and I spent an abortive two months in Hollywood in September–October 1936. David O. Selznick had optioned me to star in a planned spectacular production of *Tom Sawyer*. My life might have been very different but for the fact that bad weather in Hannibal, Missouri – where the film was to be shot – meant postponement, and it became obvious to the film people that by next spring I would have grown too much to any longer be a cute kid. So it was back to New York, back to radio, and back to "Let's Pretend." I did not feel any failure in that. I was glad to be home again.

My parents and I had long since moved from Staten Island into Manhattan, where we lived over the years in various parts of West Greenwich Village. Many other radio shows followed on both CBS and NBC, including "Bambi" with Helen Hayes, and "The Philip Morris Playhouse." After I had worked for Orson Welles in Aaron Copland's opera *Second Hurricane* I was cast by him as Lucius in his historic Mercury Theatre modern-dress production of *Julius Caesar*, which we played on Broadway (1937–38), and in repertory with the bawdy Elizabethan farce *Shoemakers' Holiday*. In that I was listed as "Boy," and spoke the prologue. Orson also used me in radio on "The Mercury Theatre on the Air," as Jim Hawkins in Robert Louis Stevenson's *Treasure Island*, and later in the Mercury's "Campbell Playhouse."

Shortly after joining "Let's Pretend" I went into my awkward years, not knowing whether I was a child or a grownup, and not feeling I fitted into either category. My voice started changing too – serious for a child radio actor. When I was called for an afternoon or evening show I knew I could carry off the 12-year-old and younger parts I was cast in, but a morning show was a problem (I knew nothing about voice warm-up techniques, of course). That was another reason I felt secure and happy on "Let's Pretend." When doing a giant or an enchanted frog, adolescent voice change was not a problem. I was gangling and bony, with a sensitive face, wavy brown hair, and slightly protruding ears.

In those days I masked my shyness and insecurity by clowning – by doing vocal sound effects and acting silly at parties, where I felt particularly vulnerable. Meanwhile, I had become quite good at singing and playing the ukulele. I constructed my own Two-Man Band ("Who's the other man?" "I'm both men"). It consisted of kazoo and train whistle mounted on a coat hanger around my neck, the uke, and various electric and mechanical bells and horns I operated with my feet.

There was occasional mischief, but it was mostly harmless. Whenever "Let's Pretend" publicity photos were taken at 485 Madison Avenue, I would collect the flash bulbs (they were at that time made of glass, and almost as large as regular light bulbs), and drop them one by one down an unoccupied air shaft from the twenty-first floor. Each one made a satisfying pop as it exploded far below. Another escapade, which could have been more serious, took place at the National Theatre, where the Mercury was now playing *Julius Caesar*, in March 1938. I had a long, boring wait in my fourth-floor dressing room during every performance, and during one Wednesday matinee I applied a match to a sprinkler head on the ceiling, expecting the metal in it to slowly ooze down. Instead, the head popped off suddenly. The water inundated the dressing room, cascaded through a fire door and down onto the main switchboard, and eventually the stage. This resulted in the only intermission there had been in any Orson Welles production up to that time. Miraculously, no one was electrocuted, and the story, which was run in every New York daily, was no doubt a help at the box office. (John Houseman in his book *Run-Through* said that I was supporting my widowed mother at the time. Actually, my father was very much alive and proud of what I was doing, with the possible exception of what I have just related.)

Nila Mack used me on some of her other CBS shows, including the Thursday "Tales from Far and Near" segment of "The American School of the Air," as well as on "The March of Games," but I was not as aggressive in looking for work as were some of the other Pretenders (and their mothers). By January 1943 this didn't matter anyway, for right after doing a commercial on "Big Sister" ("My wife washes my shirts white as snow with Rinso") and the following Saturday doing my favorite "Let's Pretend" role, King Feodor in "The Queen Who Couldn't Make Spice Nuts," I was drafted.

I played a distinctly nonstarring role in the U.S. Army Air Corps for over three years, but whenever I was home on furlough Nila would always write in a part for me, such as a mysterious voice which could be done in an isolation booth or behind a screen. She felt, and rightly, that a soldier in uniform shouldn't be seen on a children's radio program.

Jack Grimes

Of all the Pretenders, Jack Grimes was the most successful in his radio career. Rather than trying to catalogue his credits, it would be easier to mention those shows he did not do. The list would be much shorter. In fact,

Jack Grimes, age 11, in Studio 1, ca. 1937. Photo by the author.

during the years 1937 to 1943, Jack and Kingsley Colton, another Pretender, between them probably played close to 90 percent of the male child parts in New York radio.

As a child Jack was small for his age. He had blue eyes, sandy brown hair, freckles, a button nose, and an impish grin – a cheerful, altogether likable typical American boy type. He also had a great facility for understanding the script and reading lines intelligently, and was a quick study.

In April 1937 Nila Mack went to see a new Broadway play, *Excursion*, with Shirley Booth and Whitford Kane, at the Vanderbilt Theatre. Jack was in the cast. She went backstage and asked him to come and audition for "Let's Pretend." (Jack, incidentally, had not long before celebrated his tenth birthday in Tulsa, Oklahoma, while on the road with Helen Menken and Judith Anderson in *The Old Maid*.)

When Jack did the dog script, one of great pathos, as part of his audition, he cried real tears – sobbed, in fact, Nila told him he would be used on the show. "Okay," said Jack, "but I don't want to do any of that sissy stuff – any of those princes." And she never did cast him in any romantic parts – he was much better at other things anyway. For instance, he always played the long-suffering Fisherman in "The Fisherman and His Wife" who has to go back time after time, more and more embarrassed, to the Magic Floun-der (always Albert Aley) each time his wife (usually Gwen Davies) de-mands a bigger house, then a castle, ad nauseum. He was Terry in the Hans Christian Andersen story "The Flying Trunk" – a charming con artist who uses his wits and his good luck to gain great riches and the hand of a princess.

Another of his favorite roles was the brave Jack in "Jack and the Beanstalk." In fact, his specialty on "Let's Pretend" became feisty parts that called for great energy, and which usually made use of his great talent for comedy. Jack found these much more fun than the child parts he played on other shows – the conventional cliché roles that all of us were called upon to do – orphans who cried, or kids who were constantly physically or emotionally abused. Sadly, it cannot be said that all dramatic fare in those dear old golden days of radio was necessarily great.

The contradiction in the Jack Grimes story is that, to hear him tell it, he didn't enjoy this at all. Jack came from a close-knit Irish Catholic family in which family ties and family support were all-important. In the early 1930s the present network of government assistance as we know it did not exist. Families took care of their own. Once it became apparent to Jack that his talents could bring in money, he became a juvenile workaholic.

There was need enough in the Grimes family. Jack's two female first cousins had been orphaned in their teens and had joined the household. Then there were Jack's older brother Pat, his younger sister May, and his father and mother. Mr. Grimes's carpet business was a casualty of the Depression. He was laid off by the carpet departments of Namm's, then Gimbel's, and suffered a complete nervous breakdown while still in middle age. And so Jack, starting at age ten, was eventually supporting seven peo-ple, including himself. There was no turning back. He had to keep working. And so, as Jack tells it, he withdrew from parochial school and simply stopped being a child.

In the post–Depression years, with unemployment widespread but radio work expanding, there were many households partly or even com-pletely supported by the child actor in the family. The Grimes family was one of them.

(A devastating comment on this was made at the time by Parker Fen-nelly, best known as Titus Moody on "Allen's Alley," but a fine actor in many other roles. One day Parker was sitting reading a newspaper on the third floor at NBC when the entire juvenile cast of Madge Tucker's "Coast to Coast on a Bus" came trooping by, towed by their proud mothers. Without looking up, Parker took his pipe out of his mouth only long enough to say quietly, paraphrasing the well-known Biblical quotation, "And a little child shall feed them.")

In spite of his full-time radio acting, Jack achieved an education. He transferred to the Professional Children's School, but since he was only in class about two hours a week, he did his work by correspondence, sometimes using a piano top in a radio studio for a desk. Later, after graduating from high school, he somehow found time to complete four years at Columbia University.

A typical week for Jack meant working seven days and doing at least 15 shows and at times more than 40. A child actor in radio was a miniature grown-up, generally paid the same money as adult actors, but always subject to the same responsibilities. That was one reason why his weekly hours with "Let's Pretend" came to mean so much to Jack. Nila Mack and the other kids were a second family, with a family's friendship and support but without the sibling rivalry that often goes with it. The only radio association that even approached this closeness for Jack was that he felt for the cast of "Second Husband," which starred Helen Menken. Jack was on that show from 1938 until the mid–1940s when it went off the air, as a member of the Cummings family, which included Miss Menken (Brenda), Joe Curtin (Grant), Jack (Dick), and Charita Bauer (another Pretender) as Jack's sister Fran.

Meanwhile, William Paley, the president of CBS who ran the company very much as a personal operation from his office on the twentieth floor, had taken an interest in Jack. He had a few actors under personal management contract, and Jack was one of them, but Paley never collected any commission from him. When Jack was 12 years old and beginning to grow, Bill Paley had a sign posted in the lobby at 485 Madison:

CONGRATULATE JACK GRIMES TODAY –
HE'S WEARING HIS FIRST LONG PANTS

When Jack began on "Let's Pretend" he wore matching tweed jacket and shorts, like other schoolboys his age, and a small tweed cap with a little visor in front. He showed up one Saturday morning in a pork-pie hat with a brim, with which he was so pleased that he refused to take it off, even for the broadcast.

As Jack grew into his teen years people thought he was becoming more and more cocky. Besides the built-in insecurities any actor has, working or not, Jack explains that he was always introverted and shy, especially because of his height. The cockiness was a cover, and a very successful one, and it certainly helped get him a lot of work he might not otherwise have had. During his teen years his idol was Mickey Rooney. "If he can do it, so can I," thought Jack. Rooney after all was only five feet tall, and Jack was not much taller.

The early 1940s brought important transitions to the lives of all the Pretenders. The child actors inhabiting Nila Mack's world of make-believe had turned into adolescents, and were now almost adults. Many of them disappeared from the show and from radio as their voices and their interests changed. But there was no aging-out for Jack. His phone continued to ring.

Jack Grimes had great energy, and as we have seen, even greater motivation. The feisty little Irish kid was a survivor. He successfully made the transition from cute kid parts to mature adult roles, and could now reasonably expect to remain active and successful in radio for many years to come.

Kingsley Colton

Kingsley, having a methodical turn of mind, knows for a fact that his first "Let's Pretend" appearance was on July 31, 1937. As a small child (born in 1924) he was already busy as a commercial model, signed with the John Robert Powers Agency. That came about when Kingsley was in a school play in Flushing, Long Island, and the father of a fellow cast member told his father that Johnson & Johnson was looking for a kid to pose for an ad – a little boy crying, with a dog. (More childhood pathos, but it kept many of us working, and sometimes quite lucratively.)

Kingsley was what in those days was called a beautiful child, with hazel eyes and brown, curly hair. He once did a screen test for the lead in the motion picture *The Yearling*. When Claude Jarman was chosen, Kingsley was not heartbroken. Though he did enjoy being a child actor ("It was okay – it was pleasant enough," he says) he was never emotionally involved with it, either positively or negatively, as were some of the other Pretenders. Kingsley was (and still is) rather shy and low key, though not painfully so.

He had an appealing quality and was energetic, intelligent, and dependable. If a radio director in the late 1930s wanted a feisty kid who could talk fast and project excitement, he would very likely call Jack Grimes. But if a more laid back, earnest, even cultured quality was wanted, he would use Kingsley.

In 1938, acting on a personal referral from a friend, Kingsley's father contacted the casting director of the BBD&O advertising agency, and as a result Kingsley started having a very busy full-time career on network radio, starting with their shows, which included "The March of Time" and

"Cavalcade of America." Mr. Colton had diligently followed up the lead. And this recalls the fact that Kingsley Colton was the only one of the Pretenders to have a father, not a mother, promoting his career.

Due to word-of-mouth referrals from directors and casting directors, Kingsley soon had a running part on the daytime serial "Valiant Lady," and another on "John's Other Wife." For over a year he was Betty Garde's little boy on "My Son and I." This was the poignant story of a vaudeville trouper who was widowed, and struggled to keep her self-respect while raising her small son.

The suspense was once prolonged for several weeks on that show when both mother and son were held captive in a cave by Mexican banditos.*

On "Let's Pretend" Kingsley always played straight parts, not comedy and not character voices. His sincerity and earnestness made any magical situation believable. He and Sybil Trent played the husband and wife Yeng-Ki and Hatsu in "Princess Moonbeam." It is the beautiful story of a poor Japanese couple whose prayers for a child are finally answered by the Moon Goddess. She sends a tiny baby whom they find in the bell of a flower. In the classic story of "The Little Lame Prince," which we did every year, Kingsley always played the title role.

After returning in 1946 after three years in U.S. Army Signal Corps Intelligence, Kingsley determined that the insecurity of an actor's life was not for him. That decision, he said, may have been made when one day he saw several grey-haired actors on the third floor at NBC waiting to audition, and he visualized himself at their age, still knocking on casting directors' doors. Though his life after V-J Day went in a very different direction, Nila Mack continued to call him for "Let's Pretend" as long as he was available.

Betty Jane Tyler

Betty Jane Tyler, born in 1928, probably first appeared on "Let's Pretend" in 1937, when she was nine years old. She, her father, mother, and older brother lived in Washington Heights in upper Manhattan, and it appears that Betty Jane broke into radio through the connections provided by a local dancing and dramatic school and the periodic showcases of its students for whatever casting people could be persuaded to attend. These tenuous connections were always augmented by a strong network of

*"My Son and I" was one of several radio programs first heard as weekly segments on "The Kate Smith Show." Another was "The Aldrich Family." The same device was used on "The Rudy Vallee Hour." They were the equivalent of out-of-town tryouts of stage plays which might or might not later reach Broadway.

ambitious mothers, who would exchange tips on whom to see and who was casting in the magic world of radio.

Her first running part was little Midgie, Marge's daughter, on "Myrt and Marge," when it moved to New York from Chicago and became a daytime serial. She was also the Norths' niece Susan on "Mrs. and Mrs. North," and had long before made her professional debut in movie shorts starring the fast-talking news commentator Floyd Gibbons. "Let's Pretend," was an important part of Betty Jane's career. She was particularly valuable to Nila Mack because even in adulthood she could still do a little-girl voice. I remember when she was a small child doing the title role in "Thumbelina," and standing on a platform to raise her to microphone height, as so many of us did in our early years.

There was a long period during which Betty Jane was not available for the show, beginning in 1944 when she won the part of Isabel, one of the leads on "Land of the Lost." This was another Saturday morning children's program, and was on the ABC network. One of Betty Jane's fellow cast members on that was Art Carney, who played Red Lantern, a magical talking fish.

The world of live radio was as glamorous for child actors as it was for grown-up performers. There you were, acting your heart out in a tall skyscraper on Madison Avenue, or the RCA Building in Radio City, for an unseen audience of possibly millions. You were being complimented, flattered, and well paid. None of us realized at the time, though, that the pressures we were under could be traumatic and damaging. A child radio actor had to be a miniature adult—a little businessman or businesswoman. Betty Jane was dealing with directors and casting people at a very early age. She had to be charming, and sometimes had to ask them to grant conflicts.* Even a simple "just thought I'd check and see if there's anything I'm right for today" phone call involved aggressive salesmanship and the possibility of rejection that is part of any actor's career. But for a ten-year-old child it could be traumatic. (Gwen Davies's mother used to give her one dollar's worth of nickels, and send her to Whelan's Drug Store to make calls to casting directors.)

In addition to this, you were expected to be no less than perfect on the broadcast. There were no recordings or retakes in radio in the 1930s and 1940s, and directors would no longer call anyone, child or adult, who fluffed their lines too often or did not observe promptness and studio discipline.

*Conflicts in radio meant the overlapping of the end of an actor's broadcast with the beginning of the rehearsal for his next engagement. Sometimes an actor would be granted a conflict on condition that he hire another performer to be his stand-in at the rehearsal he would miss. The other actor would be delighted. He would not only get paid for the rehearsal time but it would also serve as an audition for the director, and a possible entrée to his list of favored actors.

Added to this pressure was Betty Jane's constant awareness that her mother was proud of her and tremendously anxious for her to succeed. With all these things going on, something was left out. There was no time for Betty Jane to simply be a little girl.

Though the glamour of radio carried with it the pressures we have seen, especially for child performers, "Let's Pretend" was somehow different. It was, after all, fairyland. And when Betty Jane, as tiny Thumbelina – threatened with an unwanted marriage with a mole – was rescued and flew through the air on the back of a friendly swallow, musically whistled by Henry Boyd to the tune of "Birds and the Brooks," the stresses and strains of being a miniature grown-up simply vanished in fairy dust.

Bill Lipton

Bill Lipton was yet another Pretender from Brooklyn, born there in 1926. His start in radio came from the fact that his mother knew Floyd Neal, an announcer at station WOR, and Neal introduced Bill to Bob Emery, the producer of "Rainbow House," another kiddie talent show. When Emery heard Bill sing and then read some lines, he told him, "You're not a singer – you're an actor." So at age 11 Bill did his first radio work appearing in sketches on the show, and getting up at 4:30 A.M. every Sunday to make rehearsal.

After passing his audition for Nila Mack in 1938, he got his first call for "Let's Pretend." It was relayed by a neighbor, as the Liptons did not have a telephone. The message was "Be at CBS between 2:00 and 5:00 on Thursday (we were then broadcasting midweek, with a 5:30 P.M. air time). So Bill got there between 2:00 and 5:00, choosing 4:00 P.M. for his arrival. Naturally, the rehearsal had started at 2:00, so Bill's introduction to "Let's Pretend" was not a pleasant one. He remembers two other things about his first show: that it was "The Princess on the Glass Mountain," with Lester Jay doing the handsome Prince, and also (Bill could not have been feeling very good about the rehearsal call mix-up) that one of the girls flashed a lovely smile his way: it was Sybil Trent. Bill was instantly smitten, and has ever since had a heartfelt affection for her.

Though there were sometimes other feelings of affection between the Pretenders, from the surviving members I have talked to, it appears that they were always secret. Sybil, for instance, early on had a crush on Albert Aley, who usually played princes. "To me, he personified what a Prince was," she said. Her affections later shifted to Kingsley Colton – she pinned his picture over her bed – then to Jack Grimes. I had amorous thoughts about Pat Ryan for some time. We even went out on a date once. But there were no serious romances between "Let's Pretend" cast members. By the time we were adults and our respective teenage crushes had subsided we had formed such long-standing brother and sister relationships that anything closer would have seemed unnatural.

Bill, with his mother's help and guidance, became a busy child radio actor, and the family moved to Manhattan, on West Fifty-Sixth Street. His father, meanwhile, had his own problems. Mr. Lipton was not able to support his family as a singer, for which he had been trained, and so instead went into the scrap metal business. When that enterprise was no longer successful, there were several years when his son's radio earnings were the family's entire income. This was possible because Bill was now on the Air Features casting roster, and by 1938 was doing dozens of network shows.

As a child he played Skeezix on "Gasoline Alley," later progressing to the lead in "Chick Carter, Boy Detective" on the Mutual network (a spinoff from "Nick Carter"), and eventually going on to older parts such as Dr. Malone's son David on "Young Doctor Malone," and another doctor's son, John Brent, on "Road of Life." (Remembering those last two shows, incidentally, brings to mind the old French proverb which translates: "The more things change, the more they are the same." After 60 years, and the transition from radio to television, daytime serials are still preoccupied with doctors, hospitals, and serious illness. The only difference is that now you can *see* the suffering.)

Bill, in addition to his flourishing career on daytime serials and nighttime programs such as "The March of Time," continued on "Let's Pretend," playing not only romantic leads but character parts as well, and, like Jack Grimes and Kingsley Colton, interspersing his radio work with studies at Columbia University.

Looking back on his career, Bill is particularly proud of the sustaining programs he did for the networks. The reason, he says, is that they were not bound by sponsors' strictures or ad agencies' fears but could afford to be experimental. The ones he remembers best are "The Columbia Workshop," on which he worked several times, and "Mrs. Miniver," the CBS wartime serial on which Judith Evelyn played the lead and Bill was her son.

Some of Bill's busiest radio years were just after Pearl Harbor. By then he was playing 18- and 19-year-olds, and young GIs. Soon his own military service would be inevitable, so Bill decided to join the Navy while he still had a choice. Ironically, this came just at the time when his blue eyes, blond hair, and square-jawed good looks were becoming more and more of an asset. In 1943, the day after he was sworn in, 20th Century–Fox called from Hollywood and offered him a contract. But for the time being show business, and Bill's happy memories of "Let's Pretend," would have to be put on hold.

Bob Readick

Bob Readick (called Bobby when he was a child) was the last one to be added to Nila Mack's permanent roster before we became sponsored. He joined "Let's Pretend" in 1939. Little Bobbie did not break into show business via the proud mother route. He did it completely on his own, by bluffing.

Bob was the fourth generation of a theatrical family. His great-grandfather, George Randall, was an actor. Before that he had been a cavalry private in the Civil War, assigned as the groom to the horse which had been the only survivor of the Battle of the Little Big Horn. Bob's grandmother was the original female lead in the 1922 Broadway long-running classic *Abie's Irish Rose*. He lived for years with his mother Dorothy Randall Readick, who was separated from his father Frank Readick, one of the busiest and best-known radio actors of the 1930s and 1940s.

Bobby was rather thin and gangly. He had grey eyes, a longish nose, and a pale complexion. It apparently never occurred to either his mother, or his father whom he saw occasionally, to "put him into show business." One day in 1939 his mother, who had a radio show to do at CBS, left her little 11-year-old boy in Colbee's Restaurant, downstairs at 485 Madison. In Colbee's he saw many boys his own age who were obviously radio actors. He followed them upstairs to the studios, where each went in to audition, came out with a script, and threw it in a waste basket in the reception room. Bobbie fished out one of the scripts, and when the last child emerged went in and announced that he was there to audition too: and he got the job. It was a running part on a daytime serial. His pay was $24 a show, and, with no help from his mother, he was launched.

Having now become a professional actor, Bob appeared in two Broadway plays, first as the pesky little kid Raymond in *George Washington Slept Here* (1940), and later, at age 16, in *All in Favor* (1942).

Bob was a clever and versatile actor, and Nila cast him in a wide range of parts, from the addlepated King in "Rumpelstiltskin" who couldn't remember why he had asked the maiden to spin the flax into gold, to the wicked Bluebeard in the scary classic of that name from *The Arabian Nights*. After Pearl Harbor, too young for the draft but with quite a mature and resonant voice, he was able to fill the roles on "Let's Pretend" and on many other radio shows usually done by those who were away in uniform. It was then that Bob came into his own as a steadily working actor in adult parts, and seemed destined for a long and successful career.

There were other Pretenders during the pre–Cream of Wheat years, each of whom was for a time as important to the show as any of the long-termers just described, but who left for various reasons. One of the first and most prominent was not one but two, the Mauch twins – Billy and Bobby – born in Peoria, Illinois, in 1922.

Their mother brought them to New York when they were ten, and modeling and radio jobs followed, including "Let's Pretend" and "The March of Time." In 1936 Billy was hired to play Fredric March as a child in the Hollywood film *Anthony Adverse*, and Bobby was his stand in. The twins did not tell the director until the picture had finished shooting that they had taken turns playing the boy Anthony. Billy and Bobby both were great successes in 1937 with Errol Flynn in *The Prince and the Pauper*.

The twins were then in the picturization of Booth Tarkington's *Penrod and Sam* in 1937, and in two forgettable sequels in which Penrod and his twin brother were juvenile detectives. When the twins returned to New York for a visit they were welcomed back to "Let's Pretend" and given maximum CBS publicity coverage. Their film acting careers eventually faded, but they remained in southern California, and both found new careers in and near Hollywood, as film editors.

Billy Halop, born in 1920 to a lawyer and a professional dancer, made his first radio success as the lead in "Bobby Benson and the H Bar O Ranch." "Let's Pretend" was only one of his many radio shows. In 1935, already in his teens, he originated the role of Tommy, leader of the gang, in the Signey Kingsley Broadway hit play *Dead End*, then went on to Hollywood in 1937 to repeat it in the film, starring Sylvia Sidney. From then on he was known, and typed, as a "Dead End Kid," and he and some of the other boys from the original cast made a long series of highly lucrative but assembly line–formula films based on the same characters. In the early days he made a few trips back to the East Coast, and was always welcomed back to our show by Miss Mack and the rest of us.

After a stint in the Coast Guard in World War II, he returned to Hollywood and the disappointment of being unable to get out of the Dead End Kid type of role. After a bout with alcohol, threats of suicide, and a nervous breakdown, he gave up drinking and went into training as a registered nurse to care for his wife, who had multiple sclerosis. He did bit parts toward the end of his career, including Mr. Munson, owner of the taxi service which employed Archie Bunker, in "All in the Family." He died in 1976.

Nancy Kelly, born in Lowell, Massachusetts, in 1921, had, like Sybil Trent, already done several films as a small child when she came to "Let's Pretend," and had played Dorothy in a serialization of Frank Baum's most famous book *The Wonderful Wizard of Oz*, on the NBC network. She played in *Susan and God* with Gertrude Lawrence at age 16, interspersing her Broadway plays (a total of 13) during her teens and early adulthood with a great variety of radio shows, including "The March of Time." She also specialized in screams for adventure programs such as "Gangbusters."

She eventually became an important actress in Hollywood, repeating there in 1956 her performance as the mother in *The Bad Seed*, for which she had won a Tony Award on Broadway. By then, her childhood acting on "Let's Pretend" had become just a memory.

Patricia Peardon was another Pretender who grew up in radio. She had a round face, blue eyes and curly, flaxen-colored hair. She started on "Let's Pretend" at the age of ten, appearing on such other shows as "Orphans of Divorce," "Second Husband," "The March of Time," and "Cavalcade of America." She had a soft and most sympathetic-sounding voice. Nila Mack always cast her in romantic leading roles. Meanwhile, after appearing in an undistinguished Broadway play called *The Hook-Up* at age 11 in 1935, she created the part of Judy Graves in *Junior Miss*, one of the biggest hits of the 1941 season. She became a star at the age of 17.

Patty's long run in *Junior Miss* (two and a half years on Broadway, and a coast to coast tour) was followed by 14 months in the same role overseas for the USO, and by the time she came back she had decided there would be no more radio in her life. She temporarily retired from acting, got married, and bore two daughters, Christine and Anne. She returned to the theatre in 1955 as Cindy, the spitfire daughter in the Tony Award–winning Broadway production *The Desperate Hours*. Among her many other distinguished acting credits were several seasons at the Stratford, Connecticut, Shakespeare Festival, and yearly Shakespearean roles with Arnold Moss at the Library of Congress in Washington.

Patricia Peardon made a surprising career switch about 1961. She became quite a successful sculptor, with several prominent exhibitions and many private commissions to her credit. At the time of her death in 1993 she had for some time been specializing in small cast bronzes of dancing and flying sprites—lovely groups of magical beings. It is easy to imagine that they were inspired by the fantasies of "Let's Pretend."

Little Lorna Lynn's first "Let's Pretend" appearance in 1941 was an abortive one. Only six and a half years old, she was fired by Miss Mack after one performance, she said, because she could not read the script. Six months later she had learned to read, and worked on the program many times after, as well as on Ed Wynn's program "Happy Island." She landed a running part on "The Brighter Day," and did many other radio shows.

Lorna also appeared in twelve Broadway plays. In 1961 she married, and is now quite content managing some of the business affairs of her husband, who owns gas wells in Texas.

Eddie Ryan was a regular on our show in his childhood and early teens, but left for Hollywood in 1943, under contract to 20th Century–Fox to play opposite Ann Baxter in the wartime epic *The Sullivans*, the true story of those five heroic brothers who went down with their ship. (It was later retitled *The Fighting Sullivans*.) He costarred with Thomas Mitchell in *Within These Walls*, then later played important roles in five other films, was on "The Charlotte Greenwood Show" on the radio for two years, and then formed a vaudeville act, which toured the country for two seasons.

It was in the early 1950s that Eddie decided on a career switch, which has worked out very well. He went into sales and marketing, and has now been successful at it for 40 years. "I found," he said recently, "that acting and selling are the same business."

Unfortunately, Roddy McDowall must be listed, not as a Let's Pretender, but as an almost Pretender. A child refugee from the London blitz in 1940, he had already appeared in films in England. After he had auditioned for her, Nila Mack cast him in several of her radio programs, and would have used him on "Let's Pretend," but his English accent was too distinctive.

Arnold Stang known in radio and later in television and in three Broadway plays as a comedian, played some of the same talking animal and other character roles I did in numerous prewar "Let's Pretend" broadcasts.

Sidney Lumet, born in 1924, was a Let's Pretender during his teens, until he entered the Navy in 1942. A child of the distinguished actor Baruch Lumet, he had done several Broadway plays during his childhood, one of the earliest being *Dead End* in 1935, followed by the sharply contrasting religious epic *The Eternal Road* and William Saroyan's hit *My Heart's in the Highlands*, but did not do much radio except for our program. When I worked for him in the Phoenix Theatre production of Shaw's *The Doctor's Dilemma* in 1955 Sidney was already a successful CBS Television director (for example, "You Are There," "Omnibus," and "Alcoa Theatre"). It was thanks to his experience directing live television that he was able to complete *Twelve Angry Men*, the first of his brilliant screen successes, in just 20 days. It is certain that none of us on "Let's Pretend," including Sidney, could have guessed that his radio acting days would be little more than a hint of things to come.

Jimmy Lydon, a freckle-faced, cute, red-headed kid born in 1923, was on "Let's Pretend" only three years – 1937–39 – before a motion picture he made in New York, *Back Door to Heaven*, propelled him to Hollywood, under contract. He started there by playing teenage roles, including the lead in a series of nine Henry Aldrich films, which lasted from 1941 to 1944. Jimmy acted in over 100 Hollywood motion pictures, but found that he enjoyed life behind the camera much more than in front of it. He now produces, writes, and directs for his own company, Spectrum Productions.

It would be oversimplification to say that Nila Mack had built a repertory company of child actors. It simply would not stay built. There was constant turnover from the day she directed her first broadcast until the last show she cast before her death. First, not all of those whose careers I have outlined were always available. Then there was the group who had defected to Madge Tucker's camp over at NBC, after that lady's ultimatum that they could not play both sides of the street, or in this case, the dial. And last, there were those whom Nila would phase out as she decided they were no longer suitable as Let's Pretenders.

Besides those I have profiled or will mention elsewhere, there are certain to be others who are left out because they were on "Let's Pretend" only occasionally, or perhaps once, and so are not included in any surviving records. Those actors I have been able to document, though, who were on the show at some time during its 24 years (25 including its predecessor "The Adventures of Helen and Mary" before Nila Mack took over) add up to a total of 175 (see Appendix B). This does not include CBS staff announcers, who were assigned by the network and not cast by Nila.

The motivations of the Let's Pretenders' parents included dreams of glory for their children, extreme economic necessity, or a combination of both. The children's motivations probably ranged from obedience to what Mommy wanted, to the desire to experience the fun of acting out fairy tales, with many gradations in between.

Nila Mack, I am sure, had no idea when she started out how successful she would be in molding this extremely varied group into a good radio acting company. That it became so successful was a tribute, not so much to our individual talents as to the lady who brought them all together every Saturday morning and who built "Let's Pretend" into the institution it became.

Chapter 9

Please Send Me
Free a Fairy

"Let's Pretend" was now attracting fan mail, press notices, and awards. Nila Mack was also much in demand to give interviews and make speeches before women's clubs. In May 1934 someone cooked up the idea of having her write a weekly column called "The Child's Hour," which appeared in *Radio Guide* (5 cents a copy).

Our director was highly touted in the introduction to the first column: "Nila Mack, director of all children's programs at CBS [is a] friend to children ... one of the outstanding students of child temperament and authority on juvenile behaviorism."

Nila herself wrote this disclaimer: "Let me begin by putting my readers at ease. I am not a child psychologist. Children have taught me everything I know about them."

The subject of the first article was how to cure thumb-sucking, and contained the advice to use a metal thumb guard, or for older children a rough adhesive bandage. It concluded, "Take from thumb-sucking the comfort, solace, contentment and cheer it gives, and you have broken the habit." Later articles discussed such things as shy and imaginative children, the highly strung, tense child, the lazy child, and the spoiled child. By implication, some of these were personality problems supposedly afflicting the Let's Pretenders. Though some of us were rather complicated, high-strung children, no one reading these articles who knew Nila could believe that this bat guano was anything but ghost written, though it is possible that the actual writer consulted with her from time to time.

Radio Guide (later *Radio and TV Guide*) was a pulp-paper magazine which every week featured complete program listings, gee-whiz feature articles, photographs of star personalities, and a fictionalized murder mystery. "The Child's Hour," which lasted for 8 months, gave it a touch of class it otherwise sorely lacked, and also of course helped publicize CBS and "Let's Pretend."

From the first, the ending of each of our broadcasts had always included an invitation to the children listening to "Write to 'Let's Pretend' in care of your local station, and ask for your favorite story." Miss Mack said, "It's not only good for the children to get used to writing letters, but it's also good for me. They never leave me in doubt as to what story they want to hear." It also reminded the local affiliates of how popular the program was.

As our show developed into an institution, the mail volume grew. By 1940 we were receiving over 1,000 letters weekly. They were in three categories: requests for stories, requests for photographs of the Pretenders, and requests for auditions. From their early teens onward, Albert Aley, Gwen Davies, Miriam Wolfe, and Daisy Aldan would help in the office by opening and handling the fan mail. When Nila was interviewed she would usually mention some of the more interesting letters received recently, and that way a few of them have survived. From eight little girls: "We like all the stories except the stories we don't like, but you make them so good that we like them." And then there is this: "Dear Let's Pretenders: I've had almost every germ you can get, and now I have the mumps, but I think I would feel better if you played 'Snow White and Rose Red.' I like all the stories you have played. Thank you."

In August 1938 the office was literally deluged with mail, 5,334 letters, in response to a single announcement of a prize for the best letter on "Why I Listen to 'Let's Pretend.'" The prize was $10.

Not all of the letters requesting stories were necessarily charming. One little boy wrote: "Dear 'Let's Pretend', If you do not play 'Snow White and the Seven Dwarfs' I will never tune in again. If it takes too long, you can have it continued. I am 10 years old, but I still like 'Snow White.' If you do not have it I will tell everyone not to tune in again. I have a lot of friends, and they do everything I tell them."

Many other letter writers had very definite ideas of their own: "Dear Actors, If you get a letter from James please don't play that story because I think you played it. Therefore I got a better story, and here it is – 'Aladdin and His Magic Lamp.' I like it because my teacher read it to me. So long, actors."

Nila answered a fan who requested "Snow White," telling her we would play it later, but evidently a friend of the writer became impatient: "Dear Let's Pretenders, You told a listener friend of mine that you would play 'Snow White' later. Well, now it is later. I have to eat my supper now, so goodbye."

Other letters ranged from poignant to grasping. One of the most unsettling ones came from the mother of a girl, age undetermined, who hoped we would interrupt the broadcast to send a personal message. The letter read: "She has always listened to your program. Please tell her, wherever she is, to come home to her heartbroken mother."

Nila would often take the time to dictate personal notes to the writers of the letters. One letter she took particular trouble with came from a little girl named Phyllis Knapp, age 11, in Utica, New York:

> Dear Let's Pretenders, I do think your fairy tales are grand.
> I love the music that is played while we're in Fairy Land.
> And Nila Mack, I want to say how much I love your plays. (The ones you write yourself, I mean, for special holidays.)
> I have one wish I'd like fulfilled, and it is simply this:
> If you could act "The Snow Queen" I'd be such a grateful miss.
> And then if you tired of our wishes never ending,
> Just act a play to suit yourselves, despite the notes we're sending.
> And here was Nila's reply:
> Dear Phyllis Knapp, just past eleven, your poem put me right in heaven.
> How very nice to take the time to put your story wish in rhyme.
> But oh my dear, I'm in a spot (but tell me nowadays, who's not?)
> I have "The Snow Queen" in my files, but it's too long by miles and miles.
> To try to shorten to present it, I'll leave out parts, and fans resent it.
> But maybe on some magic day, I'll try again to find the way.
> And when I do, I hope you'll hear, and write some other poems, dear.
> I really think you have the knack. My love to you, Miss Nila Mack.

Among some other letters were these: "Please send me a baby sister." "I love your hour." "I like it, but it made me have bumps on the neck." "Dear Let's Pretend: I wish for $80."

The all-time favorite, though, of Nila and indeed all of us was this letter from a little girl in Chicago, which showed not only childish innocence and trust but also, incidentally, the power of radio to completely involve its listeners: "Dear Lespertend: Please send me free a fairy."

As the CBS publicity department ground out each new press release about "Let's Pretend," it would never fail to mention the many awards and popularity polls we had won. There were such a large number of them that the network had reason to be proud. One of our first was the Motion Picture Daily Award for best children's program on the air. "Pretend" won this award five times in the six years from 1938 to 1944. *Radio Daily* gave us its award for the years 1939, 1940, 1944, 1945, and 1946. In 1939 we won a grand slam of three awards as top children's radio program from *Motion Picture Daily*, the Women's National Radio Committee, and the 600 radio editors polled by Scripps-Howard Publishing. Winners in various categories in the Scripps-Howard poll, announced in February 1939, were:

Favorite Program and Best Comedian	Jack Benny
Quiz Program	"Information Please"
Light Orchestra	Guy Lombardo's
Male Popular Singer	Bing Crosby

Female Popular Singer	Frances Langford
Classical Singer	Nelson Eddy
Symphonic Conductor	Arturo Toscanini
Dramatic Program	WABC "Radio Theatre"
Announcer	Don Wilson
Sport Announcer	Ted Husing
News Commentator	H. V. Kaltenborn
Favorite Quarter Hour	"Amos 'n' Andy"
Outstanding New Star	Orson Welles
Children's Program	"Let's Pretend"

Each new award was always acknowledged by a letter of thanks from Nila and mentioned during the opening of the following week's broadcast. Sometimes she would make a brief speech of thanks on the air (her only radio performances in the last years of her life), then hurry back into the control room to direct the rest of the show.

The count of awards and polls won by our program varies with each CBS press agent's telling, and has gone as high as 60. Undoubtedly, the most prestigious was the Peabody Award, known as the Pulitzer Prize of broadcasting. The awards, established by the University of Georgia School of Journalism in 1940, were named for George Foster Peabody, a Columbus, Georgia, native who was a successful New York banker and philanthropist, and one of the university's trustees. "Let's Pretend" was the first winner in the new category of Outstanding Children's Programs, established in 1943. The citation read:

> The award for outstanding children's program goes to "Let's Pretend." Directed by Miss Nila Mack, this dramatization of great fairy tales has contributed both to entertainment and education, both to the passive and active development of children. The dramas are played chiefly by children, themselves. In addition to the merit of this program's direct contribution to the imagination of American children, it has become one of the most unusual child-acting schools of the air — numerous veterans of its "troupe" have gone on to play remarkable juvenile parts on Broadway.

As each new plaque, figurine, or citation came in, Nila would put it on a shelf or on the wall in her office, no doubt with satisfaction – and would then get on with the day's business of preparing for next Saturday's broadcast.

Every newspaper or magazine feature story about "Let's Pretend" would mention these awards, and usually add its own tribute to the quality of the program, its appeal to youngsters, and the lessons and moral values it taught them. The closest thing to a straight critique I found was in the trade paper *Billboard*, in 1938, and that was not entirely a rave. It concerned our dramatization of "Dick Whittington," who by pluck, ambition, and good luck became Lord Mayor of London:

Script was good, clear and well-balanced. Dialogue and clean continuity made it an easy one to follow. Nevertheless it was not suited for the juvenile cast of fifteen-year-olds who played it. Youngsters were not capable of handling the Irish and English brogues and dialects to make the script sound authentic. Script contained enough action to prevent youngsters from terming it a sissy show. An undercurrent of sympathy which shied away from anything approaching pathos made it simple to follow and a natural to be approved by parent-teacher groups.

My favorite follow-up comment was, naturally, more complimentary. It appeared in New York's newspaper PM in September 1940. After mentioning the latest awards on this, the program's tenth anniversary since Nila Mack took it over, the tabloid called us "the blue-ribbon children's show on the air," continuing:

Most radio programs for children face a particularly thorny dilemma. What the children like, the parents usually don't like, and vice versa. One kid program, however, on which both children and parents as well as child psychologists, PTAS and all sorts of air-minded busybodies see eye to eye is CBS' "Let's Pretend."

"Let's Pretend" is a program by children, for children, which goes on WABC at 12:30 P.M. on Saturdays. It hollers no hotcha, and sells no cereal or Dunko-Malt. It just acts out fairy stories, a shade professionally, but extremely well.

It was in 1940 that Nila was approached by two songwriters who wanted her to hear a new pop tune they had written called "Let's Pretend," with the thought that perhaps it would become our new theme song. Our director invited them to let us all hear it. And so one Saturday morning they both came to Studio 1, and during a rehearsal break the composer Abner Silver played it, while Gerald Griffin sang the lyrics. (Abner Silver was the composer of "Farewell to Arms," and "My Love for You," among many other song hits, while his collaborator Gerald Griffin's solo efforts included "It's Only a Step from Killarney to Heaven.") All of the Pretenders listened politely and attentively, and Nila told them she would let them know. Though hers was, of course, the ultimate decision, we all agreed that the song was very nice, but that our instrumental "Fairy Tale" was still the best. Although Nila Mack's mind was not closed to experimenting, her formula for a successful children's radio program had now become firmly established, and even when we acquired a sponsor in 1943, the basic format of "Let's Pretend" never changed.

Chapter 10

CBS and WABC

The world of which "Let's Pretend" was a part was that of network radio. This huge new industry was the product of technical advances which made two things possible: first, clear radio broadcasting over long distances; and second, the transmission of broadcasts nationwide by many stations simultaneously, due to their being joined into networks by long-distance telephone lines. The United States, now in the midst of a major Depression, was ripe for an entertainment medium which was cheap, and radio provided it. You didn't have to go to a theatre and buy tickets for radio. The entertainment and information, in great variety, came to you for free.

The economics of radio were originally based on stations being owned either by manufacturers of radio sets or department stores that sold them. The more and better programming available, the more sets people would buy. Eventually, that proved inadequate in paying the costs involved, and stations then began offering time for sale to sponsors. Sponsors would pay the costs of putting on the programs, and thus be identified with them, and this increased their sales and their importance. It worked marvelously (and still does, of course).

The sponsors got results, the stations and networks reaped income from time sales, and the listeners got free entertainment. Part of the system was that those time slots that were not sold were filled with sustaining programs* such as "Let's Pretend," which helped the network keep the loyalty of its affiliated stations and its listeners by providing, presumably, high-quality programming. Our children's show fitted ideally in that category. It was the best of its kind in radio, and generated enormous good will both for the network and the affiliates.

Better still, because our production costs were so low, the Columbia network was under no great pressure to find us a sponsor—nor did it want to, once the program started winning national radio editors' awards and

---

A sustaining program was just what the name implies: until a sponsor could be found, the show's production costs would be sustained by the network.

became so closely identified with the network by its loyal audience. Like the CBS "American School of the Air," which was broadcast into classrooms five days a week, and like the NBC Symphony, "Let's Pretend" was not for sale.

There were many other sustaining programs on CBS and the other networks in the 1930s and well into the 1940s, especially dramatic shows, which did very fine work precisely because they were not sponsored. CBS had on its payroll such highly creative people as Norman Corwin, Max Wylie, Jerome Lawrence, Irving Reis, and Charles Jackson, and it encouraged them to try new ideas in radio drama. Such programs as "The Columbia Workshop" could never have been produced by advertising agencies, whose main goals were not excellence but simply large numbers of listeners to move large quantities of merchandise off dealers' shelves.

The whole shift of radio program control from the networks to the advertisers had not yet taken place. It was lucky for Miss Mack and for "Let's Pretend" that it had not – she was given complete freedom by CBS to do her own experimenting.

Columbia Broadcasting was named the "Tiffany Network," no doubt by its own publicity department. Bill Paley was proud of providing quality programming for all of America. He had already boasted in the early 1930s of having the country's largest radio network. NBC had more stations than the 116 of CBS at the time, but they were divided between the Red and the Blue networks, so the CBS claim was in a way true.

WABC "860 on your dial" was the New York flagship station of the Columbia network, and the originator of much of its programming, which was fed to member stations by AT&T long lines.

These telephone networks were a marvel of American technology, although occasionally lines might go down due to extreme weather conditions or someone could switch a program to the wrong circuit.

(A human error of a different sort occurred once in the 1940s when a telephone lineman who had climbed a pole somewhere west of Denver to check some circuits found that he had connected his headset to the line carrying "The Romance of Helen Trent." He listened a minute, then made a specific suggestion to Helen Trent as to what she could go and do. Little did he wot, as Shakespeare would have put it, that he was broadcasting on the entire Western section of the CBS network.)

In the mid–1930s CBS began leasing Broadway theatres to broadcast shows with studio audiences, but 485 Madison remained its New York headquarters. There were (and still are) two sets of elevators in the building. The three on the left as you entered went to the lower floors, and served non–CBS tenants in the building. The three on the right went from the fourteenth to the twenty-third floors, and served only CBS. The fourteenth floor contained the offices of Nila Mack and the other directors, as well as the staff writers and the casting director, Marge Morrow.

(Note: the fourteenth floor at 485 was actually the thirteenth floor, but no one called it that. To this day, in many of the newest, glitziest New York office buildings, you will find no thirteenth floor. Even in this time of enlightened thinking, triskaidekaphobia is not dead.)

Nila Mack's office was no larger than 10 x 12 feet. Just like all the other production department offices, its walls and door were frosted glass, framed in dark-stained oak. It was high over Madison Avenue and sunny, with a western view. From its one large window Miss Mack could see the back wall of Best's department store and St. Patrick's Cathedral on Fifth Avenue, and beyond them the towers of Radio City, which contained the NBC studios, and her rival, Madge Tucker.

Other floors up to the nineteenth contained CBS business offices, and on the twentieth were President William Paley and his top executives.

CBS had seven studios at 485 Madison Avenue ranging in size from Studio 6, which had been converted from a coat room, to Studio 1, the largest, which could and sometimes did accommodate a full symphony orchestra, and was up a flight of ten steps from a cheerful, north-lit reception room on the twenty-second floor. It was raised in this way to provide extra ceiling height for Studios 3 and 5, on the twenty-first floor below. All the CBS radio studios were on these two floors, with two exceptions: the News Room on the seventeenth floor (later expanded when the Columbia news division began to make a name for itself with its pioneering overseas broadcasts before and during World War II), and Studio 7, about the size of someone's not too large living room, and isolated from the others on the third floor. Master Control was near the top of the building, on the twenty-third floor.

CBS had created a broadcasting center in a medium-sized office building (120 feet frontage on Madison Avenue, and 100 feet on East Fifty-Second Street) most unsuitable for such a use – but it worked surprising well. Those ten steps leading to Studio 1 were the only real problem, especially when a grand piano or a heavy sound effects console had to be lugged up or down.

When I started working on "Let's Pretend" in 1936, the studios at 485 had recently been redecorated. They originally had walls papered with art deco murals of skyscrapers, bridges, and ocean liners. The microphones had mostly hung from the ceilings – very impractical, as this meant they could not be moved around to suit the needs of each program. Part of the redecorating scheme was that large areas of the studio walls now had walnut paneling, extending from wainscot to ceiling, and full-length beige curtains.

The paneling and the curtains, besides being handsome, had an important acoustical use. The studios, or any part of them, could now be made "live" or "dead," depending on whether the curtains, which were soft and sound absorbent, were pulled back, exposing the hard and sound reflecting panels, or were pulled over them. Other parts of the studio walls and the doors, which had large semicircular stainless steel push panels, were painted in not unpleasant warm grays and blues. There was modern, recessed ceiling lighting. Reception rooms were done in art deco style, with mirrors, light walnut paneling, receptionists' desks with rounded corners, and large, handsome, built-in, brown leather sofas.

This new and modern layout was no doubt in response to NBC, which had recently (November 11, 1932) moved into its spectacular new studios in the RCA building of Rockefeller Center, then called Radio City (the old NBC headquarters had been on the top floors of 711 Fifth Avenue, at Fifty-Fifth Street).

During my first two years on "Let's Pretend" we always broadcast from Studio 1. This was the studio where Orson Welles originated his weekly "Mercury Theatre on the Air" broadcasts, including the famous or infamous "War of the Worlds," and where Fletcher Markle later originated his "Studio One" radio drama series in 1947 (the name was kept for the later, very successful live TV show).

The large, single door at the top of those ten steps was on the left side as you entered. On the left-hand (north) wall was the raised control room, three steps up, which one entered by first going through a glass-windowed sound isolation booth. This could be used for clients to view the broadcast, or as a mini-studio for actors whose voices were on echo, or on filter.*

Two-thirds of the distance from the control room to the opposite wall, slightly to the director's right, was a large, round supporting column, which was sheathed in stainless steel. It didn't interfere very much with the director's view, but it was yet another reminder that when 485 Madison Avenue had been designed no one had radio studios in mind. Bill Paley and associates had signed a ten-year lease on the space just in time to have the studio floors redesigned (high ceilings, no windows, mechanical ventilation) before the building was completed in 1929.

High on the studio's east wall was a large art deco clock which had metal bars in place of numbers. Beside the clock was a semicircular scale, half green, half red, with a movable pointer which could be regulated from the control room. When it was moved all the way to the right (3 o'clock, on the red side) that meant that the broadcast was one minute ahead, and to

---

*Filters, like echo chambers, were very effective in radio. They are still used in television drama and all sorts of audio productions. A filter usually eliminates the low frequencies from a designated microphone circuit, leaving a rather rough and high-pitched effect. Filters are used, for instance, for voices on the telephone. Since no telephones existed in the Land of Let's Pretend, filters on our program were used for people's inner voices, or for people who had been enchanted and were unable to speak normally.

If you were an actor "on echo" or "on filter," you would stand behind a sound-deadening screen or in a little isolation booth, so that your microphone would not pick up other actors' voices, and you would have earphones so that you could hear your cues.

slow down. All the way to the left (9 o'clock, on the green side) meant a minute behind, and to speed up, and there were many gradations in between. But in all the years I worked in Studio 1, I never saw the device used. It was completely impractical. Everybody in radio had learned to depend on hand signals from the control room, and no electric gadget could replace eye contact between the director and the performers.

Restaurant, watering hole, and the center of a good deal of the off-mike social life of people who worked at CBS was Colbee's (originally called Lebus, but hardly a soul is now alive who remembers that). Though the main entrance to Colbee's was on the building's Fifty-Second Street side, you could enter directly from the lobby, through double doors and down a narrow flight of stairs (485 Madison was built on a hillside). I remember going down them many times, and finding myself in a noisy, friendly place which smelled of food, liquor, and cigarette smoke.

While there I could telephone casting directors about jobs, use the men's room, or call my message service* free of charge on a direct line (beepers, of course, were unknown). Then I would often have lunch at the large oval bar in the center. My favorite was a chicken salad sandwich with lettuce, on white toast with a pickle on the side, and a chocolate milk shake.

Though the food at Colbee's would not have won gourmet prizes, it was good and hearty. Jack Grimes remembers that you could get a great bowl of black bean soup there for 25 cents. You could eat, or drink if you were of age, either at the bar or in one of the booths which lined the walls. Nila Mack would regularly hold court in one of them. She did not plan it that way; it was just that her many friends would naturally gravitate to her booth to say hello or exchange the latest jokes when they saw her there. And for those of her friends who were actors, these meetings were also a subtle way of asking for jobs. Between Nila's popularity as a person and the fact that she was a director, it is surprising that she had time to get any nourishment at all in Colbee's. In fact, a reporter who once tried to interview her there almost gave up, there were so many interruptions.

A more sedate establishment was Louis and Armand's, just one door east on Fifty-Second Street, on the ground floor of a brownstone. I never set foot in there in my childhood days – it was strictly for grownups. The food, the atmosphere (wood paneling, dim, shaded lights) and the prices were all more upscale than Colbee's. CBS executives were among its best customers, as were some of the more successful actors.

---

*Telephone message services were the radio performers' lifelines. Anyone at all active in the business was seldom home during the day, because of either performing or being out on auditions or other appointments. There was Reg, the actors' nickname for Radio Registry, started by Doris Sharpe; Lex, which stood for Lexington 2-1100; and later Artists' Service and Billie's Registry, both started by former operators from the other two. All of them are still in existence, though I will guarantee that none of them relay calls any more for "Our Gal Sunday" or "John's Other Wife."

Both Colbee's and Louis and Armand's had one thing in common: if you came in at all regularly, the staff knew you and would greet you like family. In the exciting but insecure world of radio, both restaurants were important contact points for many actors – places to make themselves visible and perhaps pick up casting tips or wave to a director. They knew that whether they were working or not, they would always find a welcome within these little enclaves, or at least someone to share a cup of coffee or a drink, and agree that the business was going to hell.

Child actors as well were welcome at Colbee's. Smaller children would go there for lunch with their mothers, and the older ones alone. As miniature grown-ups, we too were on the lookout for possible passing directors, as well as for a good lunch, and Colbee's was a way station for the Pretenders as much as for everyone else who worked at CBS.

485 Madison Avenue and 30 Rock, as the RCA building at 30 Rockefeller Plaza was called, were the foremost creative headquarters of network radio in the United States for at least 20 years. The main difference between them was that at CBS the activity was all concentrated in a smaller space. In the CBS building you could almost feel the excitement, the energy, and the creativity moving and pulsating – in the studios, the elevators, the offices, the reception rooms, the hallways, and certainly in the restaurants. If you were a child actor growing up in radio, it was an exciting time to be there, and even more so if you were on "Let's Pretend."

Chapter 11

New Times, New Studios

With the almost explosive development of radio programming, beginning about 1930 when Nila Mack joined CBS, came great variety. There was a wide range of programs affording listeners experiences completely outside those available in the theatre or motion pictures.

First, there was music – both classical (NBC and CBS both maintained symphony orchestras) and popular ("And now, from the Grill Room of the Hotel Taft, here is Vincent Lopez"). There were top comedians, incisive news commentators, quiz programs, church services, exciting play-by-play sports, and round-table discussions of social issues, not forgetting the amateur hour craze of the mid–1930s. But what we are most concerned with here is the great variety of dramatic programs – especially those for children.

Some of the earliest children's radio programs had been those that told stories; Ireene Wicker, "The Singing Lady" on NBC (who started on station WGN, Chicago, in 1931) and "Let's Pretend" on CBS. Also on the networks and locally, there were numerous uncles and aunts who spun yarns for small children.

Beginning in 1932, broadcasting companies and especially advertising agencies started to develop a new breed of children's programming: dramatized adventure serials, most of which were broadcast in the late afternoons or early evenings, Monday through Friday. Though there was a great variety of subjects and heroes and heroines, all of these shows had these elements in common: there was danger, adventure, sometimes physical combat or gunshots, and all were continuing stories. This meant that the hero or heroine was always in some kind of peril or danger, and the situation was never resolved at the end of a 15-minute episode. In the infrequent instances in which one particular villain or villains had finally been brought to justice, there was always a new danger introduced, either in the wrap-up of the current adventure or in the announcer's teaser for the next episode.

These were true cliffhangers, as were the old movie serials our parents had watched at the Bijou on Saturday afternoons, in which Pearl White would literally be left hanging from a cliff at the end of an episode. Back then the children had to beg a dime from their parents to see the next one, meanwhile being kept in suspense for a whole week. What the next generation's children had to beg was permission to tune in to the next day's program.

Eventually, educators and parents' organizations began to protest about the effect the adventure shows were having on children. Though it may not have been typical of heartland America, a study was made in 1936 by Azriel Eisenberg of more than 3,000 children in the New York metropolitan area. The study found that children listened an average of more than six hours a week (piddling compared to recent surveys of TV watching by young people today), and that among their favorites were "Buck Rogers," "Bobby Benson," "Little Orphan Annie," "Jack Armstrong," "Skippy," "The Lone Ranger" and "Let's Pretend." Of these, our program was the only one not of the law and order, violence, cliffhanger type.

More important, though were the children's reactions to the programs reported by Eisenberg. He stated that 27 percent of them had told of lying awake at night thinking about the shows they had heard, 43 percent said they had dreamed about them, and 72 percent of these dreams were unpleasant. All of the programs except "Let's Pretend" were broadcast in the late afternoon, or, in the case of "The Lone Ranger," early evening (7:00 P.M. Eastern time).

Marilyn Boemer in her excellent book *The Children's Hour*, about children's radio programs from 1929 to 1956, tells us that a survey by the *Ladies' Home Journal* found 63 percent of the women of America thought some of the programs were too exciting for children. However, they did sell a lot of Wheatena, Cocomalt, and Ovaltine, and for years broadcasting companies and ad agencies preferred to ignore the cristicism.

However, to quote another readable radio history, *Don't Touch That Dial* by J. Fred MacDonald:

> By 1938 the pressure against mayhem on the air became overwhelming. The adults assailed adventure series aimed directly at youngsters – programs like "Jack Armstrong," which featured an athletic teenager fighting pirates, hostile natives, and diabolical gangsters; "Jungle Jim," an adult character who struggled against enemies similar to Armstrong's rivals, "The Green Hornet," an urban vigilante whose programs included beatings, shootings and murder, and "Howie Wing," an aviator and do-gooder who usually encountered crime and brutality. These programs often relied on fistfights, loud action and death to add spice to the plot. They also featured cliff-hanger endings guaranteed to draw kids back to the radio the following day. . . .
> Groups like the Parent-Teachers Association argued that this programming left children on edge, upset their normal upbringing by placing destructive ideas in their young heads, and generally made them violence-prone.

Children, as might be expected, did not share these feelings. One early survey (1933) of children in Scarsdale, New York, reported that almost half (47 percent) preferred thriller-type programs, and one child specifically requested "a blood-curtle murder." The networks finally became nervous about all the protests. They did not want to offend listeners, sponsors, and particularly the Federal Communications Commission, which had the power to refuse to renew stations' licenses, and they responded by dusting off their standards for children's programming. The credo of CBS, adopted in 1935, had apparently gathered a lot of dust. Children's programming was not, it said, to exalt as modern heroes gangsters, criminals, and racketeers. Disrespect for parental authority was not to be encouraged, nor were cruelty, greed, or selfishness. Conceit, smugness, or an unwarranted sense of superiority over others less fortunate were not to be presented as laudable. Recklessness and abandon should not be falsely identified with a healthy spirit of adventure. It also stated that programs that caused nervous reactions in the child (a bit hard to define?) were not to be presented.

Williams Paley went further. CBS had an advisory board on children's programming, and it advised him to simply cancel what he called the "blood and thunder" children's programs. The order went out, and this was done. However, as he later related in his autobiography *As It Happened*, "Our sponsors deserted us on the replacements. The children deserted us too, turning to the same type shows on other networks." One of the replacements of the "blood and thunder" shows was "Let's Pretend," and in January 1938 we were shifted to two broadcasts a week, late afternoons on weekdays, and from a great variety of studios.

First it was Tuesdays and Thursdays from 6:00 to 6:30 P.M. (New York time). In April we started doing the show half an hour earlier. In October our days were changed to Mondays and Thursdays, and in January 1939 the time period was again changed, this time from 5:15 to 5:45 P.M. These midweek broadcasts meant that all the Pretenders had to leave school early on broadcast days to make early afternoon rehearsals – something positive or negative depending on one's attitude toward school. We were all pleased, however, that the fee had been raised from our former $3.50 per show to $5, and those of us who did both broadcasts in a given week were making out fabulously, at least percentage-wise.

During July and August 1938 and 1939 we would do our broadcasts from one of the several Broadway theatres that CBS had under lease. It was vacation time for schoolchildren all over the United States, and just a couple of announcements about sending in for free tickets brought thousands of requests. For the first time we in the cast had the experience of playing to audiences of hundreds of enthusiastic youngsters who filled every seat, cheering and clapping when Hugh Conover or Jackson Wheeler would make the opening announcement.

The shortage of studio space being what it was, there were also times in the winter months when we did the show from a sunlit studio on the top floor of the Steinway Building on West Fifty-Seventh Street that had been the original home of the Columbia Phonograph Broadcasting System before it had been bought by Bill Paley and Company.

I enjoyed the afternoon "Let's Pretend" broadcasts most when we were in Liederkranz Hall. This large, old four-story red brick and brownstone building at 115 East Fifty-Eighth Street had been built around the turn of the century by the Deutscher Liederkranz, a German-American music society organized in New York in 1847. By 1938, the average age of their membership now being on the high end, the society was no doubt very pleased to get a steady rental from Columbia Broadcasting for their spacious ballroom on the third floor.

(A good-sized photograph of the old building appears in *Orson Welles on the Air*, published by the Museum of Television and Radio. "The Mercury Theatre on the Air" moved there from Studio 1 because Liederkranz had become Columbia's largest single studio space. I am sure that the rococo, old-world style of the building appealed to Orson's sense of the dramatic. I had also imagined his being able to finagle sumptuous meals from the German kitchen downstairs, but diligent inquiry proved I was wrong. It turns out that Orson always had his Mercury rehearsal break meals sent over from Toots Shor's.)

The ballroom must have been magnificent at one time. It had at least a 30-foot ceiling. The lower parts of the walls were covered with red figured brocade, interspersed with long, narrow, vertical mirrors. The upper walls were decorated with now dingy murals of classic scenes such as zaftig maidens sporting with flute-playing centaurs.

The network made some changes. First, movable black curtains, to control acoustics, were attached at a point about two-thirds up the walls, and huge basketball court lights with wire guards were hung from the ceiling, which no doubt had once been graced by crystal chandeliers. Also, a soundproof control room was built within the ballroom. From a decorator's standpoint, the place was ruined, but it was just what CBS needed – a large studio in a midtown location. Furthermore it had excellent acoustics, especially for music. Many records were later cut there for the Columbia label.

It was an adventure doing "Let's Pretend" in Liederkranz Hall, climbing the two flights of wide, gently curving stairs with their oak banisters. There were also temptations. Though CBS had the upper floor, the club still maintained its business, including a full dining room, on the floors below. As you peered over the stair railing outside the ballroom, two floors below was an old, bald German waiter tending his stacks of clean dinner plates, ready to fill them with wiener schnitzel from the fragrant kitchen. One day, during rehearsal break, Mickey O'Day and I could not resist pouring little droplets of water from paper Dixie cups down onto the plates, then pouring more as the old waiter, perplexed, took each plate away to wipe it off with a clean napkin. Shortly after, an announcement was made by Miss Mack from the control room that whoever was doing this had better cut it out. So, back to business.

Bill Paley's experiment in good citizenship had ended when on April 22, 1939, we returned to broadcasting on Saturdays from our old home in Studio 1, on the twenty-second floor at 485 Madison Avenue, this time in the 12:30 to 1:00 P.M. time period. It was not until July 13, 1940, that we made another studio move – this time to the new, seven-story Studio Building at 49 East Fifty-Second Street, which was now ready for occupancy.

This building at 49 East had originally been constructed in 1908 by the Vanderbilt family as a guest house. It was designed in English Renaissance style, with brick front and handsome (though by 1940, old fashioned) carved stone window lintels. In 1924 it had been sold to the Juilliard Music Foundation as auxiliary space for its school. The former guest rooms, now classrooms, were oval in shape, and in each Juilliard had installed two Steinway grand pianos.

CBS was lucky to get the building, located as it was directly across the street from 485 Madison. Still expanding, the network badly needed more studio space. Besides leasing the Liederkranz Hall ballroom, by then it was even using studios of a New York local station, WMCA, which was then on Broadway between Fifty-First and Fifty-Second streets. Its size and location made the new building ideal for radio studios, more so than the original space ever was. CBS bought it from Juilliard in 1939 and completely transformed it into what *Architectural Forum* described as "the last word in broadcasting design."

For better soundproofing, the windows on the building's front were completely eliminated, except for those on the top floor. The front was otherwise completely plain and covered with white stucco. The only variation was that the ground floor was covered with rectangular blue and grey terra cotta tiles. There was a simple, modern marquee over the entrance on the right side, with "CBS" in small bluish neon letters above it. The whole effect was starkly modern and quite striking.

Inside the architects created eight studios, two of them quite large, meant to be used for audience shows. They were Studio 21, one flight down from the softly lit lobby and reception room, and Studio 22, one flight up. Each of these could seat an audience of over 300. Upstairs, reached by two elevators, were six smaller and also ultra-modern studios, as well as plenty of space for the sound effects department, for acoustical research, and for equipment storage. Columbia now had eight additional studios, and they were larger and had better laid-out space.

"Let's Pretend" broadcast from Studio 21. The double doors for the audience were at the front, at the foot of the wide stairs from the lobby. At the back end of the studio was another door to the control room and the playing area, for which a raised stage was built in sections so that it could be easily disassembled.

To prevent sound waves from bouncing around randomly, the ceiling was made in a shallow zigzag pattern. And on the rear and left-hand walls of the studio were what CBS called "Acoustivanes"—handsome, three-feet-wide vertical walnut panels which reached from floor to ceiling and were pivoted, so that when they were closed, sound was reflected from their hard surfaces, and when open, it was absorbed by a soft cloth backing behind them.

The control room was three or four steps above the studio floor level so that everyone could see the director better. Painted surfaces in these studios were those same cool CBS blues and soft greys, the whole effect being perhaps a little less friendly than the old studios, but the new building was a vastly more efficient place to work. It was to be the home of "Let's Pretend" for the next three years.

It was on Tuesday, December 24, 1940, that all of us, busy with our radio careers and happy in our "Let's Pretend" security, got a rude shock. Gwen Davies (still Estelle Levy in those days) telephoned all of us to say that Miss Mack was in the hospital.

Gwen, who lived only two blocks away, had been passing that evening, and saw fire engines in front of 55 West Fifty-Third Street, the brownstone where Nila's third-floor terrace apartment was located. Miss Mack had been there, about 8:00 P.M., opening Christmas presents, in front of a cheerful fire in the fireplace. As she opened each package she threw the wrappings into the fire. But one box was apparently filled with shredded paper padding, called excelsior, and this instantly flared out into the living room, setting fire to Nila's chair. She attempted to throw the flaming chair out of the window, which set fire to the curtains, and then to her dress.

Apparently, Maud Wilson was not much help. Nila later did an imitation of her frightened maid standing by the door, wringing her hands and saying, "Oh, whatever are we going to do? Why doesn't somebody help us?" Eventually, the neighbors did come and help, and the New York Fire Department put the flames out. Our director was taken to Roosevelt Hospital with second-degree burns about the face, hands, and arms. She was not back in the studio for two weeks.

It was also in 1940 that CBS had started making noises about "Let's Pretend" acquiring a sponsor. Radio was becoming bigger and bigger financially.

The actors, singers, and announcers had become unionized (the American Federation of Radio Artists, known as AFRA), and for this and many other reasons, programming was becoming more expensive. The idea of having so many sustaining programs for prestige and to keep local affiliates' loyalty was now less attractive to the networks. However Nila, being in charge of all children's programming originating in New York, and having the loyalty and respect of the CBS top brass, had for all practical purposes the right of refusal of any potential sponsor, though it was surely not spelled out in her employment contract.

Miriam Wolfe, Gwen Davies, and Sybil Trent, to whom I am indebted for so many facts about Nila Mack and "Let's Pretend," remember that once CBS had let it be known that the program was available for sponsorship, there were many suitors for the honor, but that for at least three years she had turned them all down as not being suitable. Though the program being under sponsorship would mean much more income for her personally, she felt a responsibility to the children in her audience and to their parents, refusing to allow "Let's Pretend" to be identified with any product that would cheapen it or cast it in a bad light. She could afford to wait.

Meanwhile, I had been thinking for some time that it was really unfair for a national network program, a prize-winning, top dramatic show, to be paying its actors a fee of $5, while other sustaining programs exactly comparable to ours, with the same number of rehearsal hours, were paying their actors $21. The reason was the Children's Program Waiver provision in the network's contract with AFRA, which stated that if more than 75 percent of the cast were children, regular union minimums did not apply. But we long-time "Let's Pretend" regulars mentioned earlier had by this time reached an average age of 16½, and more than half of us were 20 or older. Bona fide children were not now by any stretch of the imagination more than a small minority in our cast.

I called George Heller, executive secretary of AFRA. (Heller, formerly a dancer and an actor, had done many Broadway shows, the last of which was *You Can't Take It with You,* in the role of Ed.) When I explained the fee situation, his reply was, "They can't do that to you! I'll see about this, Arthur." The result was a compromise: a month later our fee had been raised to $10. This did not take place without some anxiety on Nila's part, however. The network management had apparently told her they were not at all sure they were willing to pay what turned out to be an average of $60 in additional talent fees per broadcast. I never told her or anyone else that I had blown the whistle to AFRA. There is no way of knowing whether my complaint to the union and the resulting higher fees played a part in her decision, but when Cream of Wheat came along in 1943 Miss Mack, like Goldilocks and the three bowls of porridge, decided that this one was just right. The nine years of their sponsorship (1943–52) made some changes in the program, mostly for the better, great changes in our lives (and pay checks), and marked one of the strongest product identifications in the minds of listeners ever known in radio.

Chapter 12

Cream of Wheat Is So Good to Eat

On August 18, 1943, the following item appeared in *Variety*:

13-Yr Old Sustainer Lands a Sponsor
After 13 years on the air as a sustainer, Let's Pretend, Nila Mack's kid dramatic series Saturday mornings on CBS, has been sold commercially. Cream of Wheat will bankroll the show when it resumes [incorrect, as we did not go off the air in the summer] Sept. 25 in the same 11:05–11:30 time slot.

Deal calls for the show to air over the full CBS network on a 52-week basis, with 13-week cancellation periods. Miss Mack, currently on vacation, will continue to write and direct the series. B.B.D. & O. [Batten, Barton, Durstine, and Osborn] is the agency.

The marriage between Cream of Wheat and Let's Pretend was an ideal one. Cream of Wheat touted itself as the great American family cereal, and, like the product, ours was a family program, suitable for all ages, not just for children. The company itself was an old American institution, started in Minneapolis, Minnesota, in 1896. It only made one product, a smooth white farina which came from the heart of the wheat berry, called choice middlings. Enriched five-minute Cream of Wheat, a quick-cooking variety, did not come along until 1938. The company was operated along very conservative lines. For years two of the principal stockholders would take turns being president. Every summer the entire plant would be closed down for two weeks for employees' vacations.

Cream of Wheat's only previous experience with network radio had been when it sponsored Alexander Woollcott, the writer and commentator known as The Town Crier, on the CBS network for one season in 1933. The association with Let's Pretend was destined to last a lot longer.

Though our program had since 1934 been important because of the prestige and good will it created for CBS, it was now bringing in revenue as well. The show was sold to the sponsor as a package. The network

121

figured its costs, including transmission charges to the member stations, and added a lump sum which was its profit. Because of this, CBS could also afford to budget more money for publicity. The institution that was Let's Pretend was never better known or better promoted than during those sponsored years.

As we have seen, Miss Mack was not disposed to allow any sponsorship to change the character of her show or cheapen it. We may be sure that conferences were held between her and the BBD & O people in New York to determine the new format, and how the commercials would be integrated into the program. First of all, the familiar Komzak theme music Fairy Tale was now given lyrics, written by Nila Mack, to be sung by our Sybil Trent (melody) and Gwen Davies (harmony):

> Cream of Wheat is so good to eat
> Yes, we have it every day,
> We sing this song, It will make us strong
> And it makes us shout *Hurray!*
> It's good for growing babies,
> And grownups, too, to eat,
> For all the family's breakfast
> You can't beat Cream of Wheat!

The music, which had always been played rather lethargically, was now given a more sprightly tempo, and the key was taken down one-fourth from D to A, so as to be in a comfortable range for the singers.

The music was much improved by our sponsorship because the budget now allowed for original music, composed especially for each broadcast. It was written, arranged, and conducted by Maurice Brown, who for years had been the cellist in our orchestra. Leon Goldman, our former conductor, stayed on as first violinist. No longer did we use standard works from the music library. Brownie, after reading the script, would write bridge music for each scene break. He had a genius for creating a musical button for the scene just ended, then a segue to set the mood for the next scene, all in an average time of about 15 seconds. The old standards, *"Dark Eyes"* or *"Estrellita"* were now used only if they fitted in with the mood which needed to be created.

Just how valuable the new format was to the program became evident once when Brownie's contract came up for renewal. He asked for a raise, and the sponsor was not willing to give it to him – until he reminded them that in the contract the original music remained his property, and could not be used if the contract was not renewed. Brownie got his raise.

I remember a lovely waltz he wrote for the scene in which Cinderella first dances with the Prince. In the last scene, as the Prince discovers that the poorly dressed girl by the doorstep who was forbidden by her stepmother to try on the glass slipper is indeed the maiden he had fallen in love with, the waltz sneaks in again under the dialogue. The glass slipper fits perfectly. As the scene ends the music swells, segues into the triumphant notes of Mendelssohn's wedding music, and that in turn into the Let's Pretend playoff theme denoting the end of the story. It was a superb example of how effective music could be in radio drama.

Another improvement in the show which came with sponsorship and more money in the budget was the addition of a narrator to help tell our stories. What we had had in the sustaining days were various CBS staff announcers, who would merely introduce the program in the beginning then read the cast and other credits at the end. Once we had decided how we would travel to the land of Let's Pretend there would be music and the story would start cold: that is, with no further introduction or explanation. This could be confusing, especially for some of our younger listeners.

Now Nila was able to hire Bill Adams, to be known on the show as Uncle Bill, a choice she would surely have made years before if she had had the budget for it.

William Perry Adams was born in Tiffin, Ohio, in 1887. He attended Heidelberg College in his hometown for pre-law courses, then decided upon a singing career, for which he began studying at the College of Music in Cincinnati. While there he was hired by the celebrated Shakespearean actors Edward Sothern and his wife Julia Marlowe, who needed a young actor for their Cincinnati engagement. In 1912, right after graduating from the College of Music, he joined their company with a long-term contract.

From then on Bill was a busy actor, stage manager, and later a director. He was with John Barrymore in a production of *Peter Ibbetson* which also starred Constance Collier, played with Barrymore in 101 performances of *Hamlet* on Broadway for Arthur Hopkins, and then directed Barrymore's own production of *Hamlet* in London. A list of his other stage credits would fill a page.

When he became our narrator-spokesman for Cream of Wheat, Bill, now 56 years old and the father of a grown daughter, had long since ceased to depend on the theatre for his income, and had for 15 years been occupying a comfortable niche in radio.

Bill Adams was the epitome of a working actor – never starred and seldom featured, and in radio usually not even identified by name, but always working. He gave solid, believable performances in whatever show he was cast. His running parts went back to Uncle Henry on "The Collier Hour," first broadcast in 1927, and included "Pepper Young's Family" (Sam Young), "The Story of Mary Marlin" (Franklin Adams), and Big Town (Fletcher). He was often called for one-shots on important shows such as "The Light of the World" and "Cavalcade of America," but until he became

Uncle Bill he was best known in the business for his many roles in the dramatized news events of "The March of Time," and especially for his faultless impersonation of Franklin Delano Roosevelt.

"Show us how he spoke," asked an interviewer. "He didn't speak," said Bill, "he sang." And indeed, if you listen to a recording of one of FDR's speeches before a large crowd (not his fireside chats), you will recognize that Roosevelt's was indeed a singing voice. Bill said the president had a two-octave speaking range, compared to a normal one of less than one, which held this entire nation (or at least the Democrats) spellbound for almost four terms. Bill, being a lifelong Republican, personally had no use for the man.

When not performing, Bill Adams was active in the New York local of AFRA as a board member, later as president. He enjoyed smoking cigarettes, sharing a drink with his friends at the Lambs Club, and shooting pool, at which he was an expert.

If you were inventing an Uncle Bill you could not have found a better type than Bill Adams. Rather tall, he had a long nose, a kindly, creased face, naturally wavy gray hair, and most important for radio, a beautifully resonant voice. Besides his warmth and believability when he narrated our stories, Bill was also the delight of the ad agency and the Cream of Wheat people. You could not help but trust that what he told you about Cream of Wheat ("Yes, Pretenders, it's full of phosphorus, to build strong bones") was the absolute truth.

Because the stories were what Let's Pretend was all about, we now had a time problem – a double one. First, the nation was on a war footing, and since April 1943, CBS had been broadcasting five minutes of news at 11:00 A.M. on Saturdays, which took five minutes out of our broadcast time. And our commercials cut further into the time available for the actual story.* That had been over 27 minutes in our sustaining days, and was now pared down to 18.

Did the stories suffer because of our new time limits? To some of us who remembered Nila's original radio versions they did, but this may have been our own prejudice because we knew the scripts so well from having performed some of them so many times. (Indeed, there are some lines which the few surviving Pretenders still remember, and repeat to each other for a

---

*During all broadcasts there was a production man at the director's elbow, who had made timing notations at 15-second intervals in the margin of each page of the script at dress rehearsal, and would tell the director whether the broadcast was "on the nose," or whether to give the cast a "stretch" signal or a "speedup."

Opposite: On the air: Gwen and Sybil sing "Cream of Wheat is so good to eat" while Miriam Wolfe, right, awaits her cue. In background: Violinist Leon Goldman, actress Betty Jane Tyler (hidden), conductor Maurice Brown, and pianist Sidney Raphael. ©1944 CBS Inc. Used by permission.

Ca. 1949: "Uncle" Bill Adams and Jimsey Somers (note platform). Billy Rose
Theatre Collection: the New York Public Library for the Performing Arts
Astor, Lenox, and Tilden foundations.

sort of word game when we get together.) But compromises obviously had to be made.

In "Rapunzel," for instance, the first two scenes were cut entirely. In the first a husband, John, and his wife, Marian, who is ill, are looking out of their window at the garden of a witch, who lives next door. She is growing beautiful lettuce, which Marian is sure will make her well. The Witch refuses to sell them any, threatening to put a curse upon them if they bother her again. The husband climbs over the garden wall that night to take some of the lettuce. As he does so he is caught by the wicked Witch. As the price of saving them both from a terrible curse, she forces him to agree that if the couple should ever have a daughter, she will belong to the Witch. "Now take the lettuce," says the Witch grimly, "and go back to your wife and tell her the good news!" (Ominous music, segues into "Rockabye Baby"). The (cut) commercial script begins with the third scene, which Uncle Bill introduces only by saying that a happy couple are trying to decide on a name for their new baby girl. After this is established the Witch suddenly bursts in to claim the child. Nila inserted new dialogue which explained why in just 30 seconds. Establishing the menace of the Witch next door, and how it came to be that the husband and wife are in her power – the scary scene of the husband pounced upon in the dark while taking the lettuce – all were lost. The cut material in this case equaled almost exactly five minutes – enough to accommodate all the Cream of Wheat commercials. Though it was a shame to lose the two scenes, it was a good cut. It meant that the remaining scenes could be done intact, and the listeners did not miss what they never knew had once existed.

In "The Donkey, the Table and the Stick," the innocent, good-hearted hero Jack is given magical gifts by the three artisans to whom he is apprenticed in successive years. The first two, a donkey whose ears drop gold coins at the word "Bricklebrit," and a table which is covered with a sumptuous meal at the words, "Little table be covered with food of my choice," are stolen by a dishonest innkeeper. The scene in which Jack receives the third gift, a magic stick which beats unmercifully whomever he tells it to, was cut. We never find out how he got it. All we know is that in the last scene he uses it to punish the rotten innkeeper and force him to return his loot. By then the story had gained its momentum, and this omission probably mattered very little to the radio audience. Meanwhile, a much-needed three minutes had been cut from the script.

(There was another problem with this story which had nothing to do with timing, but with Nila's rapidly maturing actors. The magic words to make the stick fly into action were originally, "Up, stick, and whang the life out of him!" But there was much giggling during rehearsals, because we adolescent sophisticates were always reversing the words "stick" and "whang" when not on mike. It eventually became such an "in-joke" among the cast that

Nila, much as she probably enjoyed it herself, changed the line to "Up, stick, and *beat* the life out of him!" and it stayed that way forever after.)

Each script that had to be cut to accommodate the shortened commercial format presented a new challenge, but our director, who by now had 13 years of radio writing experience behind her, surmounted each one successfully, preserved the show's charm and character, and if anything made it better.

Once the new format had been set for Let's Pretend under Cream of Wheat sponsorship, it hardly varied for the nine years they were with us. The opening was Gwen Davies and Sybil Trent singing the Cream of Wheat jingle, and enthusiastic applause and yelling from a theatre filled with 1,000 children and parents. Then Gwen or Sybil would tell Uncle Bill what today's story would be, and we would do our decades-old ritual of deciding how we'd go to the Land of Let's Pretend.

Once we were on our magical way, Uncle Bill, or more accurately the copywriters at the ad agency, would find a way of connecting that with Cream of Wheat. To give a sample:

> UNCLE BILL: And now, Sybil – what's the story for today?
> SYBIL: The Six Swans, Uncle Bill.
> UNCLE BILL: The Six Swans it is. And who'll say how we travel to the Land of Let's Pretend?
> SYBIL: It's Bill Lipton's turn today.
> UNCLE BILL: Well, what do you say we travel by giant rockets?
> GWEN: Bill, that's terrific. Rockets it is. One for each of you, and a great big one for Uncle Bill and me. Everybody ready?
> CAST: (Ad libs sure, etc.)
> GWEN: One - two - three!
> SOUND: (*Whiz Bang. Rockets*)
> GWEN: Gosh, Uncle Bill – did you ever in all your life see anything so fast as these rockets? And so smooth, too.
> UNCLE BILL: Almost sounds as if you're talking about our favorite breakfast treat, Gwen. Yep, Enriched Five-Minute Cream of Wheat is mighty fast, and smooth, too. You see, it cooks to full digestibility, even for babies, in just five minutes of boiling. And talk about smooth. Why, Cream of Wheat hands you the smoothest, creamiest goodness that ever came out of a cereal package. So eat a better breakfast, feel better all day. Get a better start the Cream of Wheat way. And keep listening for our special Cream of Wheat game, that comes right after the first act of to-day's story, The Six Swans.

Then came the music and narration introducing the first scene of the story.

The middle commercial, the Cream of Wheat game, always included participation by the children in the studio audience, and Uncle Bill would re-hearse them before the broadcast, with reinforcements from the cast, in case the response was weak. The game would always require three responses –

such as answers to a riddle, sound effects, animal noises, or giving the last word to a rhyme – always with a Cream of Wheat twist. Another sample:

SYBIL: Well Uncle Bill, what's cooking in the Cream of Wheat game department?

UNCLE BILL: A rootin', tootin' game about the wild and woolly West, Sybil. Okay, let's shoot: What's the cowboy's name for food?

AUDIENCE: Chow!

UNCLE BILL: Chow it is, pardners. And you can bet your boots and saddles that the best all-fired breakfast chow on the whole range is smooth and delicious Cream of Wheat. Yes siree, it's right at the head of the herd for lip-smacking flavor.

And so on. The middle commercial would always end thus:

UNCLE BILL: It's wa-a-ay up in flavor...
SOUND: (Slide whistle up)
UNCLE BILL: It's wa-a-ay down in cost...
SOUND: (Slide whistle down)
UNCLE BILL: It's pa-lenty smooth.
MUSIC: (Playoff)

The closing commercial was only about 30 seconds long, and always ended with Gwen and Sybil singing the last two lines of the jingle:

For all the family's breakfast
You can't beat Cream of Wheat.

Then as Bill Adams announced each character's name, we in the cast would in turn identify ourselves. There were closing credits for Maurice Brown and for Nila Mack. There might be an offer of free tickets to a broadcast for those who sent for them (the closest thing to a premium offer Cream of Wheat ever made). The program ended with a teaser: some tantalizing facts about next week's story, with an invitation to tune in. Then Bill would sign off with: "Bill Adams speaking." And last was the station break:* "This is the CBS Radio Network."

*Then, as now, a sponsor buying a block of time would get only that much, and no more. The cutoff deadline was inflexible. Just before the program's time was up, 24:30 in our case, as were then a 25-minute program, the director would cue the announcer to say, "This is the CBS Radio Network." This notified the stations across the country that the program was over, and they would then cut away from the network and identify themselves, as required by the FCC. There would be only seconds for them to do that, and make other local announcements, as the next network show would be starting exactly 30 seconds later.

Only once in nine years did I see Bill Adams get rattled by this inflexible deadline, and that was at the very end of one broadcast. With his network cue coming up, Bill was heard to mumble, "I'm sorry – I've lost my place." Jack Grimes bounded up to the microphone and said quickly, "This is the CBS Radio Network," thereby saving hundreds of stations across the country from utter confusion.

The comforting surety of this unvarying routine made everybody happy – the children listening, their parents, and the sponsor. And though the format did not vary, the stories naturally did, and the excitement of each one kept everyone listening until the end of the broadcast, which of course included the commercials. Though those were addressed to children, their mothers could not help being aware of them too, especially as the youngsters were always urged to "Ask Mom to put it on her shopping list today!"

How many things can you say about farina, one might ask. It is a tribute to the ingenuity of the advertising copywriters that, though the answer is not many, they constantly devised new and sometimes entertaining ways for Uncle Bill to make a few very important points about their product. I can still hear some of them, almost in my sleep: "Baby's best first solid food"; "Full of iron, niacin and Vitamin B_1"; and "Make sure you have one hot dish for breakfast, even in summer."

People did not mind hearing these things over and over again. They were put in a good mood by the story and the excitement of wondering how it would end. And that, of course, is part of the psychology of broadcast advertising.

Every sponsored radio program had to have an ad agency producer, even if the agency did not produce the program. Ours was Ed Marshall.

Edwin C. Marshall, who grew up in Chicago, had an extensive musical education, and became assistant to the stage director of the Chicago Civic Opera Company. He eventually went into radio in New York during the Depression. Before joining BBD & O he worked for CBS, supervising many of their cultural broadcasts, including the New York Philharmonic concerts, and "Of Men and Books," with Mark Van Doren.

Because of his background, plus the fact that he had a rather bookish mien – hair combed straight back, silver-rimmed glasses, and pencil-thin mustache – Nila apparently considered him a high-brow intellectual, and at first did not quite trust him. In any case, the commercials pretty much ran themselves. Bill Adams, being perfectly cast in his role of grandfather figure, storyteller, and Cream of Wheat spokesman, knew exactly what to do. And part of the sponsorship arrangement for the program was that the network, meaning Nila Mack, was to retain complete artistic control over the story portion. So all in all there was not much for Ed Marshall to do except maintain pleasant relations with everyone (he was well liked by all of the Pretenders) and act as diplomatic go-between if there should be any disagreements between CBS and the sponsor.

With sponsorship we now had the luxury of an extra hour's rehearsal, which took place at the 485 Madison studios at 5:15 P.M. on Thursdays. Nila would assign us our roles, and there would be a read-through, at which she would get a rough timing, and some idea of what special problems there might be for the Saturday broadcast. The scripts would be mimeographed at CBS, with the exception of the pages with commercials, which were mimeo'd at BBD & O and sent over to be collated.

The front page of the script, with the BBD & O logo, would list the name of the program, the date, the broadcast time, and the story's title, followed by the lyrics of the theme song. On one occasion the story was "Faithful John," below which the ad agency typist, evidently believing that he or she had a wicked sense of humor, had added: "(Or, the Plumbing That Never Broke Down)."

As soon as Nila saw this, she gave all of us an order: "Get rid of that!" This was not amusing. She knew it was possible that "Let's Pretend" scripts might fall into the hands of people in the studio audience. Fun was fun, but where the public image of "Let's Pretend" was concerned, she would not stand for it to be cheapened or ridiculed.

Besides the improvements in the show which came with sponsorship, we now had more glamorous surroundings for our broadcasts. For a short time we were housed in CBS Playhouse 4, at 254 West Fifty-Fourth Street, which had recently been leased by the network. Built in 1927 by Fortune Gallo as an opera house (the Gallo Theatre), it eventually became Studio 54, a wildly successful discotheque in the 1970s and 1980s. It was more recently restored to its former theatrical glory (ivory and cobalt-colored arches, with white cherubs and gilt decorations) as a restaurant-caberet.

By 1946 when I returned from service, the show had been moved to Playhouse 3, just around the corner, at 1697 Broadway, and there we stayed for the rest of our sponsored years. The theatre's auditorium was and still is behind a 14-story office building. Both were completed in 1927, the same year as the legendary Paramount Theatre on Times Square. The office building is in the shape of an L. The inside of the L, the corner of Broadway and Fifty-Third Street, was originally occupied by an ugly, nondescript four-story red brick building dating from about 1900. In 1960 that was torn down, and replaced by another ugly, nondescript five-story *white* brick building.

The theatre's marquee, its rather ornate and beautiful bronze doors, and its entrance lobby (and originally the box office) are on the Broadway side, while the building's lobby and elevators are on Fifty-Third Street. When I first started working at Playhouse 3, I remembered vividly having gone up those elevators to the top-floor studios of station WMCA, where in 1933 at the age of 11 I had done my first radio broadcasts on "Uncle Nick Kenny's Radio Kindergarten."

The theatre was originally called Hammerstein's. It was built as a memorial to Oscar Hammerstein I, founder of that celebrated theatrical family, by his son Arthur, and the foyer originally contained a life-size bronze statue of the great man, dressed in a long frock coat. The house was

ornately decorated inside in Gothic style, according to a contemporary account, with "mullions of ornamented plaster reaching up to the point of the dome where a great lantern is the central source of illumination."

Along the walls were a series of ten illuminated stained glass panels, depicting scenes from operas produced by Oscar Hammerstein. As it was built by a Hammerstein, the theatre was designed for musicals. Its original capacity was 1,204, with 762 seats in the orchestra and 442 in the balcony.

Unfortunately, probably due to the Depression, the Hammerstein family was not able to hold on to the house, and it passed through several different ownerships. In 1931 it became the Manhattan, and then a theatre-restaurant owned by Billy Rose, who added a pipe organ with a console that rose from the orchestra pit. After one more brief, unsuccessful period as a legitimate theatre it was leased to Columbia Broadcasting in 1936.

By the time "Let's Pretend" moved there, the theatre's former glamour had vastly diminished. The stained-glass panels had been covered, the heavy leather upholstered furniture and individually lighted oil paintings were long gone from the downstairs lounge, and who knows what happened to the statue of Oscar Hammerstein? (A partial answer to that question, and a fuller history of Hammerstein's Theatre, are in the fascinating book *Lost Broadway Theatres* by Nicholas Van Hoogstraten.)

To me the theatre had vaguely the look of a Gothic European church, and the bronze chandeliers with their fake candles were somewhat reminiscent of *The Three Musketeers* or *Cyrano de Bergerac*—not a bad atmosphere for some of the classic fairy tales of "Let's Pretend."

On Saturday mornings when the doors were opened at about 10:30, the theatre would fill with eager children, the girls usually wearing hats, and often gloves and patent leather shoes, and the boys jackets and ties. There were Girl Scout troops, teachers with their classes, as well as some older, middle-aged "Let's Pretend" fans trying to look inconspicuous.

Another audience group worth mentioning is the second-generation Let's Pretend fans. By the late 1940s some children who had grown up as our listeners were now married, and were beginning to bring their own offspring to the broadcasts. But to all of these faithful devotees, radio was still king, and this was the big-time.

It must have been rather confusing for some of the smaller children in the studio audience, who had formed clear mental pictures of the stories being enacted as they were hearing them on the radio, to come in and see what was, after all, a group of actors standing in front of microphones,

Opposite: **Thursday rehearsal at 485 Madison Avenue, ca. 1947. Left to right, behind: Michael O'Day, Jack Grimes, Albert Aley, Rita Lloyd, Sybil Trent, Bill Adams, Gwen Davies, Arthur Anderson, and Maurice Brown. At table: Marilyn Erskine, Nila Mack (who has ditched her cigarettes for the picture), Bonnie Baxter, and Joey Fallon. ©1947 CBS Inc. Used by permission.**

Heroine worship, ca. 1948: Brownies present a bouquet to Daisy Aldan. ©1948 CBS Inc. Used by permission.

holding scripts. It was just before our broadcast one Saturday morning in 1952, our last sponsored year, that I had occasion to use the men's room in the basement of Playhouse 3, the same one used by members of the audience. As I was leaving, I saw a father speaking to his little boy just before they went upstairs to take their seats in the theatre. "Now remember, sonny," he said, "it's only a radio show." I have always wondered since whether that child was expecting to see costumes, makeup, and scenery.

For most children in the studio audience the story's illusion was so strong in their own imaginations that the fact that we were in a radio studio did not matter. As Nila Mack was leaving the theatre one Saturday after we had done "Snow Drop and the Seven Dwarfs," she overheard a little girl talking to her mother on the street outside. "But she didn't eat the poisoned apple, Mother," the child was saying. "I was watching her!"

I suppose the thrill that most of the youngsters who came to our broadcasts felt was that of actuality; "There they are – that's what they look like – the actors I hear every week!" But the real excitement of radio drama is, or should be, what comes out of the speaker and goes into your ears and imagination.

As a stage presentation, a "Let's Pretend" broadcast was of distinctly uneven quality. The actors, nearest to the audience, were well lit, but both the sound effects (the most physical action there was on the stage) and the musicians were upstage, in rather dim light. Stage left (the audience's right), just in front of the proscenium was the control room, in which could be seen Nila Mack, giving cues, the production assistant Jean Hight, keeping track of time, Ed Marshall, the ad agency producer, and the engineer, who sat impassively through it all, no matter what the excitement. That, of course, was part of his job – to be impassive.

Stage right, opposite the control room was another glassed-in sound-proof room, the client's booth, in which sponsors, VIPs and relatives and friends could watch the show, smoke, and converse if they liked. Two large 10-foot-high cutouts designed by Ed Marshall on either side of the stage were the only stage setting – on one side a fairy-tale castle with soaring towers and on the other a huge box of Cream of Wheat, with its picture of the smiling black Cream of Wheat chef holding a steaming bowl of the sponsor's product. These were bathed in subdued pink and blue light when the audience entered, and brighter lights shone on the acting area during the broadcast.

The show began for the studio audience with Bill Adams's warm-up. He would welcome them, and say, "Now you know, you're all part of this broadcast. We couldn't do without you." And he would then coach the children in their responses for the Cream of Wheat game during the middle commercial. He would finish with one last admonition: "Now, you've got to be very quiet during our broadcast, so I want you to get all those coughs, and yawns, and sneezes, and foot stamps out of your system right now. Come on, everybody – let's hear it!" And a theatre full of children would all delightedly cough, yawn, and stamp their feet. Then would come momentary silence as the hands of the clock neared 11:05 A.M.

Though the "Let's Pretend" veterans had by now all become supposedly mature and sophisticated, involved as we were in the glamour world of network radio, I do not think any of us failed to get a thrill when the lights came up, the show went on the air, and the audience's enthusiastic yells and applause filled the theatre as Bill Adams said: "Cream of Wheat, the g-r-e-a-t American family cereal presents . . . 'Let's Pretend!' " Because of radio, the Hammerstein's theatre had gained yet another new life. Audiences were still enjoying themselves there, in a way that family could never have foreseen.

What was then CBS Playhouse 3 has had several other lives since its radio days. For several years it housed "Toast of the Town," starring Ed Sullivan, among other nighttime audience television programs, and in 1963 I found myself back there doing silent comedy bits on "The Jackie Gleason Show."

During its early television days the theatre was simply CBS Studio 51. It was renamed the Ed Sullivan Theatre in 1967, in honor of the host of that phenomenally successful Sunday night variety show which had a 23-year run. It was used less and less by Columbia, however, as its big-name, nighttime audience shows were emanating more and more from the West coast, and the lease was finally allowed to expire in 1981. The situation was dramatically reversed in late February 1993 when, to keep its new acquisition, "Late Show with David Letterman," in New York, the network bought both the office building and the theatre for a sum of $4 million. Completely refurbished, repainted, and rewired by Columbia under the watchful eye of the New York City Landmarks Commission, it became as much a high-tech television studio as a theatre, and was ready just in time for Letterman's first broadcast on August 30. (Columbia also announced that those ubiquitous Hammerstein illuminated stained-glass panels had been carefully removed and safely stored away.) What the Pretenders had known as Playhouse 3 thus began yet another chapter in its varied history, in which our program was by then almost a forgotten page.

Besides fond memories of many Saturday morning radio broadcasts from Playhouse 3, one particular incident that took place there comes to mind which has a "Let's Pretend" connection. One of our sound men, Vic Roubie, heard that cameramen were needed in the CBS television division, and he switched to the new medium. He was operating a camera on the stage of the theatre during an important nighttime audience show – live, of course.

"Camera 2, dolly back," came the instructions on his earphones. "Dolly back . . . dolly back" so Vic and the camera kept backing downstage, off the edge and into the audience. Luckily, a carpeted floor now covered what had been the orchestra pit – otherwise he might have been killed. But I have always imagined what a weird picture must have appeared on thousands of home TV screens as the camera and Vic careened crazily off the edge of the stage.

It was also in our beloved Playhouse 3 that another television disaster took place, which I saw myself on the air. It was on "The Red Buttons Show," for Maxwell House Instant Coffee. Every week there was a commercial showing a hand spooning some of the sponsor's product from the jar into a cup. Then steaming, boiling water was poured in, as the announcer talked about how delicious and satisfying it was. On this occasion the instant coffee was put in, but as the camera moved in for a tight closeup and the boiling water was poured, the cup shattered in a dozen pieces. A shocked "Ooohh!" went through the studio audience.

Then Buttons, not willing to let it alone, came on and began his next comedy shtick with, "Folks, this is the only coffee that can make this claim." The next week and forever after, the spoon was always left in the cup to absorb some of the heat as the water was poured in.

It was during the high-publicity, glamour days of "Let's Pretend" that Columbia decided to put the show on phonograph records. Each story was to be in an album of three 10-inch 78 r.p.m. discs – six sides, each lasting a maximum of 3½ minutes. This made a total of 21 minutes for each story, slightly more than we had on our Cream of Wheat broadcasts. As each record side had to end logically, and usually with a musical "button," this meant some minor rewrites by Nila Mack, but it all came out neatly, and was up to the usual high "Let's Pretend" standard.

We made six albums, done at Columbia's recording studios at 799 Seventh Avenue in June 1946 and June and December 1947. For those sessions we had the benefit of a slightly larger orchestra, with added reeds, brass, and tympani to give the music more body. The stories we did on those albums are itemized in Chapter 15. The records, of course, helped publicize the broadcast, and the broadcast helped sell the records, so both worked together to make "Let's Pretend" even more well known.

It is surprising how many people today assume that the "Let's Pretend" broadcasts themselves were prerecorded.* Neither our show nor any other

---

*Present-day radio and television programs are almost all prerecorded, either on audio tape, videotape, or on film, which can be edited to fit time requirements. When radio was live, however, these adjustments could only be made during rehearsal, by cutting or editing the script. Once a program was on the air, only minor timing adjustments could be made.

It is true, there is nothing that can match the excitement of live performance – it is happening now. But live performances are subject to the failings of human beings. In the days on network radio, except for some on the Mutual Broadcasting System, were pre-recorded until 1946. (Bing Crosby started the trend in that year by moving from NBC to American Broadcasting, because ABC was willing to accommodate his busy schedule by recording his show in advance.) Network programs were always live from New York, or whatever was the origination point. Stations in the Central, Mountain, or Pacific time zones might not want an East Coast program at its original broadcast hour, due to the time difference. For that reason, in the early days of network radio there was usually a "repeat for the coast," which meant the cast would go back to the studio three hours later and do the entire program all over again. No one complained about this, however, as it always meant an extra fee.*

As the networks began to relax their rigid rules on prerecorded broadcasts, acetates would be used for the repeats, but this was never done with our show. Though some people in the Pacific time zone were hardly out of bed yet on a Saturday, perhaps 8:05 A.M. was not a bad time for cereal commercials.

For the nine years "Let's Pretend" was sponsored by Cream of Wheat the company continued to be pleased with it. The whole package was a smoothly functioning blend – a good example of a radio program that was targeted for a particular audience, and gave that audience and the sponsor what they wanted.

---

of live radio there were occasional fluffs that could turn a director's hair grey overnight, such as: "And now, the NBC Symphony Orchestra, conducted by Artrusco Turanini" or "Friends, get the breast in bed." Just as disastrous, and irretrievable, in early live television performances were such things as doors that stuck, or corpses that got up and walked off the set.

Sadly, some of the artistic excitement has been necessarily erased by economic considerations. Mistakes are now left on the cutting room floor, and "perfect" programs can now be replayed an infinite number of times, resulting in greater income for all concerned.

In the days when radio programs were repeated for Western time zones, horror stories abounded concerning actors, who, especially after evening programs, had gone home for a nap or out for dinner or maybe to a movie, and had completely forgotten the second broadcast.

Chapter 13

Nila's Family Grows Up

One immediate benefit of our being sponsored was that, beginning with our first Cream of Wheat broadcast ("Cinderella" on September 25, 1943) there was no further talk of any "children's program" waivers. All the "Let's Pretend" actors received the sponsored program fee, which at that time was $47.30, including four hours of rehearsal. As new union contracts were negotiated in succeeding years, it finally rose to $71.25 in 1947. Maurice Brown and Bill Adams were paid more under their own negotiated contracts, and Gwen Davies and Sybil Trent earned additional fees because they were always in the commercials.

Agents' commissions were never deducted from our fees for "Let's Pretend" or for any other radio work, because rank-and-file performers in radio were not represented by agents. The reason was that when AFRA was first organized it had announced that it would grant agents franchises to represent its members, only on condition that they not charge commissions on union minimum fees. If they wanted their 10 percent commissions, said the union, let them obtain 10 percent above union scale or better for their clients. However, producers saw no reason to negotiate with agents for fees above union scale, unless the performer had "name value."

Sponsorship, as we have seen, caused great changes in "Let's Pretend," but another taking place at the same time, gradually and more subtly, was that Nila Mack's family of child actors had grown to adulthood. Indeed, many of our male Pretenders were now beginning to be eligible for military service. When our Cream of Wheat sponsorship started, this country was already heavily involved in World War II. Don Hughes, in the Signal Corps attached to the Air Corps and eventually sent to the combat zone in France and Belgium, was the first to leave in 1942, and he went the closest of any of us to the front lines. Bill Lipton enlisted in the Navy in 1943, and was stationed mostly at Dartmouth College, New Hampshire, in the V-12 program. Jack Grimes was in the Air Corps briefly, using his knowledge of radio to produce broadcasts by Captain Glenn Miller and his band. Kingsley Colton, younger than most of us, was in Signal Corps Intelligence, and not sent overseas until 1946.

I was in the Air Corps too, supposedly repairing radios in P-47 fighter planes in Pocatello, Idaho, but due to an acute lack of mechanical aptitude was finally transferred to work I was suited for: writing, directing, and announcing radio programs, writing newspaper columns, and putting on shows to sell War Bonds. Who would have thought that my Two-Man Band would one day help defend our country?

Returning to "Let's Pretend" early in 1946 I found many changes in the program, the much larger paycheck being among the most welcome. We had two new sound men – Art Strand, small and wisecracking, and Jimmy Dwan, large, with florid complexion, and fond of practical jokes; but in their work they were both up to the traditionally high CBS standards.

By then the second "Let's Pretend" wedding had taken place. In 1944 Albert Aley had married Maybelle Tunnicliff, originally from Florida, who was a New York Telephone Company operator. Before we were drafted, Don Hughes and I had joined Albert and Maybelle after the Saturday broadcasts for bowling at the Roxy Bowling Center on Fiftieth Street just east of Seventh Avenue, that occupied part of the building that once was the huge Earl Carroll Theatre.

Neither Don nor I had steady dates at the time, and this unlikely foursome got along very well together, even on occasions when Don and Albert would position themselves on either side of me while we were walking along the street, and I would suddenly find myself deposited in the nearest trash basket.

Meanwhile Albert, deferred from the draft because of his heart condition, had begun to find success in his early twenties as a full-time radio writer, first for "Superstition" on the ABC network, in 1942 for "Don Winslow of the Navy," and more importantly for "Hop Harrigan," who was a wartime flying ace. Albert took over the acting lead from Chester Stratton and then was made head writer.

Albert's personal life had meanwhile become very complicated. In May 1945 a daughter, Suzanne, was born to Albert and Maybelle. Five weeks later Maybelle tragically died of a brain embolism, and Albert was left with an infant to care for. Ivy Weston, a Canadian nanny who had been recommended to him by Austin Beardsley of the Young Professionals then moved into their apartment on East Forty-Ninth Street to care for Suzanne. One day in 1946 Albert met Elaine Firestone, a tall, attractive brunette. Elaine and Albert were mutually attracted, and she was willing to take on the double responsibility of a husband and a baby; so they were married several months later, when Suzanne was 15 months old. In 1947 Albert and Elaine's daughter Christopher was born.

It was a busy life for Albert. He would write the next day's "Hop Harrigan" script after Elaine had gone to bed, and deliver it at 2:00 A.M. to the doorman at the Beaux Arts Apartments, where the show's producer,

Nila Mack, ca. 1947. ©1947 CBS Inc. Used by permission.

Robert Maxwell, lived. He would go back home to sleep until 11:00 A.M., then rise and go to the studio for that day's recording. In 1952 he began what was to be a five-year association with Rockhill Productions, and became head writer of "Mark Trail," a 30-minute, three-times-a-week broadcast based on the comic strip by Ed Dodd. Mark was an outdoorsman – a man of the woods who fought the crooks, bad men, and bullies who would destroy nature. Albert also encouraged Don Hughes in writing, and Don sold several scripts to the show. "Trail" started on the Mutual network, shifted to ABC in 1951 as a five-times-a-week serial, and lasted until late in 1952. It was also in 1952 that Rockhill introduced "Tom Corbett, Space Cadet" on radio. Albert was executive producer. Before long, "Corbett" was being broadcast three times a week on radio, and two on television. Albert Aley had now become the most successful of all the Pretenders.

Though the original Pretenders were now all grown, our feeling for Nila as a mother and confidante did not cease. It was, if anything, stronger, especially among the girls, now women, who were coming to her for advice not only about careers but also boyfriends and romances. One of our newer cast members, Marilyn Erskine, who had been in radio for some time and was now playing adult roles on the show, told Nila that she was thinking of marrying a much older man.

"It's not going to work, kid," said Nila, looking at Marilyn over her glasses with those large, blue, slightly bulging eyes. Marilyn assured her that this was different. Nila told her that no, it wasn't, with words to the effect that she should not marry the man, and that if she did, to remember that she had told her not to. A few years later, when the divorce came, Marilyn did remember.

Gestures of respect and affection for Nila were given more freely by some of us than by others, but she had a real need of them. A hello kiss at first rehearsal was expected from every one of us, as was a goodbye kiss and a thank you after the show. So strong was Nila's need to receive as well as give affection that it became increasingly obvious that the frequency with which you were called had a direct relationship to your response in this department.

Marvin Silbersher (later a CBS television director as well as an actor) recalled that back in 1937, as a new child in the cast, he was physically turned off by kissing Nila (she wore too much lipstick, he said), and showed it by squirming out of her grasp. He was never called again after that incident. Rita Lloyd, new in the cast in 1948, remembers seeing the effusive greetings before morning rehearsal at Playhouse 3. She sat there not knowing what was expected. Nila turned to her and said, "Well, what's the matter with *you?*"

Playhouse 3, being a Broadway theatre, had union stagehands. (At 485 there had been only John Hosty, a redheaded Irishman who could speak Gaelic, and one other setup man, who for years had lugged heavy equipment up those ten steps to Studio 1.) One Saturday as we gathered at the control room door after the broadcast, one of the stagehands said to me disgustedly: "Now I suppose yez all goin' to kiss da director." It was certainly protocol to thank the director and say goodbye after a broadcast, but he had never seen anything like this.

Another part of the after-the-show ritual involved Don Hughes and myself. During rehearsals I had formed the habit of drawing a cartoon illustrating the week's story. I would hand it to Don, who, with grumbling expressions of reluctance, would on the spot compose a short poem to go with the illustration. Then after the show, as part of my goodbye, I would show Nila the picture and read her the poem, to which she always responded with a low chuckle.

Though Don's "Let's Pretend" verses were probably not of lasting value except as "in" jokes, they were never less than original and witty. I eventually traced the pictures and poems on heavy paper and put them in a loose-leaf book which I gave to Nila one Christmas, titled "Fairy Tales Gone Modern." Only one poem survives, and that through memory. I had drawn a picture of King Midas (of "The Golden Touch") counting his wealth, and this was Don's poem:

> There was a king named Midas,
> So they said, in days of old,
> Who had the wondrous gift of turning
> All he touched to gold.
> And as the sad result of this,
> Most all the girls in town
> Made chiming sounds like golden bells
> Whenever they sat down.

In 1947 Gwen Davies married Larry Greenhaus, a good-looking young chemical engineer, and he became part of the "Let's Pretend" family. At Playhouse 3 on Saturday mornings there were poker games during rehearsal breaks, and sometimes after the show, upstairs in one of the dressing rooms, and Albert Aley, Jack Grimes, Don Hughes, Michael O'Day, Bob Readick, the two sound men, and Larry were in on them. I was not interested in poker, though I am sure I would have been welcome to join the game if I'd wanted to.

Some of the Pretenders socialized with each other individually, such as Albert and Gwen and their spouses, Jack Grimes, Bill Lipton, and some of the actresses with each other. There were also two occasions when the entire cast chartered a party boat, the *Klondike IV*, in New Rochelle, New York, for a day's sail on Long Island Sound, including a beach picnic and swimming. I was the organizer of these jaunts, buying the food and drinks and keeping track of the money. Every Christmas we were all invited to Nila's house, and the cast would always bring her a collective present. The family feeling was indeed strongest during the Cream of Wheat years.

Meanwhile, Mae McNair, formerly the receptionist on the eighteenth floor at CBS, had become good friends with Nila, and finally moved into her apartment. She was also promoted to assistant casting director, under Marge Morrow. Another change was that Lois McQuitty, Nila's secretary, was hired away from CBS by BBD & O, our Cream of Wheat advertising agency, and became assistant to Ed Marshall, the agency producer of "Let's Pretend."

Nila, meanwhile, had become close friends with Sandra Levy, Gwen's mother, and was often invited to their apartment for dinner. After Gwen was married, she and her husband Larry would usually take Nila to dinner

Bill Lipton, ca. 1946.

at Colbee's after Thursday read-through rehearsal. It may have been partly that they realized she was lonely, but she was also witty and good company. I think that Nila's respect for Larry grew after one of those dinners, at which she apparently spoke to him in a way that to him resembled scolding. Larry said to her, "You can't frighten me, Nila. I'm not one of your kids." Their relationship was better after that.

Opposite: **August 1948: Another party, celebrating Nila Mack's 18th anniversary with CBS. Back row: Anne-Marie Gayer, Maurice Brown, Kingsley Colton (hidden), Donald Buka, Donald Hughes, Sybil Trent, Arthur Anderson, Albert Aley, Bill Lipton, and Bob Readick. Front row: Gwen Davies, Nila Mack, Patricia Ryan, Betty Jane Tyler, Miriam Wolfe, and Jack Grimes. ©1948 CBS Inc. Used by permission.**

One of the "Let's Pretend" actors' most memorable Christmas presents to our director was in 1945. It was a 10-minute take-off on the show, written by Don Hughes and entitled "Snow White Cinderella, or Sleeping Beauty and the Beast." It was recorded in Studio 1, on both sides of a 12-inch acetate.

It opened with Sybil and Gwen singing this version of the theme, in New Yorkese accents, with Mickey O'Day at the piano:

Cream of Wheat may be good to eat
But we really couldn't say,
We've sung this song for so damn long
That it makes us shout, "Oi veh!"
Perhaps the babies love it,
The sponsor does, we know,
So on and on we sing it,
We must-a stay on-a the show.
(We need the check!)

Uncle Bill tries to get the audience to shout out the name of a cereal they all love, but all he gets is "Wheaties!" and "Ralston!" He gives up and says, "All right, you little bastards. Just for that, no commercial!" (Cheers.) Don Hughes is asked how we should travel to the Land of Let's Pretend, and replies, "I do enough commuting as it is. Let's stay here."

We then meet Snow White Cinderella (Gwen Davies), who wants to go to the AFRA ball. Her Fairy Godmother (Miriam Wolfe, sounding very much like Mrs. Nussbaum from "Allen's Alley") makes her a coach from a tin can, and a coachman from a cockroach on the wall. At the ball she meets her dream man Hophead Harrigan (Albert Aley) but disappears at midnight, leaving Hophead holding her nylon stocking. He promises his sidekick Tank (Bob Readick) that he'll find the girl, and the mate to the stocking, by putting it in his radar detector.

Meanwhile, Snow White Cinderella left a little too late, and is condemned to live with a Beast (Jack Grimes) in the wilderness of New Jersey. She asks him why he has green skin, a tail, and two heads.

BEAST: Do I have two heads? Duhhh – I wondered why that guy was always lookin' over my shoulder.

We meet the Queen (played like Mae West by Betty Jane Tyler), who takes the advice of the Mirror (played by Pat Ryan with a Cockney accent), and slips her rival Snow White Cinderella a Mickey, which sends her into a deep sleep.

Hophead finds her with the aid of his radar detector. "What beautiful bumps she makes in the sheets," he murmurs. Snow White Cinderella awakes and says indignantly, "Were you tryin' to climb into bed with me? Takin' advantage of a poor sleepin' girl!" "Forgive me," says Hophead. "Well – I'm awake now," she replies. "Whatcha waitin' for?" And the cast all yells, "*Merry Christmas, Nila!*"

Don had many other facets to his writing talents. Besides "Mark Trail" scripts, he also wrote several episodes of "Tom Corbett, Space Cadet" for Albert, at Rockhill Productions. Don and I had already been coauthoring a project for television called "Date for Three," with a cast of three, including myself and Sybil Trent. The 15-minute show included songs, some of them originals written by Don, but nothing ever came of it.

Though Nila continued to audition child actors from 1943 onward, the cast was now basically adults, and replacements had to be made from time to time as people became unavailable for various reasons, the most common of which seemed to be having moved to Hollywood. With adult performers, as with the children who had been her original cast, she continued to look for people who were not only good actors but who could project the belief that fairy tales were real.

One of these was Marilyn Erskine. Marilyn called herself a "character leading lady." Blonde, with a sympathetic and appealing voice, she was able to play highly emotional parts as well as comedy. She came to "Let's Pretend" as a teenager, after doing children's parts on "Young Widder Brown" and other daytime serials. By 1950 she had left New York to do a stage play with Cesar Romero in California, and from then on only returned to the East occasionally. She later played Ida Cantor in *The Eddie Cantor Story*, and did many other films. After playing Tom Ewell's wife on his TV sitcom series, she left show business in 1962, and still resides happily in California.

Anne Francis, blonde and fragile-looking, was cast by Nila in romantic heroine roles, but left for the film capital in 1947, where she became very successful in adventure and sci-fi films for 20th Century–Fox, in roles ranging from frail young things to hardened broads.

Florence Halop had been on "Let's Pretend" as a child, with her brother Billy. After he went to the West Coast she did adult leads on our show until she too went to California. She later made a great success in Hollywood, more in television sitcoms than in films. She was the hypochondriac patient Mrs. Huffnagle in "St. Elsewhere," and was "killed off" for an even better role as Florence Kleiner, the wise-cracking bailiff in "Night Court," which she played until her death from cancer in 1986.

Rosemary Rice had a long background of daytime radio serials, including "Archie Andrews" as a teenager, then as an adult in "The Right to Happiness," "Young Dr. Malone" and a run of 12 years on "When a Girl Marries." Nila used her in leading roles such as fairy godmothers during the Cream of Wheat years. Rosemary later created the role of Katrin on

Michael O'Day, Florence Halop, Arthur Anderson, and Patricia Ryan at the microphone. ©1949 CBS Inc. Used by permission.

television in "Mama." She then launched a separate and very successful career as a writer, producer, and singer in children's records.

Joan Shepard, a British war refugee child, was by 1943 a panel member of the highly popular "Quiz Kids." Though Nila used her on our show only a few times, "Let's Pretend" helped launch Joan on a busy radio career. She appeared on Broadway in *Foolish Notion* in 1945, and in *A Young Man's Fancy* in 1947. She and her husband, actor Evan Thompson, formed Fanfare Theatre Ensemble, a children's theatre company, in partnership with John Clifton in 1970, and since 1987 they have operated a successful summer theatre, the River Rep, in Ivoryton, Conn.

Another of our new adult actresses Anne-Marie Gayer. Anne-Marie, tall, slim, and blonde, with a ready smile and great versatility, was born in the Midwest. She became active in theatre, then radio, in and near Chicago, as an ingenue and young leading lady. Then in the 1940s, since so many Chicago radio shows had shifted to New York, she moved to be where the work was.

Postwar, Anne-Marie was very successful in New York radio, including nighttime shows like "Gangbusters," and daytime serials. She also did three Broadway plays, but only one, *The Desk Set*, enjoyed a run.

She remembers Nila Mack as "our earth-mother – like a benevolent dictator." Our director cast her as the Red Queen in "Alice in Wonderland," and in a great variety of other roles. Her only negative experience with "Let's Pretend" was getting stuck in one of the cubicles in the ladies' room at Playhouse 3, just as we were about to go on the air. Jack Grimes heard her screams and yanked the door open just in time for the broadcast.

(Daisy Aldan had encountered exactly the same problem years earlier on the twenty-first floor at CBS. Alone in the ladies' room, she had desperately tugged on its door, which was stuck, until it finally opened, then rushed up a flight of stairs to the studio just as we were going on the air, to be met by Miss Mack's baleful glare from the control room. She was not able to explain what had happened until half an hour later, when the broadcast was over.)

There were many other actresses who helped bring excitement to our show during the Cream of Wheat years. One was Susan Douglas, born in Czechoslovakia in 1926, quite active on "Let's Pretend" and other New York radio programs until she began to make a name for herself on the stage in 1946.

Rita Lloyd

Rita was the last of the long-term Pretenders recruited by Miss Mack. She joined the cast in 1948. As a child she had progressed from doing imitations of Greta Garbo and Margaret Sullavan to doing the leads in school plays in her Brooklyn neighborhood, then joining "The All-City Radio Workshop" on New York's municipal station, WNYC. She studied drama under Wilson Lehr at City College and, at the age of 18, decided to become a professional.

Rita had a mature voice, good speech, and the ability to play emotional parts. She passed both the general audition at CBS ("bring 5 minutes of your own material") and the "Let's Pretend" audition. Rita had for years listened to our show, but had never dreamed of actually being on it. At her first Thursday read-through she was so nervous that she dropped her script on the floor under the table, and when she bent down to pick it up, saw everybody's feet.

"Stars have small feet," thought Rita. She was taller than most of the girls, and felt terribly intimidated. But with their help and with Nila's she overcame her insecurity and grew as an actress. Shortly after becoming active in radio, Rita obtained a scholarship in the American Theatre Wing's professional training program, and got several jobs as a result of working with directors who had volunteered to teach radio and television classes. She did "Suspense," "The Eternal Light," and running parts on "Backstage Wife," "The Romance of Helen Trent," and several others. There was only one catch: As Rita's career was blossoming, so was television, and one by one, these radio shows started to go off the air.

Rita was fond of and admired Nila, but she did have two confrontations with her. The first was when she paid a casual visit to her office. Nila got up from her desk, shut the door, and said, "I'm not going to let you leave here until I find out what makes you tick." Nila was exasperated because Rita had such a cool, unflappable exterior and did not show any nervousness. Rita explained as best she could that she had as much insecurity as the rest of us sometimes did, and that the coolness was her way of handling it – a cover.

The other run-in was when Rita had landed a nonprincipal part on "You Are There" for Robert Louis Shayon: a prestige show which all actors felt it was a privilege to be called for. At next Thursday's rehearsal Nila said, "Rita, I heard you did an extra on 'You Are There'." "Yes," said Rita. "Isn't that wonderful?" "No," said Nila. "Let's Pretenders do not do extras. Do not do an extra again, or you will never do this show again." Nila was still fiercely jealous of her own program's position in the pecking order at CBS and in radio.

On the other hand, our director was just as capable of the warmth and kindness she had always shown. Once Rita showed up at rehearsal by mistake, as a result of a mix-up by her message service. "What are you doing here?" asked Nila. When Rita explained, Nila wrote in a part for her to save her the embarrassment and the disappointment, and Rita got a check the next week anyway.

Rita found her six years on "Let's Pretend" very happy ones. She gained experience in our company playing witches, wicked queens, other character parts, and leads as well. Though on the show less frequently after Miss Mack's death, she remained a member of the family.

Today she continues as a successful working actress. She has had running parts, mostly as conniving women, on daytime television in "Edge of Night," "Guiding Light," and "As the World Turns," and has appeared on the stage in such leading roles as Lady in Tennessee Williams's play *Orpheus Descending* off Broadway and at the Bucks County Playhouse. She also learned how to lip-sync* for foreign films, and spoke in English for Giuleta Massina in *Juliet of the Spirits.* Her rather smoky voice and incisive delivery have been heard more recently narrating some of the National Geographic TV "Explorer" series.

There were many male actors, too, who Nila Mack either recruited during the Cream of Wheat years or who had been on "Let's Pretend" only occasionally as children and were now called more frequently.

The best known of these is Dick Van Patten, called Dickie when he was a child. Never used much on our show before he was grown, he had an enthusiasm and an ingenuous charm which showed more during his adult years. Besides "Let's Pretend," Dick counted 600 radio performances and opened in a total of 27 Broadway plays. His days on our show probably ended in July 1949 when he began a seven-year television run as Nels, Rosemary Rice's brother, in "Mama."

When he moved to the West Coast, Dick started a string of what is so far 30 feature films. Four have been for Mel Brooks, including *High Anxiety* and *Space Balls*, in which Dick starred. Of his TV series, the best known are "Eight Is Enough," and the more recent "WIOU." He married his former Professional Children's School classmate Patricia Poole, a dancer, and they have raised three sons. Dick remembers being in great awe of Nila (most of us were), as well as learning a lot from her, including an actor's discipline: "Never be late!"

Larry Robinson was another who had been on the show since childhood. At the age of nine he was also playing Harlan, the youngest of the Day family, in *Life with Father*, the second of his nine Broadway plays. He remembers Nila as a gruff but affectionate disciplinarian (he once got a lecture from her when he was 12 for not wearing a necktie). Not until he was 21 and had been on the show for 12 years did he feel he could call her by her first name.

---

*An actor in a recording studio speaks words which have been specially written to match the lip movements of the character on the screen, who is usually speaking in a foreign language. He may even lip-sync his own voice, or that of another actor speaking English, especially if the original recording was marred by unwanted noises, such as passing airplanes. The film (or videotape) is played back over and over, sentence by sentence, until the performer is able to achieve perfect synchronization with the picture.

When in his teens, Larry created the role of Sammy for Gertrude Berg in the television version of her radio classic "The Goldbergs." It had almost a six-year run, 1949–54. Larry remains a busy and successful New York actor. In the movie *Serpico* he played the mayor's press secretary. He works full time in radio and television voice-over commercials* and in the past 25 years has recorded over 200 books for the American Foundation for the Blind, including one on the history of radio.

Skippy Homeier, born in 1930 in Chicago, was only a Pretender for a short time. At the age of 13 he appeared as a Nazi brat in *Tomorrow the World* on Broadway, and left for Hollywood a year later to repeat his role in films in 1944. He continued to work in the film capital, in such films as *Boys' Ranch* (1946) and adventure stories such as *Halls of Montezuma*.

Donald Buka, a teenager just arrived in New York from Pittsburgh, auditioned for Nila Mack in 1940. She found that he had an interesting character voice, with a slight "edge" to it, and he became a frequent Pretender. Starting in 1945, he was featured in "The Sparrow and the Hawk," a CBS adventure series about a teenage aviator (Donald) and his uncle, a retired U.S. Air Force lieutenant colonel, played first by Michael Fitzmaurice, then by another Pretender, Lamont Johnson. Meanwhile, Donald had started to acquire what is now a long list of Broadway, television, and film credits. To this day he remains an active actor, director, and teacher.

Peter Fernandez, having served his apprenticeship in radio on Madge Tucker's "Coast to Coast on a Bus," appeared on "Let's Pretend" as a teenager during the Cream of Wheat years, while he was in the third of his seven Broadway plays, *Watch on the Rhine*. He also had the lead in a New York–made film, *City Across the River*. Peter remains very busy in radio and television voice-over work. He was the original voice of Speed Racer in that classic cartoon series. He is also a producer of English-speaking sound tracks for foreign-made films.

Bob Drew, born in 1936, auditioned for Nila when he was 15 years old. The audition was recorded on an acetate. She played it back for him and said, "You're obviously very talented, but your speech is terrible. Come back in a year and let me hear you again." Bob, who grew up in the East Bronx, says he had a Dead End Kid accent. A year later he had indeed improved his speech, and was on "Let's Pretend" often from then on, as well as many other radio shows. He is now a successful spokesman for large industrial firms at conventions and sales meetings.

There were many Let's Pretenders during the 1943–52 Cream of Wheat period who at one time or another decided that being performers was not going to be part of their long-term futures. Some of them have

---

*Voice-over is an abbreviation of a term from the film industry, "voice over film." As action is taking place on the screen, you are hearing a voice but not seeing its owner.

become very successful as executives, either in the creative end of show business or in entirely different enterprises.

One child actor briefly on the "Let's Pretend" scene at that time was Robert Evans. He eventually became head of Paramount Pictures, and returned there more recently as a producer. Another was Harlan Stone, who adopted that name professionally when he played Harlan in the Chicago company of *Life with Father*. At age 13 took over the role of Jughead on "Archie Andrews." He grew up in radio, on the stage, and in early television. After the Korean conflict and attaining a B.A. degree, he was a successful director and producer at TV stations, and then became a major producer of television commercials.

He became good friends with another Pretender, Charles Mullen. After some brief stints as a Pretender, Charles took over the title role on "Archie Andrews" in mid–April 1945, and, due to the time conflict – it being a midday Saturday program – that was the end of his "Let's Pretend" career. After a busy acting career as a young adult, he was in uniform as an Armed Forces Radio Service producer and writer. In 1950 he started to phase out of show business and joined the sales staff of the American Tobacco Company. When he retired 42 years later he was chairman, CEO, and a vice president for American Brands, American Tobacco's parent company. Acting being basically a freelance profession, he agrees with Pretender Eddie Ryan by saying that "actors and salesmen are one and the same."

Lamont Johnson we called "The Orson Welles of 'Let's Pretend'" because of his commanding vocal presence. A rather tall young man with wavy brown hair and deep-set eyes, he became a Pretender in 1943, at age 20, and remained for seven years, with time out for a USO tour of the European war theatre. His voice made him a very good leading man/hero type, but like so many of us, he also had the fun of doubling, as he described it, "as old trolls, with a scattering of elves, giants and ogres, sometimes mixed in all in the same broadcast."

Though Lamont felt somewhat self-conscious when first on "Let's Pretend" because he was a comparative newcomer, as time went on he enjoyed more and more what he called "a special camaraderie." He had fond memories of Nila Mack. "I loved her on sight," he said later, "particularly when she tried to get tough with her unruly brood, hacking into the [talkback] microphone with her nicotine-bronchitis-tinged basso and doing her best to terrorize us into order, decorum and serious work, when we were all such hellraisers at base." As Lamont could see, Nila's family had indeed grown up.

When Lamont Johnson moved his growing family to the West Coast in 1950, his greatest successes were to be as a director not an actor. From live television in Hollywood he shifted to filmed and taped television, including

Gore Vidal's "Lincoln," for which he won one of his four Directors' Guild awards, "Wallenberg" with Richard Chamberlain, and the more recent semi-documentary "Crash Landing." He has also directed 27 important feature films.

After 17 years of writing and directing "Let's Pretend," and its earlier incarnation "The Adventures of Helen and Mary," Nila Mack had grown used to losing good child performers and replacing them with just as good, or better ones. But she was to find that losing people whom she had grown to depend upon emotionally as well as professionally would be tougher to withstand. The loss of Miriam Wolfe, even though it was a gradual departure, was the first.

In April 1947 Marge Morrow, CBS casting director, had introduced Miriam to Fletcher Markle, a young Canadian who had been hired by the network to write, produce, and direct a new series, "Studio One." Miriam's first job on it was a brief appearance in "Ah, Wilderness!" From then on she worked steadily with Markle, and graduated to playing leading roles, such as Cathy in "Wuthering Heights," for which she got a rave review in *Variety*. Markle had previously offered her ingenue leads, but she refused, saying that the character roles she played were more interesting and durable.

After a year, during which she was on the show constantly, "Studio One" became "The Ford Theatre," and Fletcher Markle moved it to the West Coast, taking with him only three New York actors: Mercedes McCambridge, who was his leading lady and new wife, Bob Dryden, and Miriam.

Until then Miriam had been able to continue on "Let's Pretend," but now it was obviously impossible. She would later return to New York when "The Ford Theatre" went off the air, but for the time being Miriam Wolfe was a continent's width away, and unavailable in New York. Nila Mack was a loving mother and adviser to us all, besides being our employer, but in return for this she had been expecting, more and more, some degree of control over our lives, especially those of her young actresses, and Miriam found it necessary to rebel in order to establish her independence as an adult as well as to expand in her career.

There was in this case not much our director could do, except be angry and hurt. But two years later, in the case of Daisy Aldan, things were different. When Daisy left on her first trip to Europe in 1949, she did not realize that the rules of relating to Miss Mack had subtly changed. After she returned she was puzzled at not having received any "Let's Pretend" calls for some time. She finally went and talked to Nila, who told her that she had expected that Daisy would ask permission to take the trip. Daisy apologized. There was a tearful embrace, and her "Let's

Daisy Aldan, ca. 1942.

Pretend" calls resumed. Nila Mack was a person who had a great need to be needed.

In 1949 Nila and the program suffered another loss. Patricia Ryan had been there before Nila was, as Helen in "The Adventures of Helen and Mary." A rather plain little girl, she had matured into a lovely young woman and a very good actress. Nila and all of us rejoiced with her as she won the female starring role in "Claudia and David" for General Foods in 1941. She also continued as a busy actress in many other radio shows.

In 1944 Pat was up for a Broadway play. Since she had no stage experience, Ed Marshall helped her write a résumé featuring logical roles she might have done in a mythical stock company (this is a practice not to be recommended for actors without real credits – one never knows when casting people may ask embarrassing questions about the mythical theatre, or the other actors the young hopeful is claiming to have worked with). She got the part and was featured in *Sleep No More*, a three-act farce which opened at the Cort Theatre on August 31. Its chances were doubtful, said *Variety*. Pat was the heart interest, "a rather mild part," added the Bible of Broadway. *Sleep No More* closed after seven performances. So much for Pat's stage career.

Meanwhile, while a volunteer hostess at the Stage Door Canteen, as were several of our "Let's Pretend" actresses, she had met Bob Gibson, a British seaman. Bob was a good-natured fellow, rather short, with heavy eyebrows, blue eyes, and slightly protruding upper teeth. He bore no resemblance to the handsome prince we Pretenders might have envisioned for Pat, but she loved him and was comfortable with him, and Bob was welcomed by the Pretenders at the studio and when any of us gathered socially. Pat's mother hated him on sight. They were married in 1948, while Pat continued her busy radio career.

One of the things that endeared Pat Ryan to all of us was her complete openness and lack of guile, combined with a certain dignity and reserve that made her hard to know really well. In earlier years, when we adolescent boys started to exchange dirty jokes, we would never dream of letting Pat or any of the girls hear them. And Pat refused to share in any of their female gossip sessions. When Pat returned from her honeymoon, the girls all gathered around eagerly with: "Well? Well?" Her answer was based completely on practicality. "Whatever you do, girls," she told them, "don't buy expensive lingerie for your honeymoon. The first thing that happens you take it off, and then what use is it? You don't keep it on that long." And having known Pat, I would not be surprised if that bit of financial advice was all she revealed about her honeymoon.

When Pat found that she was pregnant, she became terrified. She came into the control room after the broadcast on February 12, 1949, and said to Nila, "I have something to tell you – just you alone," but she kept hold of Gwen Davies's hand while she said it. In a letter to Miriam Wolfe, who then was in California, Nila wrote, "Then she told me of being pregnant. And she was afraid I'd be mad. She was obviously frightened, and honest enough not to pretend she was in seventh heaven. Gwen [who had just given birth to her first child] was as usual wise beyond her years in saying that the ecstasy of motherhood was a lot of bunk, and it took time to get used to the idea, and many other things that were just what Pat needed to have said at that time, and it was so right that Gwen should be the one to tell her. We parted on a happy note as I thanked her for doing as I'd asked and 'staggered the Stork Derby' until Gwen was back in the cast."

The reader will note that this meant Nila was also timing her actresses' pregnancies so that only one at a time would be out for childbirth.

Patricia Ryan, ca. 1944.

The following Monday night Pat had an important part on DuPont Chemicals' NBC program "Cavalcade of America." Glenn Ford was starred, and Pat was playing opposite him. Others in the cast were Arlene Francis, Agnes Young, and Barbara Weeks. Ed Marshall was the DuPont BBD & O agency producer.

After dress rehearsal, in NBC's Studio 8-H, there was a supper break before the broadcast. Pat returned from it early. Ed Marshall, who by now was Pat's surrogate uncle, was sitting onstage. She came and put her arms around his neck, unusual for her, and said, "Ed, I'm dying. I feel terrible." She told him she had gone home for supper break – her husband was out – and had a can of cold pork and beans. "That would make anyone feel terrible," said Ed. "Take it easy."

During the broadcast it became apparent that there was something seriously wrong with Pat. Ironically, this "Cavalcade" show was a special Valentine's Day broadcast entitled "Valentine for Sophie," and Pat played the title role – a girl who suffered from blinding headaches. After her biggest scene she staggered from the microphone, stricken with a blinding headache herself. Two of the other actresses filled in during the intervening scenes. Pat had the last line in the show, which was essential. As the cue came she got up to the microphone and said the line, mechanically.

A doctor was found, who gave her morphine for the pain, and said she should be taken to the hospital. Ed Marshall got hold of Pat's husband Bob, who insisted that she be taken home instead, which was done. Early the following morning Bob was awakened by the barking and whining of their little dog. Pat had died in the night. When Ed Marshall received the news in his office at BBD & O, he went into the men's room, sat on the commode in one of the cubicles, and cried and cried.

An autopsy was performed, and the result was that Patricia Ryan had died of a cerebral hemorrhage. She was 27 years old.

Walter B. Cooke's largest funeral chapel on West Seventy-Second Street was filled the following Friday by the family, the Pretenders (we all contributed for a rose blanket for the casket), broadcast executives, and many other actors Pat had worked with. Her husband had decided that her body would be cremated, and the ashes sent back to England, the place of her birth, to be buried in Derby. It is easy to become maudlin, remembering our lovely, blonde Pat lying there – the Sleeping Beauty whom no Prince would ever awaken.

Nila Mack's next loss was not in the "Let's Pretend" family but in her own household. She had now had Mae McNair sharing her apartment for some years. They needed each other's company, but there were frequent quarrels. Mae was not a particularly outgoing person ("I'm sure I don't know why I keep her. I should have turned her out long ago," Nila once told her secretary, Mary Ponterio), and Nila could not always have been easy to live with. In 1951 Mae died of cancer and Nila was again alone, with only her cats and Maud Wilson part of the time for company.

During the next year two more members dropped out of the solid framework of the "Let's Pretend" structure. First, Brad Barker died of a heart attack on September 29, 1951. He had been a fixture on our program for over nine years, ever since Harry Swan had left New York and radio. Brad had been more or less taken for granted, but was always there – for a kitten's mew or an elephant's trumpet, and just as creative an actor as any of us who expressed ourselves with words. His replacement was obvious. It had to be Donald Bain.

Donald had been Brad's only real competition in radio. He was not as versatile as Brad, but made up for this by enthusiasm and flamboyance.

While Brad had been rather heavy-set, Donald, also in his sixties, was small and wiry. In fact, one radio wit said that he had seen Brad walking down Madison Avenue one day with Donald in his mouth.

Donald was a bit of a ham. When he did our broadcasts he always wore a handkerchief spread out over the top of his bald head to protect it from the sharp edges of the earphones, and rather enjoyed, I think, the bizarre visual effect this created for the studio audience.

It was in 1952 that Albert Aley, busy now as a producer for Rockhill Productions in both radio ("Mark Trail") and television ("Tom Corbett, Space Cadet" in both media) made the decision that it was no longer suitable or even humanly possible for him to also be an actor on "Let's Pretend." He came to Nila Mack's office one day and told her that he was going to have to resign from the program. Our director had now lost several important and beloved members of her radio family.

Meanwhile, there was now a shadow looming larger and larger on her horizon, and on that of every other radio producer. Its name was Television. In 1948 network radio in this country was enjoying unprecedented popularity, and was bringing in record revenues. But it was also in that year that the first intercity coaxial cables were completed, meaning that network TV was now here, and had unlimited possibilities for expansion and profit.

First Cream of Wheat, then the CBS network itself came to Nila, asking her to draw up budgets for putting "Let's Pretend" on television. The figure she gave the Cream of Wheat Company was $50,000 per show and as far as is known, nothing further was heard from them on the subject. Then (the exact time uncertain) the network practically ordered her to ready a video version of "Let's Pretend." Her reply was that the show was unsuitable for television. "When they show me how you can put a Prince on horseback climbing a glass mountain on the screen, I'll talk to them," she said to Mary Ponterio.

There were several reasons for Nila Mack's reluctance. To begin with, after 20 years, though she had an extensive and varied theatrical background, she was married to radio, and comfortable in the niche she had created for herself and for the program. The fact that she was not in the best of health was probably of less importance to her.

Miss Mack was also resisting television for a much more personal reason. She was terribly afraid that if our program were televised, it would be done by younger, video-wise people, and she would lose control of her show – her child – and with it the family of actors she had grown to love and depend upon. But anyone could see that the broadcast industry was changing, getting ready for the advent of an entirely new medium and, no matter what Nila Mack said or did, the shadow was not going to go away.

Chapter 14

The End:
Where Are They Now?

"Let's Pretend" did its last broadcast for Cream of Wheat on December 6, 1952, and reverted to being a CBS sustaining radio program. With listening habits changing and ratings no longer what they once had been, the cereal company at last gave in to what its advertising agency had been recommending for several years deciding that its advertising money should go elsewhere.

Miss Mack, who had done most of her adaptations and original scripts for "Let's Pretend" during our sustaining years, did only five more during the Cream of Wheat period. First there were "Alice in Wonderland" and "Alice Through the Looking Glass," done on succeeding weeks, April 3 and 10, 1948, for which Maurice Brown wrote delightful musical settings to the poems. "Jason and the Golden Fleece" came next, on November 10 of that year, and then "The Song of Hiawatha" done in 1950. Her last new "Let's Pretend" script, written in 1952, was an adaptation of E.B. White's *Charlotte's Web*, the story of the generous-hearted spider, done in two parts.

There were a spate of "Let's Pretend" marriages during the later Cream of Wheat years. In 1948 Don Hughes married Ann Cushman, a fellow member of the Professional Children's School Alumni Association, and the next year their son was born. In 1949 Bill Lipton, out of the service and doing very well in radio, married Joan Abbrancati, and they too had a son.

Jack Grimes, who continued not only to be busy in radio but was now commuting to Hollywood for film roles, married Joan Farrell in 1949. When Jack asked Joan's father for her hand in marriage, Mr. Farrell wanted to know how much money he made. Jack, knowing that a nonperformer would never understand our unpredictable incomes, quoted the AFRA overtime rehearsal rate, $6 an hour, which at that time was an excellent wage. Hearing that, Joan's father decided not to raise any objections.

It was in 1950 that Betty Jane Tyler married Irwin Karp, who became a prominent copyright lawyer and later authored several books on the subject. They had two children, a daughter and a son. Sybil Trent also married an attorney, French-born Andrew Nieporent, and they later had two sons. Another of our "Let's Pretend" marriages was that of Daisy Aldan, who had become successful as a poet, teacher and lecturer. In 1954 she married a fellow poet, Richard Miller.

In 1952, our last Cream of Wheat year, the agency started tinkering with the commercial format of the program. In November, with their sponsorship in its last weeks and possibly feeling they had nothing to lose by experimenting, they had changed the program's opening by eliminating Gwen and Sybil's singing of the Cream of Wheat jingle and the Komzak "Fairy Tale" theme was again being done instrumentally. After Bill Adams's introduction, a quartet now sang a new jingle, the music of which is lost to antiquity, and just as well. The words started with:

> Eat delicious Cream of Wheat,
> the hot fam'ly breakfast treat,
> Whose nourishment and flavor can't be beat.

In 1952 a new announcer, Peter Thomas, now did the commercials, while Bill Adams continued to be the host and do the narration. Peter was hired, no doubt, to liven up the show by providing a contrasting voice to attract more attention to the commercials. On one of our last Cream of Wheat broadcasts one of these commercials included the suggestion that you pour chocolate milk on your hot Cream of Wheat. No comment.

Peter Thomas, a slightly built young fellow originally from Pensacola, Florida, fresh out of military service, and new to New York, had auditioned for the agency and gotten the Cream of Wheat spokesman spot. He walked onto the stage of Playhouse 3 for his first Saturday rehearsal in tremendous awe at actually being on the legendary program he had heard as a child. He remembers his feeling of relief as Sybil Trent immediately walked over and said, "Welcome to 'Let's Pretend'." Peter had bought at Brooks Brothers for the occasion a rather fuzzy, baggy, uncomfortable woolen suit, which he at once regretted, and a new pair of yellow shoes. "Suit's all right," said Bill Adams, "but get rid of those shoes." (He later relented, saying, "Maybe they'll scuff up a bit.") Though no one knows what Nila thought of the new commercial format, she took an interest in Peter, and referred him to a special teacher to improve his speech. Peter remembers immediately being enveloped by a warm feeling of family on the program. It was a good introduction for him to New York radio.

At this writing he has been for over four decades very successful as an announcer, narrator, and spokesman, both on and off screen. (Brooks Brothers was very decent – the company took the suit back.)

Meanwhile, we continued to receive awards yearly from various

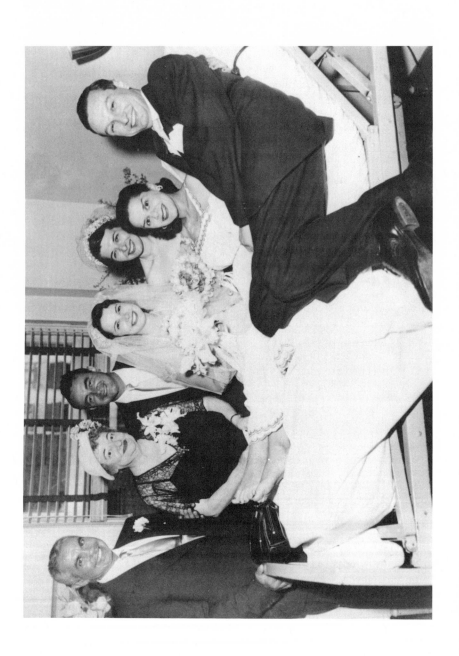

organizations as the best children's program on the air. The fan mail continued too, from children asking for stories and from parents thanking us for the entertainment and the moral lessons provided.

Casey Allen, who had replaced Ed Marshall as our BBD & O agency producer, later relayed what might be thought of as a "harbinger of change," not in "Let's Pretend" itself but in its audience. Nila arrived at the studio one Saturday morning chuckling, and told Casey of a fan letter she had just received from a little boy, which said something like, "My mother asked me to write you and say how much we all enjoy your fairy tales every week," and so on. Nila, as always, was touched – until she happened to turn the letter over. In the same childish scrawl, evidently done when his mother had left the room, the little boy had added his own postscript, a two-word imprecation starting with the well-known "f" word.

If some of our childhood audiences were becoming a bit cynical, our director herself was not immune. One day in 1952 Nila's secretary Mary Ponterio found in the morning mail almost the exact duplicate of that classic letter of some years before: "Dere Lespertend – please send me Free a Fairy." "How shall I answer this, Nila?" asked Mary. Her response was characteristically quick: "You tell that child to go to the third floor at NBC."

Meanwhile, "Studio One" had switched to television, and was being broadcast from New York. Miriam Wolfe, whose radio "Ford Theatre" engagement had meant a long stay in California, was back in New York too. In 1952 she was cast as the Virgin Mary in a special "Studio One" Christmas program. Nila had also cast her as Mrs. Santa Claus, the part she had played for years, in our own special, "The Night Before Christmas," and Miriam had thought she could do both broadcasts. Then she found that "Studio One" had scheduled both a rehearsal and a costume call on Saturday morning, a direct conflict with our broadcast time, and it was absolutely necessary that she be there. And so, the "Studio One" commitment having already been made, Miriam regretfully had to turn down "Let's Pretend."

Nila was in a rage; disappointed over her lack of control over the situation, she threatened, as she had before, that she would never call Miriam again. It was their worst disagreement and it was never resolved. On the morning of Tuesday, January 20, 1953, just a few weeks after our last Cream of Wheat broadcast, Gwen Davies called Miriam and all the rest of us, to say that Nila Mack had been found dead in her apartment of a heart attack. She was 62 years old.

Opposite: **July 29, 1951: Sybil Trent Nieporent, married an hour before, visits Gwen Davies Greenhaus, who has just given birth to her second child. Left to right: Sybil's father, Nila Mack, Andrew Nieporent, Sybil, Miriam Wolfe, Gwen Davies Greenhaus, and Larry Greenhaus. ©1951 CBS Inc. Used by permission.**

That morning Dorothy Stickney had received a phone call from Maud Wilson saying that she could not get into Nila's apartment. Miss Stickney told her to call a locksmith, and that she would be right down (the Lindsays now lived on East Ninety-Fourth Street). Gwen Davies and her mother arrived at about the same time, and they found Nila's body.

None of us were prepared for this shock, although we knew that Nila had not been in good health for some time. She had had a hospital stay the previous year, and was no longer able to function at her former pace. Both Jack Grimes and Albert Aley, though the latter was no longer on the show, would go to the office and help her edit scripts and make casting decisions for the next broadcast, while Mary Ponterio continued to loyally back Nila up and protect her as much as possible from pressures and conflicts.

It is very likely that Nila, ever since Cream of Wheat had decided not to renew the contract, had been in a state of shock. At any rate, the severe emotional stress (not to mention her years of heavy smoking) must surely have affected her heart. Being a realist, she knew that CBS was not likely to find another sponsor for the show – our listener ratings having dropped – nor was "Let's Pretend" likely to continue much longer as a sustainer. Her child was dying, and a sentimental verdict would be that she too died of a broken heart.

Nila's funeral, which filled Frank Campbell's largest chapel, was a simple affair, but hardly somber. Several old friends spoke on her behalf, and the principal speaker was Howard Lindsay. In closing, he quoted the last lines from the letter of instructions which Nila had left for him and Dorothy Stickney:

> And if at last you should get
>   to the Pearly Gate,
> Let me know you're coming,
>   and I'll bake a cake!

At Nila's last appearance she played to a full house, and exited to a laugh.

The Lindsays, as her closest friends, accompanied her casket on the train back to her birthplace, Arkansas City, Kansas, where she is buried next to her mother and father. The marker reads imply: *Nila Mac Briant.*

Nila's assets were valued by the executor at $64,193, leaving a net estate of $60,693 after the payment of her debts, which amounted to $3,500. Among these debts the executor had listed this item: "$8.24 owed to CBS for sand."

Pure guesswork would indicate that, since the network bought the sand in large quantities for the ashtrays which stood near the elevators on each floor at 485 Madison, Nila had probably been in the habit of buying a bag of sand from time to time to use for her cats.

An appraiser's valuation of Nila's personal effects does not indicate a taste for luxury or high living. Her most valuable furniture item was a George Steck baby grand piano and bench, $150. Most furniture items were marked in poor or very poor condition, and valued at $30 each, or less. She had a black seal coat with silver blue mink collar and cuffs, worth $300, and a 20-year-old black seal coat valued at $15.

Nila had left a trust fund of $15,000 to Mae McNair (whose married name had been Mary Wiggin) if living with her at the time of her death, and a lesser sum if no longer living with her, but this was meaningless since Mae had already died. She left $5,000 to Maud Wilson, payable at $1,200 annually. She also left $5,000 to Sandra Levy. Nila had telephoned Gwen Davies as the will was being drawn in October 1951 and told her, "I am giving you peace of mind." This meant that the $5,000 was to prevent Gwen from worrying about her mother's old age. However, Mrs. Levy had done very well for herself in business since her husband's death, and so she used the $5,000 for a trip to Europe. So much for peace of mind. Any cash remaining in Nila's estate was to be given to the Salvation Army.

An earlier biographer wrote that Nila had left money to her childhood friend Bonnie Nix to care for her handicapped son, but there was no mention of it in Nila's final will. Arkansas City historian Betty Sybrant guesses that she had already turned the money over to Bonnie so that it could be given to the institution where her son resided.

The Lindsays received all of Nila's books and theatrical memorabilia. They were also named as remaindermen to dispose of all her other personal effects, according to a nonbinding letter of instructions. Her closest living relatives were first cousins, apparently on her mother's side, whom she had not seen for years. There is no indication of whether any of them wanted or were given anything, but some record does exist of things which went to various Pretenders.

Dorothy Stickney wrote to Sybil Trent on February 14, after she and her husband had returned from Arkansas City and had begun the task of getting personal possessions moved out of her office. Miss Stickney told Sybil that Nila had wanted her to have her little mantel clock and any costume jewelry she might want. Miriam Wolfe and Gwen Davies received other personal items from our director's possessions. Daisy Aldan was left Nila's collection of chinaware and crystal cats, and a sterling silver pin in the shape of a little angel went to Betty Jane Tyler. However, Nila Mack's most important heritage was the "Let's Pretend" program itself and the scripts, all of which remained the property of the Columbia Broadcasting System.

As "the show must go on" in radio as well as in the theatre, her immediate supervisor at the CBS network, Zack Becker, made sure that it did. Our former "Let's Pretend" production assistant Jean Hight was promoted to full director, and staff writer Johanna Johnston was assigned to take care of the scripts.

The biggest change in the program when it again became sustaining had already taken place. We were back in the Studio Building on East Fifty-Second Street, in Studio 21, and had been shifted from 11:05 A.M. to 2:30 P.M., Eastern time. Our checks, of course, were smaller, as we were now under the union's Sustaining Program code, and the actors' fee was $43. Under this contract, two actors were allowed to double without additional fee, and I was usually one of them, as I had now taken over doing the animal sounds. The Cream of Wheat jingle was replaced by a new one Nila had written for Gwen and Sybil to sing, to the same Komzak "Fairy Tale" music, as follows:

> Hello! Hello! Come on, let's go!
> It's time for *Let's Pretend*!
> The gang's all here, and standing near
> Is Uncle Bill, your friend.
> The story is exciting,
> From start right to the end . . .
> So everyone come join the fun
> Come on and *Let's Pretend*.

Though Cream of Wheat was gone from our lives, the program retained some of the improvements that had been made under their sponsorship. We still had Bill Adams as our storyteller; Maurice Brown remained as conductor and writer of original music; and we also retained our hour's rehearsal on Thursday, which meant a much smoother show. One thing we now lacked, which we had never realized we would miss, was the Cream of Wheat commercials. With their quizzes, rhymes, and word games, they were lively and fun for children, even if they did lessen the time available for the story. The commercials were now replaced by public service spots done by CBS staff announcers Jim Campbell or Warren Sweeney, on subjects such as "Don't start forest fires," or "Be careful with electricity," while the show's ending always included a plug for some other CBS radio program. These spots ranged from mildly to deadly dull, and were also depressing because they were a constant reminder that we were no longer sponsored.

Obviously, the biggest change in the program was the loss of Nila Mack. Most of us already knew Jean Hight, who was a veteran CBS production man, having started with station WABC as an announcer in the early 1930s. He came from an old New Jersey family which had founded the town of Hightstown. We all thought Jean was a pleasant enough fellow, but he had one obvious flaw: he was not Nila Mack.

Jean did not have an easy job. He was, after all, stepping into a very large pair of shoes. Each of us, though we felt Nila's loss keenly, wanted the program, as we knew she would have, to continue to be its excellent self, and so we tried to help him, especially when there was a complicated sound effects sequence which was not obvious from the directions in the script. Also, we wanted to continue getting called. Jean, being director, now had full control of casting and could call whomever he wanted.

Johanna Johnston, the new writer, had more script time available, as we were now restored to being a 30-minute program. She filled out the extra minutes as best she could, probably not having access to Nila's original scripts from the years before 1943, or possibly she did not want to use them. I was not able to be objective, having been with the program for so long, but to me the scripts now had a slight tinge of dullness and pedestrianism. And it did not increase my feeling of good will toward her when the closing credits were changed to read: "originated by Nila Mack and written by Johanna," with no last name. This I suppose was because it was a children's program, and you're supposed to talk down to children, so you only give your first name. I was disgusted. When I gave my name in the cast credits at dress rehearsal one week after, I simply said, "Arthur." "What's the matter, Arthur?" asked Jean after the dress. "Don't you have a last name?" I apologized. However, the cutesy "Johanna" was replaced by her full name soon after.

CBS sustained "Let's Pretend" for one year and nine months after Nila Mack's death. It was still an excellent children's program, but it now lacked adequate publicity exposure and a stable time period. In 1954 the program was tossed around between several spots on the schedule. Jean Hight kept most of the original Pretenders, but added several of his own choices as well, including Roger Sullivan, Robert Morea, Marian Carr, Cameron Andrews, Ruth Last, Stanley Martin, Hal Studer, and Donald Madden. Donald was one of the best of the latter-day Pretenders. He had been highly recommended to Jean by Rita Lloyd. Donald later built an important stage career, playing 114 performances of *Hamlet* for the Phoenix Theatre, an American record. He replaced Kenneth Haigh in *Look Back in Anger* on Broadway in 1959, won a Tony nomination for *Black Comedy* in 1967, and later played Dickinson in the motion picture version of *1776*. He unfortunately died at the age of 49 of cancer in 1983.

Johanna Johnston, to her credit, created some new adaptations which, though not fairy tales – those having been pretty well exhausted by Nila Mack – were good children's radio fare. One was from the story "The Husband to Mind the House" in which a husband and wife, quarreling, agree to exchange roles for a week, with disastrous results. Others included "Ceres and Proserpine," based on the Greek legend. A rousing version of the legend of "Robin Hood" was probably her best. There was plenty of action, and I had a song in my role of Alan-a-Dale.

The status of New York radio production during the last two years of "Let's Pretend" might be indicated by the fact that during that time we received our casting calls and our checks from the CBS Television Production Center at 524 West Fifty-Seventh Street. By then it was obvious that Bill Paley's business "household" at 485 Madison Avenue was gone. He himself concluded his autobiography by writing that running CBS had never been as much fun as it was in those early great, experimental days.

The inevitable happened without much notice. At a Thursday rehearsal of "Jorinda and Joringel" we were informed that that Saturday's broadcast, October 23, 1954, one day before what would have been Nila Mack's sixty-third birthday, would be our last. We were now broadcasting in the 2:00–2:30 P.M. (EST) time period. Football season had arrived, and "Let's Pretend" was interfering with the pigskin play-by-plays.

Our last broadcast was not one of our happiest or most "up" stories, but it was of course by chance: there had been no time to plan the last show. In the story of "Jorinda and Joringel" the happy couple (Robert Morea and Sybil Trent) announce their engagement, but are warned by their friend David (Michael O'Day) not to let Jorinda suffer the same fate that befell his beloved Robina. It seems that there is a Witch (Daisy Aldan) living in a nearby castle who likes nothing better than to capture unsuspecting maidens and transform them into lovely singing birds.

Jorinda and Joringel, now newly wed, walk through a mysterious forest and come upon a pitiful mewing kitten (that was me) and Jorinda, in spite of her husband's warning, goes into the bushes to pick it up. Once there she is caught by the Witch and transformed into a nightingale (the many bird calls were once more done by Henry Boyd). Joringel then makes it his life's work to rescue his beloved and destroy the Witch and her power. An old man (my last role on "Let's Pretend" – a character man to the end) advises him of the best way to catch the Witch off guard. Joringel finally does, thus freeing not only Jorinda but all the other maidens from the Witch's spell, while the Witch herself falls from the castle tower to a well-deserved death (scream, fading off, but no body thump).

At the end of the broadcast, in the spot where there was usually a teaser for the next week's show, Bill Adams said that CBS had decided for the time being to discontinue "Let's Pretend," and that this would be our last show. There was an audible "Ohhhh" from the small audience in our upstairs Studio 28. When it was over, Gwen Davies, Sybil Trent, and I went across Madison Avenue to the Berkshire Hotel for a rather low-key lunch and a drink. (Mickey O'Day had already left, to catch a train for New Jersey.)

In spite of that "for the time being" in the script, we had no illusions. Not only was this our last "Let's Pretend" broadcast; it was the end of a weekly association which had been an important part of the lives of each of us.

A necessary postscript: For weeks after "Let's Pretend" was taken off, CBS received letters of protest. And early in 1955 we received, posthumously, two more awards as the best children's program in radio.

The reader who has followed the life of "Let's Pretend" and its cast thus far may be interested in knowing where the many Pretenders are now and what has happened to the various locales of the show.

The Columbia Broadcasting System, though not immune to recessions and the viewing and listening competition provided by other networks and other media, has continued to be one of the nation's entertainment giants. Long gone from 485 Madison Avenue, its corporate headquarters have since 1965 been in an imposing 38-story building at 51 West Fifty-Second Street, New York. Designed by Eero Saarinen, it is known in the business as Black Rock, as it is sheathed in charcoal grey Canadian granite. The north side of the building towers over and dwarfs the old brownstone at 55 West Fifty-Third Street where Nila Mack had lived.

At 485 Madison Avenue there is still broadcasting. The third floor, where Studio 7 was located, is now the home of WMXV, one of New York's contemporary music FM stations, "105 on your dial."

Across the street at the former studio annex, 49 East Fifty-Second Street, there is silence. As its need for radio studios decreased, CBS started to use the large studios 21 and 22 for recordings. Hit records were made there by Frank Sinatra, Paul Simon, and Barbra Streisand. Then the space was used to store CBS business records, and in the glassed-in control rooms where Nila Mack and the other CBS radio directors once threw cues for coast to coast broadcasts, there are now typists and file clerks.

In 1988 Number 49 was leased to the Sony Corporation, which again used the large studios for recording and needed office space as well, but that company vacated the building in 1992, and the following year CBS sold it to a real estate firm. At this writing the formerly striking stark-white stucco front of the building is painted black, no doubt for weatherproofing purposes. Above the modernistic entrance the outlines of the now-vanished neon letters "CBS" can still be dimly discerned. Meanwhile, Studio 21, the home of "Let's Pretend" for three of our sustaining years, has now been made into a discount drug store.

As for the third floor terrace apartment at 55 West Fifty-Third Street, it continued to have a life of its own after Nila Mack's body was found there. In 1964 the then tenant made an arrangement with United Artists to film extensive location scenes on the terrace, by then bordered by ornate white-painted latticework, for the Jack Lemmon picture *How to Murder Your Wife*. In the opening shots, as the camera pans leftward across the width of the terrace, you can see quite clearly the Ziegfeld Theatre on Sixth Avenue, still standing, and the steelwork going up for the new CBS Building.

Three years later, on May 1, 1967, the terrace attained another kind of notoriety. Nila's former apartment was now occupied by James Stephens, a pleasant, round-faced young actor 43 years old and very successful, mostly in television voice-over and radio commercials. After a "Christmas in May" party given for clients of the nearby United Recording Studios, Jim brought an agency producer and two girls over for barbecue and drinks on the terrace. As the party got mellower, they all started singing and swinging in a hammock, one end of which was attached to the trellis, the other end to a spike driven into a narrow, 15-foot-high chimney. Suddenly, the ancient chimney toppled over from the pulling of the spike on its dried-out masonry. It was capped by a large granite slab, which crashed down on the heads of the two men, killing them, while the chimney's bricks fell on and around them. The girls were hysterical but relatively unhurt.

As this is written, the two houses at 45 and 47 West Fifty-Third Street which housed the historic Rehearsal Club, inspiration of the Edna Ferber–George S. Kaufman play and motion picture *Stage Door*, are being torn down, to be replaced by the new headquarters building of the Museum of American Folk Art. Meanwhile, 49, 51, 53 and number 55, Nila Mack's old home, all stand empty, forlorn and boarded up, awaiting their own recycling fate, amid what is now some of the most valuable real estate in Manhattan.

As for Cream of Wheat, it has for years now been owned by Nabisco, and its business is still thriving. Besides Regular and Enriched Five-Minute Cream of Wheat, there are now many instant varieties and different flavors, which are microwaveable.

Here is what has happened since the last broadcast of "Let's Pretend" in the lives of some of the surviving Pretenders:

Gwen Davies continued to do "Casper the Friendly Ghost" and other cartoon voices, and became very busy in singing commercials, including those for Mission Bell Wine, Robert Hall Clothes, and the "Sound Off" spots for Chesterfield Cigarettes. In television she had the lead in "The Boys from Boise," the first original TV musical, done on the DuMont network.

Gwen's husband Larry became executive vice president of a large industrial firm, and her interest in him and in her three children eventually meant that she had no time for the rat race of competing for jobs. Gwen has no regrets. A grandmother now, she takes care of Larry, a dog, a cat, and a big old stone house in Pennsylvania. She continues to live enthusiastically, and has cast herself in the long-running part of the social "mother" who keeps the survivors of the "Let's Pretend" family together. Her telephone bill is tremendous.

Don Hughes found after his marriage that radio acting or writing could not provide sufficient income to feed a family, and so went to work for Commerce Clearing House, a firm specializing in tax and legislative information, in 1948. During his last years on "Let's Pretend" he now also had a new career, writing incisive summaries of new tax and other legislation for CCH. When he retired he was one of their most experienced and valued employees.

Don and I remained close friends, this relationship being one of the greatest benefits I received from my years on "Let's Pretend." I felt a great loss when he died of emphysema in May 1990.

Albert Aley, aged 35 when "Let's Pretend" went off the air, was already very successful as a writer and producer in New York radio and television. In 1956 he and Elaine moved to California, where he soon sold scripts for "Cheyenne," "Have Gun, Will Travel," "Rifleman," "Rawhide," and "Laramie," among many others. They shared a private joke that writing all these westerns was doing pretty well for a young boy who had only known the streets of Manhattan.

Afterward he wrote for Walt Disney Productions, including animal stories for "The Wonderful World of Disney," and the screenplay for *The Ugly Dachshund*. He then went on to be producer and head writer of "Cimarron Strip," and was promoted from writer to head writer to producer of the Raymond Burr series "Ironside," for which he won two Emmy Award nominations. He then produced "The Paper Chase," for which he won a third.

During most of his Hollywood career Albert was very active on committees and on the board of directors of the Writers' Guild of America West. His special interest was guiding and teaching young writers. His career was cut short by cancer in 1986, when he was 66 years old. Nila would have been proud of Albert's achievements.

Michael O'Day was already in other kinds of work before the demise of "Let's Pretend." Radio acting jobs were drying up, so Mickey, his parents, and his sister moved to what had been their summer home at Point Pleasant Beach, New Jersey. He soon had two jobs: as a Social Security representative weekdays and as a radio disc jockey on weekends, both in Asbury Park.

In 1965 Mickey and his parents moved to San Diego, California, where he continued to work for the government. He was offered work in voiceover commercials as well as voice dubbing at the film studios, but , as his sister Joanne explained, "he never wanted to do that kind of work anymore. ... He never really liked acting. He loved to draw, and art was the only thing he truly liked to do, along with playing the piano. Would have loved to have gone to art school. Never got the opportunity." Mickey, like Don Hughes, was another Pretender who never got to use more than a fraction of his talents. He died of a heart attack in 1982.

Miriam Wolfe was spending less and less time in New York when "Let's Pretend" was canceled. She now had many contacts in California radio and television, but was not happy with what she found to be its aggressive commercialism. Friends then persuaded her to visit Canada, where 2½-hour dramatic shows with full orchestra were still being done. In 1956 she moved there permanently, and was soon working on radio and television in Toronto, some days from 7:00 A.M. until midnight.

In 1957 Miriam met Canadian John Ross. They were married, and moved to France after their son was born. There she developed a method of teaching communication skills with phonetic sound games. When she returned to Canada in 1980, she was by now more interested in teaching and writing than in acting. She wrote a book, *The Sounds of English*, as part of the *Listening to Language* series. She worked with students of the Ontario Gifted Children's Program, and with the faculty of medicine at the University of Toronto. Miriam credits her years of work on "Let's Pretend" under the strict tutelage of Nila Mack for her current ability to successfully direct her pupils in good speech and group communication.

Daisy Aldan by the time of our last broadcast had developed a wide range of literary and artistic interests. While achieving her doctorate at New York University, she was also teaching at New York's High School of Art and Design, was founding the Tiber Press, and was also starting *Folder*, an avant-garde magazine which first introduced many later renowned poets and graphic artists. A major poet, she has produced seven books of poetry, as well as translations of the works of major European poets. More recently Daisy has launched herself into fiction, having written two novellas, *A Golden Story* and *Day of the Wounded Eagle*. Those and *In Passage*, her latest book of poetry, have all been nominated for Pulitzer awards.

Several years ago Daisy started creating her own shows, doing readings of her own poetry, or of Shakespearean excerpts at universities and other places, with another actor and musical accompaniment or alone – performances that go far beyond the rather dry and analytical approach that academic audiences have learned to expect.

She was recently introduced during an exhibit of her papers, manuscripts, and photographs at Yale University's Beinicke Rare Book and Manuscript Library, and when her "Let's Pretend" affiliation was mentioned the entire audience, or at least its older members, spontaneously burst into a rendition of our Cream of Wheat theme song.

When "Let's Pretend" went off the air Sybil Trent had been married three years. Meanwhile, she played Countess Marla Darnell, who stole the daughter of "Stella Dallas," shortly before that show went off the air – a role that she found a refreshing change from the sweet, virtuous parts she had played since the age of five. She played both comedy and dramatic parts on live TV shows, including "The Martha Raye Comedy Hour," and closed out her acting career doing a Charmin Bathroom Tissue commercial

("Please don't squeeze the Charmin"). The following week she joined Fifi Oscard Associates as a talent agent.

In 1973 Sybil became a casting director at Young & Rubicam, one of the nation's largest advertising agencies. Her older son is now a busy marketing executive, while her younger is a successful restaurateur, involved with both New York's Tribeca Grill and also as owner of Montrachet, a few blocks away from it. Sybil still works full time, both as a creative casting director and a loving grandmother.

Arthur Anderson, the undersigned, continued in radio, playing a talking parrot and a cat on "Mr. Jolly's Hotel for Pets," sponsored by Puss n' Boots Cat Food (another cereal maker, the Quaker Oats Company), then early in 1955 went into rehearsal for the Phoenix Theatre's production of *The Doctor's Dilemma*, directed by another ex–Pretender, Sidney Lumet. I continued actively in live television, in theatre, and did several films in New York, including *The Group*, *Zelig*, and *Green Card*.

Some of my theatre involvement during those years included a year off Broadway as the Girl's Father in *The Fantasticks*, and two years on Broadway in *1776*. Like many actors, I have also lived by doing commercials. For seven years I was Mr. Kuppenheimer, spokesman for Kuppenheimer Men's Clothiers. Much more long-lived, though, was my work for yet another cereal. From 1963 through 1992 – 29 years – I was the off-camera cartoon voice of Lucky the Leprechaun for Lucky Charms (General Mills).

In 1963 I married Alice Middleton, former actress, associate director in live television, and later a commercials casting director, and we have a grown daughter.

During the last "Let's Pretend" years, Jack Grimes, like Albert Aley, had become interested in producing. In 1962 he started doing children's stories for MGM Records, and several of us ex–Pretenders were on them. Jack also formed a film company with Peter Fernandez, and for seven years they produced educational films.

In 1972 Jack met Norman Lear in Hollywood, which resulted in his playing Mr. Whitehead, the Undertaker, in 17 episides of "All in the Family." Meanwhile, he had been commuting to California for several years doing roles in feature films, including the murder mystery *Pendulum* with George Peppard, and the later production *Cold Turkey*.

In the 1980s Jack had to give up acting due to ill health, but continued his childhood tradition of being responsible for members of the family, and personally cared for his wife's aged father during his last years. Jack's son is the senior partner in a New York advertising agency, his older daughter is the personnel director of a large bank, and his youngest is the mother of three children. Jack, now white-haired, has not lost any of his enthusiasm for his days in radio and on "Let's Pretend."

By the time World War II was over, Kingsley Colton was no longer interested in acting. He was much too busy completing his B.A. degree at Columbia University. For employment he started in the messenger room at Young & Rubicam Advertising, later switching to production assistant on their television shows. In 1951 he terminated his union membership, which took him completely out of the performing field.

Kingsley married in 1951, and he and his wife raised a boy and two girls. Meanwhile, he had switched to the business side of TV advertising, then the administrative (meanwhile achieving an M.A. degree in 1969). When he retired in 1987 he was a vice president and benefits administrator at Young & Rubicam. The sincerity and honesty that marked his acting on "Let's Pretend" had carried Kingsley to great success in an entirely different world.

Betty Jane Tyler was already into other things by the time of our last broadcast. When her two children were old enough, she completed her work for a B.A. degree at Sarah Lawrence College. She had become a writer, and put this skill to work as public relations director of the State University at Purchase, New York. Betty's performing days were by no means over, however. Now billed as Elizabeth Karp, in 1970 she started on her own Monday through Friday radio show on station WGCH, in Greenwich, Connecticut, interviewing many theatre celebrities, educators, writers, and Greenwich residents.

Betty became active as a playwright, joining New York's Ensemble Studio Theatre in 1979. One of her plays done there was *Ten Cents on the Dollar*, a partly autobiographical story about a little girl who becomes a child actress in radio. Betty had to give up her radio show in 1982 when she underwent surgery for cancer, and two years later she died. As a child actress, and into adulthood and two other careers, Betty Jane Tyler typified the spirit of gaiety, freshness, and discovery that "Let's Pretend" was meant to represent.

After his discharge from the Navy, Bill Lipton went right back to "Let's Pretend" and to many other radio shows, including a running part on "Road of Life." Bill had also become interested in politics. In the 1960 campaign for the Democratic presidential nomination, he was Stuart Symington's radio and television adviser.

At about this time he was diagnosed with Parkinson's disease, which made continuing as an actor impossible. His wife, who was in advertising, got a job in England, and the Lipton family lived there for five years, during which time Bill became a guinea pig for experimental treatments with L-dopa and other drugs. After returning to this country, he and his wife were divorced and he went to live with his brother and family in Michigan. In 1980, through the helpful efforts of Betty Jane Tyler, he moved to housing for the handicapped in Greenwich, Connecticut, his former hometown. Though this eventually became too difficult for him, he never forgot her

Bob Readick, ca. 1944. Courtesy of Anthony Tollin.

loyalty and friendship. In 1984 Bill moved to Portland, Oregon, where his son, now a judge, lives with his family. Bill keeps active as a member of the board of directors of the Oregon chapter of the American Parkinson's Disease Association.

Bob Readick was a very busy radio actor in the 1940s. Besides frequent "Let's Pretend" appearances, he had running parts on "The Second Mrs. Burton," "This Is Nora Drake," and later, in 1960, the lead on "Yours Truly, Johnny Dollar" on CBS. Then he too began to be plagued by a disability, but of an entirely different nature.

During a rehearsal of "Aunt Jenny's Real Life Stories" Bob complained that devils were after him. During a broadcast of "Cafe Istanbul," on which he had the male lead opposite Marlene Dietrich, he started throwing microphones on the floor. He received treatment for a mental illness, which Miss Dietrich paid for.

By the mid–1970s Bob was no longer working much. Rolly Bester, an ad agency casting director and a former actress herself, threw some radio commercials his way so that he could earn the minimum necessary to qualify for union medical benefits. She also recommended him to Himan Brown, whom all of us had worked for, who called him for his hour-long "CBS Mystery Theatre." But this did not last. He had become too unreliable.

In the mid–1980s Bob disappeared several times, once turning himself into the police and telling them that he was AWOL from the Army base at Fort Dix. It was on May 27, 1985, that his wife received a phone call from the police in Cherry Hill, New Jersey. Bob had been killed there, trying to walk across an eight-lane highway.

As each of the regular "Let's Pretend" cast members, and the scores of others who were on less frequently went our separate ways, it is doubtful that any of us ever thought of the contributions we had made to the program. But every one of those I have talked with had been touched in a positive way by the character of the program and of the stories we did, and particularly by the indelible personality of the woman who directed them.

Looking at it today with the objectivity which the passing of 40 years can bestow, none of us veteran Pretenders really had anything to feel sad about when the program went off the air. For a period of time ranging from 6 years for Rita Lloyd to 24 for Gwen Davies, we had had, on one program, an emotional and financial security often lacking in radio – a business where most people were freelancers, and today's broadcast was your last . . . unless some director called you tomorrow.

By the time of the demise of "Let's Pretend" all of us had either built successful careers on other shows or in other media, or had long since gone into other occupations. None of us had been dependent for some time on "Let's Pretend" checks to pay next week's bills. We had received at least as much as we gave, and had gained maturity and independence. And we had had the creative joy of participating in a delightful program under the loving, if strict, tutelage of a remarkable woman. The radio industry and CBS owed us nothing. In short: we were lucky.

Chapter 15

After the Station Break:
Memories and Re-Creations

Just as we have briefly followed the lives of some of the Let's Pretenders since the program went off the air, it might also be useful to mention the afterlife of radio itself – the medium which was responsible for our fairy-tale dramatizations being available to a whole generation of American children – and then go on to recount how "Let's Pretend" has been heard since, and still is, occasionally.

As "Let's Pretend" was dropped from the CBS roster, so were the other dramatic programs, one by one, on that and the other networks. Sponsors were not supporting them because listenership was falling off, and that was happening because there was more and more interesting programming available on television and less on radio. The networks used the large profits of their radio operations to finance the development of television programming, and the studios and equipment it needed – not radio. After the radio networks' income started declining because of the desertion of their sponsors, the programming that was left became less and less interesting. The withering and changing of American network radio thus fed upon itself.

No chronicle of the years, golden or otherwise, when radio was a dominant part of everyone's life in this country can be complete, or even truthful, unless it mentions not only the program gems that those surviving still cherish but also touches on some of the many uninspired, run-of-the-mill clinkers that probably stayed on the air only because their sponsors liked them or because nobody had thought of anything better to fill the day's schedule. But judgments such as these, of course, must be subjective. Indisputably, some of the best of radio has survived, via scripts and recordings, and a good deal of the less than the best, but it will be up to collectors and historians to decide which is which.

As a writer in the *New York Times* said in reviewing Sally Smith's biography of William S. Paley, *In All His Glory*, "To be sure there was quality programming, but it functioned as a facade behind which was a great deal of junk." Some of the enthusiastic aficionados of what is now referred to as "old-time radio" should face the fact that not all of it was great. Not all of it was good even then, before the obscuring mist of sentiment had blown in.

Radio was at first a novelty – a toy. Then it became a companion for the lonely and a source of entertainment, information, stimulation, and occasionally even inspiration. But there were enough potboiler scripts, less than inspired music, dull public service programs, and – let it be admitted by an actor – sometimes mediocre performances to more than balance the really good listening that was available. Radio was (and I am afraid television is) proof of H. L. Mencken's sardonic comment that no one ever went broke "by underestimating the intelligence of the great masses of the plain people."

After the last of the network dramatic programs disappeared from American radio in the 1960s, the only substitutes available to listeners at first were recordings of some of the better known (but not necessarily better quality) crime and comedy shows of the 1940s and 1950s. But this picture is now beginning to change.

Radio is being rediscovered by an entirely new generation of writers, producers, and performers who see its potential as the "Theatre of the Imagination" and have been disappointed by the frequent lack of that quality on the television screen. Tentative stabs have been made locally on public radio stations, and a few sponsored dramatic programs have begun to appear on commercial outlets. In fact, so much is happening in this direction that to try to enumerate the many new programs and their originators would be to render this page instantly archaic by the time it reaches the printer. Suffice it to say that a comeback of radio as a medium for drama and comedy is taking place, though no one should pretend that it will ever reach the importance it once had in the United States.

The reappearance of original radio drama has also come from another, quite unexpected source. Shortly after audio cassette tapes became popular, someone had the idea of putting books on tape: best-sellers as well as literary classics, read either by the author, by well-known actors, or by unknown actors, some of whom, incidentally, have found it a welcome sideline.

The next development in audio publishing has been dramatizing the books with actors, sound effects, and music. This has been done, for instance, with 26 of the short stories of Louis L'Amour, which, being full of action, are most obviously suitable. The L'Amour stories, edited for a one-hour radio format, have now been syndicated, which means being available for local sponsorship.

CKW Associates, the producer of this new radio venture, has also recorded a new 30-minute serial drama written especially for radio, called

"Milford-Haven." A spokesman for the company said recently, "We're trying to bring back the golden age of radio in the 1930s and 1940s." Audio
dramatizations: who would have thought of such a thing? Thus is the wheel
being reinvented.

Even without the dramatic shows there is still incredible variety in
present-day radio, but the listener in each area has to roam the dial at random among 10 or 15 stations to get it, as detailed radio program listings
are not carried any more by most newspapers. This is because many stations do not have programs – just different personalities presiding in turn
over one basic format for all of the broadcast day, which in many cases is
24 hours long. The only important exceptions are major sporting events.

As for news and special events, radio still excels. Especially in on-the-
spot coverage, radio gets there sooner, is more flexible, and, paradoxically
having only words and not pictures to rely on, gives infinitely more information than does television.

In music, radio formats range from hard rock to classical with many
others in between, including easy listening, soft rock, and country and
western. There are also religious, multi-ethnic, all news, and all talk formats. There was even at one time a station in Fort Myers, Florida, which
was all Christmas – all year.

Thus has radio made its peace with television, and carved out a
different and in most cases still profitable place for itself in the television
age. This is such a complete change from the early days of radio that no
one in the industry back in the 1930s could have foreseen the medium's
present shape. But then, who could have possibly predicted that man would
walk on the moon; that people would have themselves frozen after death,
leaving wake-up calls for a century later; and who could have forecast back
then that Broadway shows would be financed, not by Brock Pemberton or
even by the Brothers Shubert, but by a Japanese distillery?

Two more sidelights on radio's recent history are worth recounting –
one sad and one encouraging.

On August 16, 1990, almost 60 years to the day after Nila Mack
directed her first broadcast at CBS, that network announced that it had
ended its operations at station WCAU-AM, Philadelphia, which had been the
first station in Bill Paley's new network. About 35 employees were laid off.
The station's talk show and local news format was replaced with golden
oldies rock-and-roll programming, and its call letters became WOGL-AM.

On a more positive note, children's programming, confined almost ex-
clusively to stereotyped cartoon and violent adventure fare on commercial
television, has begun to flourish again on radio. Most of the new programs
are on public radio stations which, just like sustaining radio in the 1930s
and 1940s, are free to experiment and are not forced to use mass marketing
techniques and high-pressure salesmanship. Children's needs are being

listened to and, in many cases, the children themselves are now involved in the writing, production, and on-the-air performances.

Though it went off the air in 1954, such was the interest in and affection for "Let's Pretend" that it has reappeared many times since then and still does, via recordings, and re-creations of various kinds. It is among the many old-time radio shows resurrected and occasionally broadcast today. There are good recordings of it, bad recordings, and some pseudo-recordings. The following are some of the many ways our program has been heard since its last live broadcast.

Probably the best in sound quality, depending upon how they have been treated, are our 78 r.p.m. phonograph albums, recorded in 1946 and 1947. Each story was complete on three 10-inch discs, and, except for the 3½ minute time limitation on each side, was done exactly as we had broadcast it. The story titles, and the Columbia album numbers, are as follows:

Jack and the Beanstalk	Album MJ 31
Cinderella	Album MJ 32
Puss in Boots	Album MJ 33
Rumpelstiltskin	Album MJ 40
Sleeping Beauty	Album MJ 45
The Chinese Nightingale	Number unknown

Two of these, "Rumpelstiltskin" and "The Chinese Nightingale," were later transferred to a Columbia LP, number JL 8502, and it is possible that others wre put on LP records too. For avid searchers, some of these may still be found in flea markets, yard sales, antique stores, or in a neighbor's attic or basement.

An LP pressing of our January 9, 1954, broadcast of "Robin Hood," a year after Nila Mack's death, on the Radiola label, may still be found in dusty corners of some record stores. In the cast list Robert Morea's name is misspelled, as is Betty Jane Tyler's name in the caption of the cover photo. The rest of the record contains excerpts from broadcasts by Smilin' Ed McConnell's Buster Brown Gang, and also a show called "Big Jon and Sparky." These are for very young children, and are interesting only because they represent the insufferably cute "itty-bitty-kiddie" approach to children's broadcasting to which Nila Mack and "Let's Pretend" never gave in.

Of greatest entertainment and historical value are recordings of the actual "Let's Pretend" broadcasts which were both written and directed by Nila Mack. The oldest (some still do exist) were made in our original sustaining days in 1942. Recordings of our Cream of Wheat broadcasts would be those dated September 25, 1943, through December 6, 1952. Our later sustaining broadcasts were from December 13, 1952, through our last show on October 23, 1954.

These recordings were taken from acetates, recorded for reference by ad agencies, or sometimes by engineers at network origination points or member stations for rebroadcast. Copies were later made on open reel or cassette tapes, and there is a great variation in their sound quality, depending upon their sources and the care with which they have been reproduced and handled. These tapes are not available in record stores but only from individuals and dealers who specialize in collecting and selling (or sometimes trading) recordings and other memorabilia to other old-time radio devotees.

A good selection of dealers in old-time radio tapes, most of whom include "Let's Pretend" in their wares, is found in the pages of *The Nostalgia Entertainment Sourcebook* (available at bookstores or Moonstone Press, Box 142, Beverly Hills, CA 90213). Anyone interested can also join one of the old-time radio enthusiasts' organizations mentioned in this book. These organizations publish periodic newsletters and listings of old-time radio (sometimes abbreviated OTR) programs broadcast in 64 cities in 27 states. The largest of these are:

Friends of Old-Time Radio (newsletter $12 per year) care of Jay Hickerson, Box 4321, Hamden, CT 06514; and *SPERDVAC* (first-year membership $25, newsletter only, $15; the acronym stands for the Society to Preserve and Encourage Radio Drama, Variety and Comedy, Box 7177, Van Nuys, CA 91409).

Friends of Old-Time Radio holds its yearly convention opposite Newark Airport in New Jersey in late October, and *SPERDVAC*'s is held in the Los Angeles area in November. There are similar organizations in Baltimore, Chicago, Cincinnati, Denver, and several other cities. Each of them does its best to get as many members of the original casts of the classic radio shows as possible to stride – or totter – up to the microphone and re-create actual broadcasts. There are also panel discussions, with guest stars, and dealers' tables.

Interest in nostalgia in this country, especially old-time radio nostalgia, is thriving, and to mention the Kate Smith Fan Club, the National Lum and Abner Society, and the Abbott and Costello Fan Club is to only scratch the surface.

Of the "Let's Pretend" broadcast recordings available, the only ones to avoid are reproductions of those which were reedited for the Armed Forces Radio Service. Commercials, lead-ins, and cast credits have been edited out. There is an orchestra playing "Smiles," and a smarmy, patronizing announcer doing the lead-ins. Anyone judging "Let's Pretend" by these AFRS tapes would wonder why the show had ever received so much praise. The AFRS tapes can be identified by the fact that the others usually list the date of original broadcast and these do not.

In 1970 CBS leased the rights to the "Let's Pretend" name and the scripts to a Canadian firm, which recorded 50 of our stories on the Stereo Dimension label, two on each of 25 LP records, done in Toronto by a cast of Canadian actors.

How should I describe them? First, I must admit a built-in prejudice born of long association with the original. These actors are not bad but the final result is simply rather bland. There is an Uncle Ted, and children who discuss "How shall we go to the Land of Let's Pretend?", but they sound rather uninterested in the whole thing. The main interest of these records, to an ex–Pretender at least, is that the scripts seem largely intact and, if the direction and some of the performances can be discounted, the charm, originality, and excitement of Nila Mack's radio adaptations still come through.

If there is anything else to be learned from these records it is that Nila Mack's impeccable taste, discernment, and humor and her unerring skill at working with child actors, were things which no amount of money paid by the Canadian firm could buy.

Seven of the "Let's Pretend" broadcast recordings, all done after Nila Mack's death, are available for listening at the Museum of Television and Radio in New York. It will eventually have many more, donated by ex–Pretenders and by others. In the few instances where more than one broadcast of a story has been recorded, it will be interesting to compare the differences in performances of the same part by different actors, possible script changes, and the changes in our voices as we matured from children to adults.

The program was re-created by members of its original cast three times after its disappearance from the airwaves. All three performances took place during annual conventions of Friends of Old-Time Radio. The first was in October 1980 in Bridgeport, Connecticut, where we did "Cinderella."

Betty Jane Tyler played the lead, Sybil Trent and Gwen Davies were the nasty Sisters, and Rita Lloyd the Stepmother. I played the Prince, a part in which Nila would never have cast me, but this was necessity. All our regular princes had either died or were unavailable by then.

Three years later in Newark we did "The Brave Little Tailor," or "Seven at One Blow," with Larry Robinson in the lead, Sybil Trent as the Princess, and Donald Buka as the exasperated King. Jackson Beck (a seasoned radio performer but never on "Let's Pretend") and I played the two Giants. The last "Let's Pretend" re-creation was in 1988 at the same location, where we did "Beauty and the Beast." Beauty was Sybil Trent, I was the mysterious Butler, and the Beast was Don Hughes, by then wracked with coughing and not sure he could get through the performance – the last before his death – and done as a favor to me. He did get through it, and was excellent as he had always been. Miriam Wolfe was there to do not a witch, but her old part as the Voice in the Wind.

The amazing and touching thing about these "Let's Pretend" reunions was that the first took place 26 years, the second 29 years, and the third 34 years after our last broadcast, and yet as we sat at a table each time for our read-through rehearsal, it was as if the previous show had been just the week before, so smoothly and almost effortlessly did everything function. It was not as if we had all maintained intimate friendships. Indeed, some of us had not seen or heard from the others once in all that time. But we had been, after all, a radio repertory company, under a director whose feeling of caring for her actors and for her material united us still.

One more "Let's Pretend" re-creation of a different sort took place in January 1990, at the Museum of Television and Radio (then called the Museum of Broadcasting). It was a Saturday workshop for children called Re-Creating Radio, which the museum continues to hold every year. The children are given scripts and they rehearse and perform classic radio programs, playing all the parts and operating manual sound effects. The whole thing is recorded, and each child receives a cassette of the performance in the mail. I was asked to come and talk a little about children's programs on radio, and to participate in a recording of "Aladdin and the Wonderful Lamp." I played the evil magician Magi Tapha.

The children, who ranged in age between 8 and 12, took to it enthusiastically, and there were remarkably few stepped-on cues and muffed lines. There were only two microphones on the tiny stage of the auditorium, for both actors and sound effects, and I was reminded that during our radio days there had been a mystique about microphone technique – a skill that only old, experienced radio pros were supposed to know. I came to the conclusion that microphone technique could really be expressed very simply: don't forget to stay close enough to the microphone.

The children doing the Aladdin story had a fine time. Though there was very little resemblance between them and professional actors, it did not matter. They were participating in a ritual as old as civilization – telling a story. That was part of the fascination of "Let's Pretend": a good story, for both its actors and its listeners; and telling a story, after all, was how theatre began.

These children's pleasure in what they were doing suggests that, in spite of the latest fads in violence, cruelty, and destruction as seen on our screens and heard in our loudspeakers, the beauty and the adventure expressed in older forms of narrative are still attractive to children, and the old-fashioned virtues possessed by their heroes and heroines can still be exciting without being stuffy.

The praise I have given to Nila Mack is perhaps excessive. She was,

after all, only one human being, and obviously possessed no monopoly on
the art of writing for children or working with juvenile performers.
However, she was a pioneer, and very successful at doing it on radio. In
spite of the enthusiastic fan mail she used to receive from parents as well
as from children, Nila could have had no idea then of the influence which
her creation would still have today in the minds of those same children who
survive, and how strong would be their childhood memories of it. Here are
a few examples.

While I was working on this book, *Variety* published a letter of mine,
asking anyone who had been on "Let's Pretend" or who had known Nila
Mack to please get in touch. Part of my response was from several *Variety*
subscribers who were not in show business and had no information to
add, but who simply wanted to express their own fond memories of the
show.

One day a couple of years ago Jack Grimes, who was then employed in
the Queens, New York, district attorney's office, was conversing with a
coworker, when a woman's voice spoke to him from behind. He turned to
find a lady aged in her seventies, who asked hesitantly, "Were you ever on
a program called 'Let's Pretend'?" Thirty-five years had gone by, but Jack's
voice had formed an indelible impression in her memory. Besides being a
compliment to Jack and to our program, it was also a tribute to radio.
There were no pictures to watch. The sound was all, and it stimulated the
imagination in a way nothing else could do.

Much more recently, Jack received a letter, forwarded by our union,
AFTRA (the union's name was changed in 1952 to the American Federation
of Television and Radio Artists) from a man who had grown up in
Philadelphia. He had just recognized Jack's voice when playing a radio buff
collector's tape of "Let's Pretend." "Coming as I did from a working-class
background, from 1940s radio I learned to speak well, without the curse of
my family's typical Philadelphia accent," he said. He went on to thank Jack
for the many hours of radio entertainment he had provided him, both on
"Let's Pretend" and on other programs. Nila would have been very pleased –
especially at the mention of good speech.

While Miriam Wolfe was living in France, a good friend who was a
psychotherapist met her on a Paris street one day. "I shouldn't tell you
this," she said to Miriam. "I'm supposed to keep everything my patients tell
me confidential, but this American lady had her first session with me today," she went on, "and practically her first words were that, as a child, one
of the most important influences in her life was a children's program called
'Let's Pretend,' and that she was terrified by the actress who played the
witches, Miriam Wolfe."

Francis Ford Coppola, the celebrated film director, mentioned in an interview how as a child he had spent long hours confined to a sickbed with

polio. He passed the time by reading James Joyce, playing with his pup-
pets, listening to "Let's Pretend" on the radio, and beginning to fantasize
stories he might tell – another example of how the classic fairy tales, which
after all come from European folklore several centuries old, still had the
power to stimulate a young imagination in the late twentieth century,
through the medium of our program.

Sybil Trent recently visited the Tribeca Grill, where her son Drew
Nieporent is manager and part owner. Drew steered his mother to a table
where sat Robert De Niro, another Tribeca owner, Dustin Hoffman, and
their party. As she was leaving the building, she felt a hand on her
shoulder. Dustin Hoffman had run to catch up with her. "I used to listen to
you every Saturday morning on 'Let's Pretend'!" he said excitedly. "I grew
up in Los Angeles, and every Saturday morning I would be glued to the
set." Someone at the table had apparently told him of her background. And
he continued happily rambling on about how he had enjoyed Sybil and the
program as a child.

In an old *Saturday Evening Post* cartoon, a wife asks her husband if he
by any chance remembers the "Let's Pretend" theme music. And in the
Broadway Play *6 Rms Riv Vu*, a couple who are trapped in a vacant apartment with a missing doorknob pass the time waiting for rescue by singing
old radio and television theme songs: "Your Hit Parade," "Your Show of
Shows," and "Let's Pretend."

"Long ago, when radio mattered, 'Let's Pretend' was a good entertainment for children," wrote Russell Baker, beginning one of his syndicated
columns. His subject was not our program, but the fairy tales he felt the
Bush administration was telling the American public at the time.

All of these examples, taken together, suggest that if the golden age
of radio, as it existed in the 1930s, 1940s, and to some extent in the 1950s,
has become a chapter of our American folklore, then "Let's Pretend" must
surely be included as an important page.

Nila Mack once told of how as a little girl in Arkansas City, in the
garden beside the white house with green shutters, she had tied her
mother's apron around her waist for a train, pretending that she was a
beautiful princess, and her audience of geraniums had shown appreciation
by nodding their heads in the breeze. The imagination starting to grow in
her then was to bear fruit years later in radio – a medium that had not even
been invented.

Appendix A

Long-Term Let's Pretenders

(In the order of joining cast)

	Born	Joined	Cast
Davies, Gwen (originally Estelle Levy)	1922	1929	
Ryan, Patricia (Pat)	1921	1929	Died 1949
Hughes, Donald (Don)	1918	1929	Died 1990
Block, Vivian	1922	1931	Resigned 1944
Aley, Albert	1919	1932	Resigned 1952 Died 1986
O'Day, Michael (Junior/Mickey)	1920	1933	Died 1982
Wolfe, Miriam	1922	1933	
Aldan, Daisy	1923	1933	
Trent, Sybil	1926	1935	
Anderson, Arthur	1922	1936	
Grimes, Jack (Jackie)	1926	1937	
Colton, Kingsley	1924	1937	Resigned 1951
Tyler, Betty Jane (later Elizabeth Karp)	1928	1937	Died 1984
Lipton, Bill (Billy)	1926	1938	
Readick, Bob (Bobby)	1926	1939	Died 1985
Lloyd, Rita	1930	1948	

(All were on the program until 1954 unless otherwise noted)

Appendix B

The Let's Pretenders

O: Original "Helen and Mary"   (sustaining, 9/1929–3/1934)
E: Early "Let's Pretend"   (sustaining, 3/1934–9/1943)
CW: Cream of Wheat   (sponsored, 9/1943–12/1952
L: Late, through last broadcast   (sustaining, 12/1952–10/1954)

Actors

(in alphabetical order)

Abel, Edmund E
Adams, Barbara CW
Adams, William P. (Bill) E, CW, L
Aldan, Daisy E, CW, L
Alexander, Denise CW
Alexander, Janie CW
Aley, Albert E, CW (and director)
Altman, Elmer O, E
Altman, Julian O, E
Anderson, Arthur E, CW, L (and animal sounds)
Anderson, David CW
Andrews, Cameron L
Artist, Michael E
Ashley, Mary Ellen CW
Ayers, Jack (Jackie) CW
Bain, Donald CW (animal sounds)
Barker, Brad E, CW (animal sounds)
Barker, Ethelmae CW
Barry, Lloyd E
Bashner, Lila O, E
Bauer, Charita E

Baxter, Bonnie CW (Phyllis Chalzell's daughter)
Bellin, Charles E
Benkoil, Maury E
Bishop, Adelaide E, CW
Blakeman, Robert E
Block, Vivian E, CW (and vocal sounds: baby cries)
Blume, Ethel O, E
Boyd, Henry O, E, CW, L (bird whistler)
Bruce, Edwin CW
Buka, Donald E, CW
Cameron, Marlene CW
Carney, Art CW
Carr, Marian L
Case, Richard L
Cavell, Maurice (Butch) CW
Chalzell, Phyllis E
Chapman, Pattee E, CW
Collins, Lillian L
Colton, Kingsley E, CW

Cooper, Ben CW
Cort, Bob E
Cury, Ivan CW
Dante, Jean E
Danton, Ray CW
Davies, Gwen (Estelle Levy) O, E,
  CW, L
Dayton, Jean E
DeGore, Janet E
Dengler, Ronnie CW
Diem, Peggy CW
Donnelly, Andy E
Donnelly, Jimmy E
Donnelly, Tommy E
Douglas, Susan CW
Drew, Bob CW, L
Dreyfuss, Michael CW
Eaton, Evelyn E
Eaton, Warren E
Englander, Alec E
Engler, Elaine E
Erskine, Marilyn CW
Etlinger, Dick E
Evans, Robert CW
Fallon, Joey CW, L
Fernandez, Peter CW
Fields, Elvin E
Flicker, Joan Patsy CW
Francis, Anne CW
Gates, Joyce E
Gayer, Anne-Marie CW
Gilman, Toni E
Glass, Mary Ellen CW
Goodwin, Patricia E, CW
Gordon, Dorothy E, CW
Greenhouse, Martha E
Grimes, Jack (Jackie) E, CW, L
  (and vocal horse effect)
Hagen, Edna E
Hale, Diana L
Halop, Billy E, CW
Halop, Florence E, CW
Hastings, Bob E, CW
Homeier, Skip E, CW
Hughes, Donald (Don) O, E, CW, L
Hughes, Tommy CW
Ives, Burl E

Jay, Lester E
Johnson, Lamont CW
Jordan, Jack (Jackie) E
Jouvin, Regina CW
Juster, Evelyn (Evie) CW, L
Kahn, Lillian L
Kamen, Milton E
Kane, Ronald (Ronnie) L
Kane, Sugar E
Karen, Barbara L
Kassel, Arthur L
Kelk, Jack (Jackie) E
Kelly, Nancy E
Last, Ruth L
Lazar, Joan CW
Lee, James L
Lee, Madeline O, E
Lee, Robert (Bobby) E
Levy, Estelle: *see* Davies, Gwen
Lipton, Bill (Billy) E, CW, L
Liss, Ronald (Ronnie) E, CW
Lloyd, Rita CW, L
Lockser, Judith CW
Loring, Lynn L
Lumet, Sidney E, CW
Lydon, James (Jimmy) E
Lynn, Lorna E, CW
McCallion, James (Jimmy) E
McGonaole, Robert (Bob) E
Mack, Nila O, E, CW
McKee, Margaret E (bird whistler)
Madden, Donald L
Martin, Stanley L
Mauch, Billy E
Mauch, Bobby E
Merrill, Howard O, E
Miller, Hope E
Monks, James E
Morea, Robert L
Mullen, Charles (Charlie) CW
Nelson, Bill CW
Nye, Louis CW
Ober, Muriel E
O'Day, Michael (Junior/Mickey) E,
  CW, L
O'Shea, Patsy CW
Patterson, Patricia E

Peardon, Patricia E
Peterson, Nancy E
Philson, Betty E
Porter, Paul, Jr. E
Raphael, Gerrianne CW
Readick, Robert (Bobby) E,
  CW
Redfield, William (Billy) CW
Reed, Lydia L
Rice, Rosemary CW
Robinson, Larry E, CW, L
Roe, Raymond E
Rose, Donald L
Rose, Teddy CW
Ross, Arthur E
Ryan, Eddie E, CW
Ryan, Patricia (Pat) O, E, CW
Schneider, Mildred O, E
Shay, Alan CW
Shepard, Joan CW
Silber, Roslyn O, E
Silbersher, Marvin E
Somers, Jimsey CW
Stang, Arnold E

Stickney, Dorothy E
Stone, Harlan (Hal) CW
Studer, Hal L
Sullivan, Roger L
Swan, Harry O, E (and animal
  sounds)
Sydell, Amy O, E, L
Taylor, Charles L
Tetley, Walter O, E
Tetzel, Joan E
Thatcher, Lynn CW, L
Thorne, Susan CW
Trent, Sybil E, CW, L (and vocal
  sounds: baby cries)
Twamley, Mack CW
Tyler, Betty Jane E, CW
Van Patten, Dick E, CW
Van Patten, Joyce CW
Wallach, George E
Warren, Nan E
White, Robert E
Wigginton, Sandra Ann L
Wolfe, Miriam E, CW, L
Worth, Diane CW

(Total as of 1994: 175)

Appendix C

The "Let's Pretend" Stories
Written or Adapted by Nila Mack

(Alphabetical, with Date of First Broadcast)

Aladdin and the Wonderful Lamp (9/13–20/30: 2 parts; adapted from Yolanda Langworthy script)
Ali Baba and the Forty Thieves (11/21/31)
Alice in Wonderland (4/3/48)
Alice Through the Looking Glass (4/10/48)
Babes in the Wood (4/25/31)
Beauty and the Beast (8/18/31)
The Blue Light (3/12/32; blended into The Tinder Box 11/8/47)
Bluebeard (4/11/31)
The Bluebird (Maeterlinck) (10/14, 10/28, 11/4/33: 3 parts)
The Brave Little Tailor (or, Seven at One Blow) (8/3/35)
The Bremen Town Musicians (10/1/32)
The Bronze Ring (9/19/31)
Brother and Sister (The Enchanted Stag) (7/2/32)
The Bushy Bride (11/5/32; rewritten as The Terrible Heads, 6/18/49)
The Castle of Hatred (Nila Mack original; 6/1/35)
Charlotte's Web (1952: 2 parts)
Childe Roland (3/18/33)
The Chinese Nightingale (or, the Emperor's Nightingale) (6/30, 7/7/? 2 parts; edited into single broadcast, 5/24/41)
Christmas Story – Sick Girl – Portrait (Mack original or Yolanda Langworthy adaptation 12/31/30)
Cinderella (8/22/31)
The Crystal Coffin (12/9/33)
Dick Whittington and His Cat (5/9/31)
Dog of Flanders (only done once; 12/15/38)
Donkey Skin (4/2/32)
The Donkey, the Table and the Stick (6/24/33)
Douban the Physician (7/11/36; also done on "School of the Air" with adult cast, 10/26/30)

Drakestail (7/16/32)

East of the Sun, West of the Moon (10/1/32)

The Elves and the Shoemaker (1/30/32)

The Emperor's New Clothes (7/8/33)

The Enchanted Canary (2/4/33)

The Enchanted Frog (7/9/32; Nila noted: "Rewrite stuttering girl")

The Enchanted Toystore of Fairyland (1938: 2 parts; by Flora Spiegelberg)

Fairer Than a Fairy (Halloween; 10/31/31)

Faithful John (2/13/32)

The Ferryman and the Mermaid (1/23/32; Nila's note: "n.g. Rewrite." Done only once since)

The Fisherman and His Wife (1/2/32)

The Flower Queen's Daughter (12/5/31; by Flora Spiegelberg)

The Flying Trunk (11/26/32)

The Frog Prince (5/23/31)

Fur Ball (9/17/32; later blended with Donkey Skin)

The Giant Who Had No Heart (10/20/34)

Gigi and the Magic Ring (4/28/34)

The Golden Blackbird (4/14/34)

The Golden Touch (King Midas and) (7/8/39)

Goldilocks and Prince Charming (8/20/32)

Goldilocks and the Three Bears (6/27/31; Nila's note: "n.g. Rewrite." Done, 11/5/49)

Goody Two Shoes (11/6/31; Nila's note: "n.g." Done only twice since)

The Goose Girl (and Falada) (3/14/31)

Graciosa and Percinary (3/28/31)

Gulnare of the Sea (8/25/30; Nila's second broadcast, Adaptation of Yolanda Langworthy script)

Hansel and Gretel (12/12/31)

Heart of Ice (11/17, 11/24/35: 2 parts. Done only once since)

Heavenly Music (Easter: Nila Mack original; 3/30/34. Done yearly since)

Hop o' My Thumb (6/13/31)

The House in the Wood (5/18/35)

The House of the World (New Year: Nila Mack original; 12/23/33. Done yearly)

How Six Traveled Through the World (1/26/36)

The Invisible Kingdom (2/3/34)

Jack and the Beanstalk (5/7/32)

Jason and the Golden Fleece (11/20/48)

Jorinda and Joringel (5/28/32)

Junior Meet the Artist (Thanksgiving: 11/19/32; Nila's note: "Fooey!" Never done again)

The Juniper Tree (4/8/33)

The King of the Golden Mountain (2/24/34)

The King of the Golden River (9/22, 9/29/34: 2 parts)

King Thrushbeard (4/23/32)

The Leprechaun (Nila Mack original; 3/17/31)

The Little Black Pot (5/15/37; by Jean Barhydt)
The Little Lame Prince (1/24/42)
The Little Mermaid (10/15/32)
Little Red Riding Hood (11/28/31)
The Little Soldier (1/6/34; possibly a rewrite of The Little Tin Soldier)
The Little Tin Soldier (12/26/31)
The Magic Carpet of Baghdad (10/24/31)
The Magic Cuckoo (date missing)
The Magic Horse (ca. 1931–32)
The Maiden Without Hands (7/28/36)
Melilot (3/10/34)
The Night Before Christmas (date missing)
The Nuremberg Stove (10/26/35)
Old Pyres and the Dryad (3/16/36)
One-Eye, Two-Eye, Three-Eye (5/3/31)
Palace of Tears (11/16/30; Nila Mack original)
Prince Agib (9/27/30; adapted from Langworthy)
Prince Codadad (10/4/30; adapted from Langworthy)
Prince Darling (2/27/31)
The Princess and the Pea (10/3/31)
Princess Goldenhair and the Wonderful Flower (8/6, 8/13/32: 2 parts; by Flora
    Spiegelberg)
Princess Miranda (1930)
Princess Moonbeam (5/13/33)
The Princess on the Glass Mountain (11/14/31)
Puss in Boots (3/1/31)
The Queen Who Couldn't Make Spice Nuts (9/16/33)
Rapunzel (4/18/31)
The Riddle (9/23/33)
Rosanella (8/5/33)
Rumpelstiltskin (3/24/32)
The Rusted Knight (8/19/33)
The Silver Knight (4/27/35; by Patricia Ryan)
Sinbad the Sailor (8/18/30; adapted from Langworthy. Nila's first broadcast)
The Six Swans (5/16/31)
Sleeping Beauty (8/29/31)
Snow Drop and the Seven Dwarfs (8/15/31)
The Snow Queen (8/11, 8/18/34: 2 parts; rewritten into one as of 4/2/49)
Snow White and Rose Red (9/5/31)
The Song of Hiawatha (ca. 1950)
The Three Feathers (7/23/32)
The Three Golden Hairs (6/25/32)
The Three Snake Leaves (6/9/34)
The Three Spinners (12/10/49)
The Three Terrible Heads (6/18/49)
Thumbelina (8/1/31)
The Tinderbox (9/3/32)

The Twelve Dancing Princesses (5/4/32)
The Twelve Months (5/20/33)
The Water of Life (4/29/33)
The White Cat (1/14/33)
Why the Sea Is Salt (9/26/31)
The Winged Princess of Bronze Mountain (4/16/32)
The Wishing Ring (7/22/33)
The Yellow Dwarf (7/11/31)
The Youth Who Learned to Shiver and Shake (3/25/31)

Nila Mack conscientiously noted, in longhand in a large spiral-bound book, every broadcast of each story. There may be another book, now lost, but the last entry in this one is 4/29/50.

When a story was broadcast in two or more installments, each broadcast is counted as a separate script. The total of Nila Mack's "Let's Pretend" scripts, including both originals and adaptations, is 133.

Select Bibliography

Books

Boemer, Marilyn Lawrence. *The Children's Hour*: Metuchen, N.J.: Scarecrow, 1989.

Buxton, Frank and Bill Owen. *The Big Broadcast: Radio's Golden Age, 1920–1950*. New York: Viking, 1972.

Dunning, John. *Tune in Yesterday: The Encyclopedia of Old-Time Radio 1925–1976*. Englewood Cliffs, N.J.: Prentice-Hall, 1976 (revised edition in progress).

Fornatale, Peter, and Joshua E. Mills. *Radio in the Television Age*. Woodstock, N.Y.: Overlook, 1980.

Hoogstraten, Nicholas Van. *Lost Broadway Theatres*. New York: Princeton Architectural Press, 1991.

Julian, Joseph. *This Was Radio*. New York: Viking, 1975.

Lamparski, Richard. *Whatever Happened To?* New York: Crown, 1974 et seq.

Landry, Robert J. *This Fascinating Radio Business*. Indianapolis: Bobbs-Merrill, 1946.

Lawrence, Jerome, editor. *Off Mike – Radio Writing by the Nation's Top Writers*. Chapter by Nila Mack. New York: Essential Books, 1944, Dist. by Duell, Sloan & Pearce.

MacDonald, J. Fred. *Don't Touch That Dial!* Chicago: Nelson-Hall, 1979.

McGill, Earle. *Radio Directing*. New York: McGraw-Hill, 1940.

Mack, Nila. *Animal Allies*. Julian Messner, 1942.

_____. *Let's Pretend*. Niles, Ill.: Whitman, 1948.

Mott, Robert L. *Radio Sound Effects*. Jefferson, N.C.: McFarland, 1993.

New York Times Directory of the Theatre. New York: Arno, 1973.

Paley, William S. *As It Happened*. New York: Doubleday, 1979.

Settel, Irving. *A Pictorial History of Radio*. New York: Grosset and Dunlap, 1967.

Skinner, Cornelia Otis. *Life with Lindsay and Crouse*. Boston: Houghton Mifflin, 1976.

Slate, Sam J. and Joe Cook. *It Sounds Impossible*. New York: Macmillan, 1963.

Smith, Sally. *In All His Glory*. New York: Simon and Shuster, 1990.

Stickney, Dorothy. *Openings and Closings*. New York: Doubleday, 1979.

Wylie, Max. *Radio Writing*. Rinehart, 1939.

Articles

Jelf, Steve. "Nila Mack – The Great Pretender." *SPERDVAC Radio Magazine: 1987 Convention Edition.* Society to Preserve and Encourage Radio Drama, Variety, and Comedy. Van Nuys, Cal.

Mack, Nila. "Writing for Children." In *Off Mike: Radio Writing by the Nation's Top Writers*, edited by Jerome Lawrence. Essential Books, 1944. Dist. by Duell, Sloan & Pearce.

"Nila Mack." Biography in *Notable American Women.* Cambridge, Mass.: Harvard University Press, 1980.

Sybrant, Betty. "CBS's Nila Mack." *Little Balkans Review: A Southeast Kansas Literary and Graphics Quarterly* (Spring 1983).

Index

I

I Get a Kick Out of You 73
I Love You from Coast to Coast 83
I Wear My Glasses to Bed Every Night 86
I Wish There Were a Radio Up in Heaven 83
The Iliad 38
"I'll Find My Way" 31
I'm H-A-P-P-Y Cause I Am S-A-V-E-D 80
I'm Planting Little Onions 86
In All His Glory 177
In Passage 172
In the Dark Hour 33
"Information Please" 104
Inherit the Wind 74
"Inside a Kid's Head" 50
"The Invisible Kingdom" 38
"Ironside" (TV) 171
Isolation booths 88, 110
"It's Only a Step from Killarney to Heaven" 106
Ivans, Elaine 49, 73
Ives, Burl 29, 189
Ivoryton, Conn. 149

J

"Jack and the Beanstalk" 38, 60, 90, 180
"Jack Armstrong (The All-American Boy)" 114
"The Jackie Gleason Show" (TV) 136
Jackson, Charles 74
Jameson, House 50
Jarman, Claude 92
"Jason and the Golden Fleece" 160
Jay, Lester 15, 79, 80, 95, 189
"The Joe Penner Show" 3
"John's Other Wife" 93, 111
Johnson, Lamont 152, 153–54, 189
Johnson & Johnson Co. 92
Johnston, Johanna 166, 167
Jolson, Al 29
Jordan, Jack (Jackie) 13, 79, 189
"Jorinda and Joringel" 55, 168
Jouvin, Regina 189
Joyce, James 185
"Joyce Jordan, Girl Interne" 21
Juilliard Music Foundation 117
Juliet of the Spirits 151
Julius Caesar 87, 88
Jumbo 82
"Jungle Jim" 114

"The Junior Bugle" 49
Junior Miss 68, 99
"The Juniper Tree" 40, 64
Juster, Evelyn (Evie) 189

K

Kahn, Lillian 189
Kaltenborn, H. V. 105
Kamen, Milton 79, 189
Kane, Ronald (Ronnie) 189
Kane, Sugar 189
Kane, Whitford 89
Karen, Barbara 189
Karp, Elizabeth *see* Tyler, Betty Jane
Karp, Irwin 160–61
Kassel, Arthur 189
Kate Smith Fan Club 181
"The Kate Smith Show" 18, 21, 83, 93
Kaufman, George S. 170
Kay, Howard 59
Keep 'Em Rolling 82
Kelk, Jack (Jackie) 13, 15, 16, 23, 77, 189
Kelly, Nancy 98, 189
Kenny, Charles 86
Kenny, Nick 86
"King Midas and the Golden Touch" 48, 143
Klaas, Isaac 59
Klondike IV (charter boat) 143
Knapp, Phyllis 104
Knight, Felix 15
Kollmar, Richard 21
Komzak, Karel 58, 66, 122, 161, 166
Kool cigarettes 65
Kreisler, Fritz 58
Kremer, Ray 53
Kuppenheimer Men's Clothiers 173

L

Ladies' Home Journal 114
"The Lady Next Door" 15, 29, 69
Lafferty, Perry 18–19
Lakewood, Me. 73
Lambs Club 125
L'Amour, Louis 178
"Land of the Lost" 94
Lang, Andrew 35, 38
Langford, Frances 105
Langworthy, Yolanda 5, 7, 11, 35, 46
La Palina cigars 7, 22